Reader's Digest

Complete A-Z of Medicine & Health

VOLUME THREE

Coma to Food allergies
and intolerances

Reader's Digest

Complete A-Z of Medicine & Health

VOLUME THREE

PUBLISHED BY THE READER'S DIGEST ASSOCIATION LIMITED
LONDON • NEW YORK • SYDNEY • MONTREAL

Coma

Damage to the brain or brainstem can cause coma, a state of unconsciousness from which a person cannot be woken. Coma may progress to the vegetative state, in which people open their eyes but remain unconscious.

People in a coma do not respond to external events. They do not move, speak, feel pain or open their eyes. They may not have control of automatic functions such as breathing and heart function and so may may require life support on a ventilator. They have very little brain activity and any responses they do have are very basic reflexes. Such a state of unconsciousness may be caused by an illness such as **stroke, meningitis, diabetes** or **Alzheimer's disease** in its later stages. Coma may occur as a result of a head injury or poisoning by, for example, narcotic drugs or carbon monoxide. Coma may also result where oxygen supply to the brain has been interrupted for several minutes – for example, in a heart attack or as a result of the blocking of the windpipe when a person chokes.

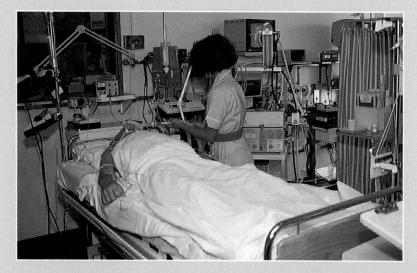

▲ **Coma monitoring**
The condition of a person in a coma is regularly examined for signs of change by a nurse or doctor using intensive care equipment.

A coma may last for as little as a few hours, and have few long-term consequences, or it may continue for days or weeks. It rarely lasts for more than a month – if a person does not recover or die, he or she usually progresses to the vegetative state.

When coma lasts for longer than a few hours, there is a high chance of very severe brain damage and, even if the person regains consciousness, he or she is likely to suffer some form of permanent after effect such as difficulty with speech, loss of memory or movement impairment.

COMMUNICATING WITH A COMA PATIENT

When the brain is functioning normally, sensory stimulation such as noise, smell or touch sparks off activity in the nervous system and this activity spreads to many areas, including parts of the brain that generate awareness. When someone is in a coma, sensory stimulation may still produce neural activity, even if it does not extend to awareness. This neural activity helps to keep the brain alive – in some people it may make the difference between their falling into a deeper coma or returning to consciousness.

Methods of promoting neural activity include talking gently to the person; playing music at the bedside; wafting strong or familiar smells (such as a favourite perfume) under the person's nose; massaging or stroking the legs and arms, and perhaps even stinging or pricking his or her skin; moving the person's legs and arms and grasping his or her hands.

COMPLICATIONS OF COMA

People in a coma are kept under close observation in hospital. Their inability to move may cause bedsores to develop, so hospital nurses turn people with coma regularly to prevent this happening. Patients in coma usually lose the muscle tone in their limbs, but as time passes the limbs become rigid. They can become permanently deformed, unless physiotherapists manipulate the limbs to prevent them 'setting' into an abnormal position.

Inactive people are susceptible to **pneumonia**, and coma patients, whose cough reflex is weak or who have to breath through a breathing tube (tracheostomy tube), are especially vulnerable.

When coma is the result of a head injury, there may be bleeding into the brain, and swelling and congestion of the damaged tissue. An operation may be required to remove the blood clot and decrease pressure in the skull.

Sometimes, the coma state improves but further complications arise such as the development of epilepsy, or bone formation in the muscles.

THE VEGETATIVE STATE

People in coma either die or enter a Vegetative State (VS), in which they have no awareness of

Home care for a coma patient

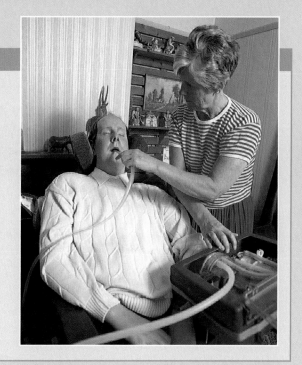

Once medically stable, some people in the vegetative state can be taken home. Carers must make a major commitment.

It is important to arrange for sufficient back-up if you are planning to care for a relative or friend in the vegetative state. You will need to provide 24-hour care and will usually need support from community nurses and doctors – many vegetative people have conditions such as epilepsy or require medication for neurological problems.

Family and care staff should be trained in general nursing duties – for example, how to turn the patient regularly, move the limbs to prevent their deterioration, feed using a tube, manage bowel movements and emptying of the bladder and use hoists, suction devices and other equipment.

---

their environment but retain the 'lower' brain functions needed for the body to survive. They breathe unaided; their heartbeat, circulation and digestion are normal; and they show a normal sleep/wake cycle. This may be a temporary or permanent state.

A disturbing aspect of VS is that people in this condition often appear to be aware of their surroundings. They might grip an object placed in their hand, or grimace and smile, which can mislead carers into thinking that the person is aware. But the behaviour seen in VS patients is produced reflexively by activity in the brainstem and other 'lower' brain regions and does not signify recovery.

The minimally conscious state

Some patients emerge from the vegetative state into the minimally conscious state, in which their responses to stimuli are above reflex level. For example, they may follow somebody's movements with their eyes or even be able to blink or move their fingers – sometimes on command.

A rehabilitation team experienced in the assessment of profound brain damage should judge the level of a patient's awareness.

OUTLOOK

The outcome for coma and vegetative state patients depends on the cause, location, severity and extent of brain damage, and ranges from total recovery to death. It is difficult to predict what might happen in any individual case.

For those who remain in coma for several weeks and enter into the vegetative state, the outlook is not favourable. Some patients recover, but usually they have some disturbance of memory and some physical disability. Others

remain severely physically and mentally impaired and a small number remain unconscious. The chances of recovering from a short-lived coma, however, are generally good.

WARDING OFF DIABETIC COMA

Diabetics, especially those treated with insulin, are vulnerable to coma caused by unstable blood levels.

Blood sugar too high

Warning signs include increased thirst and urination, tiredness, breath smelling of nail varnish, and, eventually, unconsciousness.

Seek medical attention immediately as insulin and fluid will be needed. If detected early, increasing the insulin dosage can prevent the condition from worsening and control the diabetes

Blood sugar too low

Warning signs vary but often include feeling shaky, sweating, tingling lips, paleness, heart pounding, confusion, irritability and faintness leading rapidly to unconsciousness.

If the person is already unconscious seek medical attention urgently. A conscious person should take a sugary drink, followed by a starchy snack, such as a sandwich.

SEE ALSO *Brain and nervous system; Concussion; Consciousness; Head and injuries; Magnetic resonance imaging (MRI)*

Locked-in syndrome

Some people emerge from coma paralysed and unable to signal their 'return'. Their condition is called locked-in syndrome.

People with locked-in syndrome are often misdiagnosed as being in the vegetative state. They can hear and see, but apart from the ability to look upwards they are totally paralysed. Using the latest technology, such as eye-blink or eyebrow-controlled switches, they can use computers to write out messages, switch on the TV or radio or close the curtains – they can perform any activity that can be controlled by an electricity supply.

CONTACT **Royal Hospital for Neuro-disability** West Hill, Putney, London SW15 3SW (020) 8780 4500 (www.rhn.org.uk)

Community care

Community care means that individuals in need of care and support are looked after at home and in local day centres or surgeries, rather than in long-stay residential homes and hospitals, to help them remain independent.

The community care system has many merits – primarily that it enables people to live in their own homes with care and support tailored to individual circumstances. The services help people with mental illnesses, mentally handicapped people (now more usually referred to as people with learning disabilities), and physically disabled and elderly people.

WHAT ARE COMMUNITY CARE SERVICES?
Care is usually available locally from a number of sources run by statutory, private and voluntary organizations. All services are subject to an assessment of needs and the ability to pay towards the costs. Services vary from one local authority to the next. Ask your authority's social services department what community care is available in your area.

Home adaptations and equipment
If you are disabled, chronically ill or recovering from a major operation, a few well-planned adaptations at home can make the difference between your being able to live there safely and having to move or remain in hospital. An occupational therapist may visit your home to assess your needs. Possible adaptations include installing a stairlift, lowering kitchen worktops or adding handrails in the bathroom. There may be grants available to pay for alterations (see Your community care assessment, page 320).

Your local health authority may also loan equipment to help you in your home or to

Factfile

The many faces of the community care team

Specialists and general helpers combine to provide care in the community services.

Behind the scenes, the care manager ensures that health workers are in place and services ready when you need them. The care manager is available to help you if you want to discuss your package of services or need community care advice. In a single day, your package of services might bring you into contact with a care worker at a day centre, a care assistant when you return to your house and a community nurse, either in a health centre or at home. In some areas, direct payments for community care are made to those eligible for help. This is to pay for services from approved private providers.

Care manager

Following your community care assessment (see page 320), the care manager is responsible for drawing up a package of your needs. She or he will help you with any benefits you can claim.

▶ **Special needs worker**
In some areas the special needs team works with the education authority to provide support for children with learning disabilities.

▲ **Care worker**
Staff and volunteers in day centres and luncheon clubs provide a friendly face as well as helping people with everyday tasks such as getting up and down and using the toilet.

improve your mobility when you go out. Examples include a bedroom commode, walking aids and wheelchairs or hoists for getting out of bed or into a car.

Home help and day centres

Most authorities supply care assistants, either directly or through the voluntary or private sectors, to assist you in domestic and personal tasks. They may pop in two or three times a day or be present for the entire 24 hours if you have no other carers. You may also be able to travel in a local authority-funded bus, taxi or ambulance to a day care centre for companionship, meals and care.

Respite care and night-sitting

If a relative or friend cares for you at home, relief may be available in the form of respite care – a local authority carer will join you at home for a few hours each week or for a spell of a few days. This will give those who normally care for you a break. Night care can also be arranged. Night-sitters provide companionship and perform simple services such as turning you in bed or helping you to use the toilet. They are not normally medically qualified and so cannot carry out medical procedures, but they will be present to call assistance if necessary.

Meals on wheels and lunch clubs

Many local authorities provide a Meals on Wheels service. Meals are delivered to your home at lunchtime each day. In some areas, instead of Meals on Wheels precooked frozen meals are delivered for you to heat up at home. In other regions, authorities provide transport to a central lunch club. If you have special dietary needs, discuss them with your social worker, if you have one, or with the social services department.

Other services

Some local authorities provide a laundry service and incontinence pads. Washing is collected from your house and returned the next day. This is an important aid if you or the person for whom you are caring is incontinent. Authorities may also provide televisions, radios and library books to some chronically sick or disabled people. Some disabled people also qualify for a holiday at the expense of the local authority or in a local authority holiday home.

Health care

A major part of community care are the health care services provided by Primary Care Trusts through GP surgeries, community nurses, health centres, NHS hospitals and so on. NHS services available in your area will probably include

Other care workers

- Physiotherapist
- Community mental health nurse
- Occupational therapist
- Speech therapist
- Respite carer

▼ **Care assistant**
Home helps assist with domestic jobs such as cleaning, ironing and shopping or with personal tasks such as washing, shaving, drying and combing your hair or eating.

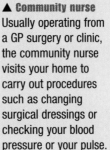

▲ **Community nurse**
Usually operating from a GP surgery or clinic, the community nurse visits your home to carry out procedures such as changing surgical dressings or checking your blood pressure or your pulse.

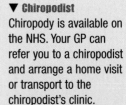

▼ **Chiropodist**
Chiropody is available on the NHS. Your GP can refer you to a chiropodist and arrange a home visit or transport to the chiropodist's clinic.

physiotherapy, and home visits by occupational therapists, chiropodists and community nurses. If you have a mental health problem you will be cared for by an NHS community psychiatric health nurse. When you have your community care assessment (see below) the social worker or other assessor should make note of your health needs and pass on the information to your GP and other relevant health professionals.

Care in residential and nursing homes
If after your assessment your local authority decides that it cannot economically support you in safety in your own home it may offer you a place in a residential/nursing home.

Will I be forced to leave home?
Government guidance to local authorities says that they should have the following priorities when they plan community care services: first, to try to support people at home; second, to provide a more suitable home, for example, sheltered housing; third, to move people to and support them in another household, such as that of a relative or close friend; only then, to move them into a residential/nursing home and only as a last resort, to recommend long-term hospital care.

However, after assessing your needs your local authority is permitted to offer the cheapest package of services that meets those needs. This means that if you need help, say, with washing and dressing in the morning, preparing your meals, taking your medicine twice a day, using the toilet, and preparing for bed at night, the authority might offer you a residential care place on the grounds that this is more economical than providing round-the-clock care in your home.

APPLYING FOR COMMUNITY CARE SERVICES
Contact your local authority if you feel that you need help under the community care system. You can apply on behalf of a relative, friend or neighbour if you have their permission to do so. If you care for another person, you can apply for community care support on your own behalf as a carer. The authority will perform an assessment to determine what your needs are and which services, if any, it can provide for you.

Your community care assessment
The assessment is carried out differently in different areas. It will usually take place as a face to face meeting in appropriate surroundings and time will be taken to answer your questions. Occasionally, certain details are discussed beforehand by telephone to establish the urgency of the situation. At the end of the assessment your care needs are clearly defined and if further help is needed an agreement is reached with the person, provided he or she is mentally capable.

In some areas, a social worker will perform the assessment, if appropriate, with the help of specialists such as a physiotherapist or an occupational therapist. In other regions, community nurses are responsible for assessments. The assessment can also usually be carried out in hospital if you are recovering from an operation, say, and preparing to be discharged.

The assessment focuses on your most pressing needs – these may be physical or learning disability, mental health problems or short-term incapacity after an operation. If you are an elderly person and find it difficult to walk around your home or have trouble managing stairs, the assessor will discuss with you the aids and adaptations that might enable you to overcome these difficulties. He or she will ask you what kind of help and services you want.

The assessor will also ask you how much help you receive from carers, family or friends and whether these people are willing to continue helping you. Because you may have to pay for some community care services, the assessment will include questions about how much money you have. If you qualify for benefits, the assessor will tell you which ones and how to apply. At the end of the assessment, he or she will usually ask you to sign a written statement of your needs.

Preparing for your assessment
The assessment gives you the chance to have your say about the kind of help you want. Be sure to explain your difficulties fully – for example, if you find it hard to lift things, think of all the daily activities that are affected. Some people find it helps to make a list of activities they find difficult. Another tip is to keep a diary of what you can and cannot do on good and bad days.

Your care plan
If you are approved for community care services, you should receive a written care plan, detailing

▼ **An adapted vehicle**
The UK charity Motability helps people with physical disabilities choose and afford adapted wheelchairs and cars. Motability offers advice on vehicles and practical adaptations. It runs hire and hire-purchase schemes and mobility benefits can be used to pay for the vehicle. Since its creation in 1977, Motability has helped provide more than 1.4 million vehicles to disabled people.

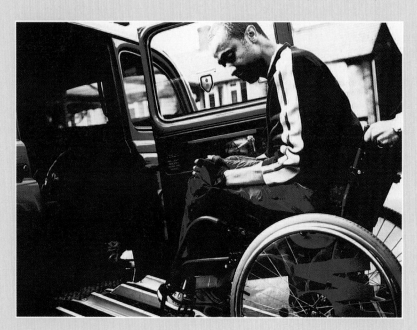

Help with paying for care

In the UK those in need of care may be entitled to a number of benefits that make it easier to meet the costs of services.

TYPE OF HELP	AVAILABILITY
Attendance allowance	Attendance allowance is payable to people over the age of 65 who have been ill or disabled for at least six months. Depending on the degree of illness, it provides for either 24-hour, or just day or night help.
Disability living allowance	A benefit payable to people under the age of 65 who need help with personal care, have been unable to walk or have great difficulty in walking, and/or have needed someone to watch over them for more than three months because of their physical or mental disability.
Aids and adaptations grants	In some circumstances, existing dwellings can be made suitable for disabled people through aids and adaptation grants to install stairlifts, downstairs toilets, ramps across single stairways and so on. If you are disabled you may be able to claim this assistance under the Chronically Sick and Disabled Persons Act 1970.
Available support	Assistance may be available through your local authority under the Chronically Sick and Disabled Persons Act 1970 in the form of services, including meals, disability aids, adaptations (to make areas of the home, such as the bathroom, easier to use), provision of television and transport. If you are disabled, you have a right for an assessment under the Act, and you must be provided with services if they are needed.
Other benefits	You may also qualify for means-tested benefits such as Income Support or Housing Benefit. Ask for advice at your local Citizens' Advice Bureau or GP surgery or contact voluntary agencies such as Help the Aged.

which services you will receive, the agencies that will provide them and a contact to deal with problems outside office hours.

If your circumstances change – for example, if you have a chronic illness and your condition worsens – you or your carer can apply to have your community care needs reassessed.

DISAGREEING WITH YOUR ASSESSMENT

Each local authority is required by law to provide a complaints procedure and a designated complaints officer. If you are unhappy with your assessment you should first talk informally to the person with whom you have been in contact at your local authority – most complaints are sorted out at this stage. If necessary you can make a written complaint and the complaints officer must reply within 28 days with an explanation. If you are still not satisfied, you can take the case to a

local authority review panel. You should also be invited to attend the meeting of the review panel to state your case. You can take a friend along for support or seek advice from the Citizens' Advice Bureau.

If the authority will not assess your needs
Some local authorities perform a 'screening' process to filter out people who ask for community care – perhaps by asking questions over the telephone. If you are given a brief interview of this sort and then refused a full community care assessment and you still feel that you need community care services, write to the authority and ask for your case to be reconsidered. If the authority refuses a second time, you may decide to use the complaints procedure. Under the law you are entitled to a full assessment if you are disabled, a carer or if you 'appear to the local authority to be in need of community care'.

MEANS TESTING

Most services provided by the NHS are free. But local authorities can charge for many of the care services they supply and a financial test is part of the community care assessment.

If you move into a residential or nursing home, you are not expected to pay for nursing care but you do have to pay for personal care and accommodation. If your main asset is your home, fees for the first three months of your stay in residential or nursing accommodation are waived. Thereafter, in order to meet the continuing cost of care, local authorities in England, Wales and Northern Ireland can make charges against the value of your property, provided your resources do not fall below a certain sum, which may vary annually. In Scotland, however, local authorities pay for the personal care costs of elderly people. There is no question of the family home being taken over while close relatives continue to occupy it. By arrangement, other members of your family may contribute to the costs of residential and nursing care.

CONTACT Age Concern Astral House, 1268 London Road, London SW16 4ER; helpline 0800 009966 (www.ageconcern.org.uk) **Disabled Living Foundation** 380–384 Harrow Road, London W9 2HU; helpline 0845 130 9177; textphone (0207) 432 8009 (www.dlf.org.uk) **Help the Aged** 207–221 Pentonville Road, London, N1 9UZ (020) 7278 1114 (www.helptheaged.org.uk) **Royal Association for Disability and Rehabilitation (RADAR)** 12 City Forum, 250 City Road, London EC1V 8AF (020) 7250 3222 (www.radar.org.uk)

Complementary therapies

There are more than 100 different health treatment systems that can be classed as complementary therapies. They all aim to treat the whole person on a mental, emotional and physical level.

Complementary therapies, also widely known as alternative therapies, can be used in conjunction with conventional medicine or, in some cases, in place of it. Many are recognized by the medical establishment and are available on the NHS, while others are on the fringes of credibility. In the 1970s it was regarded as very alternative to see an osteopath for a bad back, but today osteopathy is one of the more widely accepted complementary therapies.

The interest in alternative therapies has increased to such an extent that in some countries there are now more registered complementary therapists than there are GPs. Americans made twice as many visits to complementary practitioners during the 1990s as they did to their family doctors. Around half the population of the USA and Australia and one-third of people in the UK use complementary therapies of some sort.

Research shows that most people who choose to be treated with complementary therapy do so out of frustration with the available orthodox medical treatments, are satisfied with the results, and feel more in control of their illness.

HOW COMPLEMENTARY THERAPY WORKS

Whether you visit a chiropractor, reflexologist, acupuncturist or any other good complementary therapist, he or she is likely to spend a large part of the consultation listening to what you have to say. The therapist will search for the reason behind your health problem in addition to giving you symptomatic relief for the pain or disorder that brought you to seek help in the first place.

One of the biggest differences between orthodox and complementary therapies is that you and your therapist are seen as partners in your recovery. You are not the passive receiver of medical care, as is often the case in conventional

◀ **Healing herbs**
A vast range of plants is available to both the medical herbalist and the aromatherapist. Leaves, root, bark, seeds, flowers or berries may be used in herbal remedies or massage oils depending on their specific properties.

medicine. Imagine that you have arthritis, for example. A GP is likely to prescribe a synthetic drug to soothe the pain and reduce the inflammation, following a short appointment lasting perhaps ten minutes. A complementary practitioner, on the other hand, would usually spend an hour on a first appointment, take a detailed medical history, and would adopt a broader approach both to tackle the arthritis from different angles and to find out what is causing it. A medical herbalist, for example, would treat the pain or inflammation with herbal medication, and provide some soothing herbal poultices for use at home. The herbalist would talk to you about various issues.

■ **What you eat** The herbalist may suggest that you cut out foods that could aggravate your condition, such as red meat. You may also be referred to a nutritionist or clinical ecologist (a medical doctor who has undergone extensive further training in nutrition), who could check whether you have any of the food intolerances that can be linked with arthritis, and advise you on adapting your diet.

■ **Your job and lifestyle** The therapist may be able to help you to identify specific areas where your daily stress load could be reduced, or suggest stress-reducing techniques to suit you. This may help to alleviate certain symptoms of the arthritis and also enhance your overall well-being.

■ **Exercise or movement** The therapist may recommend appropriate gentle exercise, such as swimming, to help you to keep your body moving and prevent stiffness.

CHOOSING THE RIGHT THERAPY

The range of available therapies can seem bewildering, especially since many of them are said to help with a wide variety of different problems. The table on page 324 provides a rough guide to the complementary therapies that can be used to help common conditions. This should help you get the most out of your sessions.

Some forms of complementary therapy are available on the NHS via GP referral. Most British medical insurance companies will fund treatment by the major complementary therapies if recommended by your GP or a specialist. However, even if the therapy is being paid for by the NHS or a medical insurance company, you may still need to find the therapist yourself.

It is worth taking time to do a little research. Find out more about your condition and read up on the appropriate therapies, so that you can make an informed choice about the right one for you. Many complementary therapists belong to a professional association, which will often provide information about the therapy and its suitability for specific conditions. There are also helplines and support groups for many conditions. These can be a good source of information both about the condition and the treatment options available.

FIND A THERAPIST YOU TRUST

Many people find a therapist through word-of-mouth or by contacting the relevant professional association. Personal recommendation is usually the best indication of a trustworthy therapist, but remember that what suits a friend may not suit you. The Institute of Complementary Medicine can provide contact details for therapists. Talk to the therapist for a few minutes over the phone before you make an appointment. Ask about their qualifications and where they trained, and check these out with the relevant body.

Work with your therapist

Whichever therapy you choose, give it some time to work. You may begin to feel better after the first session, but many therapies take a couple of weeks or longer to take effect. Ask the therapist how long it is likely to be before you see results.

Be an active participant in getting well. Follow any extra dietary or lifestyle advice or relaxation techniques that the therapist gives you. Ask questions about your treatment.

In the UK there are 40,000 registered complementary therapists and 36,000 GPs.

Checklist

To help to make your experience of complementary therapy a positive one, try following these steps.

Do

✓ Ask what is in any remedies or medicines that you are given – and expect an intelligible answer.

✓ Trust your instincts. If you do not feel comfortable with a practitioner, no matter how impeccable his or her qualifications, discontinue the treatment.

✓ Tell your GP if you are having complementary therapy.

✓ Tell your complementary therapist which prescription drugs you are taking, and whether you are receiving any other forms of complementary therapy.

Don't

✗ Choose a practitioner who promises you a 'cure', or who will not give an estimate of how many sessions you might need after the first in-depth consultation.

✗ Expect instant results.

✗ Stop taking prescription drugs without checking with your doctor first.

The variety of complementary therapies

So many forms of complementary therapy are available that the choice can be bewildering. The following lists are not all-inclusive but should provide you with a starting point. It is important to be aware that you should always contact your GP or hospital if you have any conditions that require either surgery or an emergency life-saving procedure.

Common complaints

There are some generally useful complementary therapies. These include:

- **acupuncture** – (left) can help to relieve headaches, insomnia and tiredness;
- **Ayurvedic medicine** – has been used to treat eczema, asthma and arthritis;
- **Chinese herbal medicine** – treats eczema, hay fever, asthma, bronchitis and menstrual problems.
- **herbal medicine** – treats many of the same kinds of problems as Chinese herbal medicine;
- **homeopathy** – can be used to treat a wide variety of complaints, including colds, coughs and allergies;
- **naturopathy** – useful in treating arthritis, emphysema, ulcers, allergies, rashes and colds.

Muscular and skeletal problems

Back pain, sciatica, neck pain, joint problems, sports injuries and related problems, such as some headaches, may be treatable by:

- **Alexander technique** – by training the body to adopt the correct posture, all manner of muscular and skeletal problems can be improved. It also helps respiratory and digestive disorders;
- **Bowen technique** – light, precise movements can release tension in the muscles and realign the body, so easing pain and disorders in the muscles, joints and spine;
- **chiropractic** – can relieve pain through joint manipulation. Can be used for slipped discs, sciatica, lumbago and tennis elbow;
- **cranial-sacral therapy** – subtle manipulation of the head can help back and neck pain as well as migraine;
- **Feldenkrais technique** – lessons in the correct movement of the body can help to ease back and neck pain and muscle injuries;
- **massage therapies** – gentle manipulation and deep tissue work can take muscles out of spasm and improve the blood supply, so enhancing the healing process;
- **osteopathy** – treats mechanical problems associated with the spine, joints and muscles. Used for neck and back pain, sports injuries and osteoarthritis;
- **rolfing** – deep tissue massage helps realign the body and so eases pain and tension in spine and joints.

Stress-related problems

Stress can be linked to a wide range of conditions. Complementary therapists believe that these conditions can often be improved by working to relieve underlying stress:

- **acupuncture** – the purpose is to restore the body to a state of balance, which naturally relieves any stress;
- **aromatherapy** – scented oils and, perhaps, gentle massage relax or stimulate the body and mind;
- **autogenic training** – mental exercises tackle stress through autosuggestion;
- **Bach flower remedies** – aim to release emotional blocks and so enhance a person's sense of well-being;
- **colour therapy** – aims to improve mood and relieve stress through the use of colour;
- **homeopathy** – individualized remedies can treat emotional problems and stress;
- **massage** (above) – relieves stress by inducing a feeling of deep relaxation;

- **reflexology** – massaging certain points on the feet and so rebalancing the body's systems promotes relaxation and relieves stress;
- **reiki** – a Japanese form of healing based on chanelling energy, it usually helps the recipient to feel deeply relaxed;
- **shiatsu** – a firm massage focusing on particular pressure points can improve vitality and release tension and stress;
- **tai chi ch'uan** – this gentle exercise involves graceful flowing movements that can relax the body and mind, so banishing stress. It also enhances the circulation and breathing.

COMBINING ORTHODOX AND COMPLEMENTARY MEDICINE

Many forms of complementary therapy are compatible with orthodox medicine: you do not necessarily have to choose between them. However, you should check with your doctor and the complementary practitioner if you wish to combine treatments.

If you have a chronic health problem such as asthma or arthritis, it may respond best to two or three therapies simultaneously, as well as some sensible self-help measures.

Safety

Complementary therapies generally work more gently and subtly than much of orthodox medicine. The therapist will seek a more complete understanding of the patient as an individual and involve him or her in the treatment. But some treatments can still cause harm if used inappropriately or by a therapist who has not been properly trained. For example, manipulation techniques such as those used in osteopathy and chiropractic can damage nerves and vertebrae, and there is even the risk of a stroke. If acupuncture needles are inserted incorrectly they may cause pain, swelling, bleeding and, very occasionally, nerve damage.

There is no reliable information about the incidence of adverse side effects from most complementary therapies; however, studies suggest complication rates ranging from 3 to 24 per cent.

The orthodox view

The medical profession is increasingly receptive to complementary therapies. There is enthusiasm especially about integrated medicine, combining orthodox and complementary treatments.

■ Ten per cent of GPs now treat their patients with complementary therapies themselves. For example, one in five Scottish GPs has a basic training in homeopathy.

■ Complementary therapies are a growing part of multidisciplinary services in NHS hospitals on palliative-care units, such as pain clinics and cancer units. Acupuncture is now used in most NHS chronic pain services.

■ Four out of ten GP practices in the UK were providing some form of complementary medicine services for their patients in l995. It is estimated that by 2001 the figure was nearer 50 per cent.

RESEARCH INTO COMPLEMENTARY THERAPY

The Research Council for Complementary Medicine in the UK, which has worked with both the Office of Alternative and Complementary Medicine and the National Institutes of Health in the USA, has a database of 1500 randomized controlled trials. The majority of these support the efficacy of complementary therapy. But more research is needed. Certain factors limit the extent to which complementary therapies are researched.

■ **Methods** It is difficult to research many forms of complementary therapy using the techniques employed for evaluating orthodox medicine. Because of this, most orthodox doctors feel that much of the research available is not of a sufficiently high standard.

■ **Language** Large bodies of published research on traditional Eastern systems of medicine, such as Ayurveda and acupuncture, do exist. But most of it has not been translated into English.

■ **Funding** There is a lack of funding available for research into complementary therapy. Drug-based trials are backed by pharmaceutical companies, but there is little incentive for these companies to fund natural remedy trials. The government-funded Medical Research Council, the other major source of backing for research in the UK, spent no money funding complementary therapy research in 1998. Medical charities, the only other significant source of research funds, spent 0.05 per cent of their combined total research budgets on complementary therapies in 1999.

The placebo effect

Many orthodox doctors suggest that much of the success of complementary medical treatments is due to the placebo effect, rather than the fact that the therapies genuinely work. Others take the more pragmatic attitude that even if this is true, the reason why a therapy works is less important than the fact that it does so.

The word 'placebo' comes from the Latin for 'I will please'. In medical terms, the placebo effect occurs when someone is given an inactive pill, liquid or powder that has no treatment value, but the person feels better afterwards because he or she expects to do so.

When scientists are researching the effectiveness of a new drug, they usually test it against a placebo and do not tell the trial participants which one they are being given. An average of 30 per cent of people in any clinical trial will experience the placebo effect, and the figure can be as high as 90 per cent.

SEE ALSO *Individual therapy entries*

CONTACT **Institute for Complementary Medicine (ICM)** PO Box 194, London SE16 7QZ (020) 7237 5165 (www.icmedicine.co.uk). Answers queries and provides information on courses, practitioners and careers.
Research Council for Complementary Medicine Email: info@rccm.org.uk (www.rccm.org.uk) The council offers a research database and can help with finding and choosing a therapist.
British Complementary Health Medicine Association (www.bcma.co.uk)

Concentration, loss of

Concentration is when we focus our attention on one task to the exclusion of others, such as when we write a letter or play the piano. Concentration is thought to be a function of parts of the brain directly behind the forehead. People lose concentration temporarily and variably when they are tired, anxious, emotionally upset or when infections or serious illnesses affect brain function. More specifically, consistent loss of concentration can be a sign of brain disorders such as **dementia, depression** or psychosis. Children with **ADHD** are easily distracted and find it very difficult to keep their attention on particular activities (see **Behaviour problems in children**).

SEE ALSO *Alzheimer's disease, Brain and nervous system*

Conception

Conception is the moment of fertilization, when a sperm breaks through the outer layer of an egg in one of the woman's Fallopian tubes. The nuclei of the two cells fuse to create a single cell with the potential to develop into a baby. This cell contains 46 chromosomes – 23 from each parent – which determine the baby's genetic make-up. The fertilized egg, called a zygote, divides into two identical cells, and continues to grow by splitting into four cells, then eight, 16, 32 and so on, eventually forming three layers (the ectoderm, mesoderm and endoderm), from which the fetus develops. There are around 10,000 million cells in the adult human.

SEE ALSO *Contraception; Genetics and genetic disorders; Infertility; Pregnancy and problems*

Concussion

Concussion may occur after a brief period of unconsciousness following injury to the head or neck, but severe whiplash or shaking may also produce concussion. Unconsciousness may only last for a few seconds and after this the concussed person may fall over or stagger about looking vacant. Other symptoms may include headache, confusion and loss of memory.

People with concussion experience symptoms because their injury has disrupted electrical activity in the brain. In simple concussion this rights itself quickly, but thinking and sensation may be affected for several minutes, making the person confused and dizzy. If brain activity does not resume, the person goes into a **coma**.

The disruption of normal activity in the brain prevents the memory recording what happened immediately before concussion and as a rule people with concussion do not remember how it happened. It is also quite common to be unable to recall any events in the hour or two before the incident that caused the concussion.

COMPLICATIONS

Most cases of concussion are associated with bleeding or bruising in the brain and the destruction of some nerve tissue. These are potentially dangerous and need immediate medical attention, so a doctor should always be consulted as soon as possible after concussion.

TREATMENT

If there are no immediate symptoms, the affected person should rest quietly for 24 hours under observation and contact a doctor if the following are experienced:

- vomiting or nausea;
- breathing difficulties;
- visual disturbances.

▶ **Egg race**
During sex a man may deposit up to 1000 million sperm at the upper end of the vagina. Of these a few thousand may swim into each Fallopian tube, a few hundred may reach the egg and one may penetrate the egg's outer layer. Within 30 minutes of this, the egg's outer layers are impervious to other sperm.

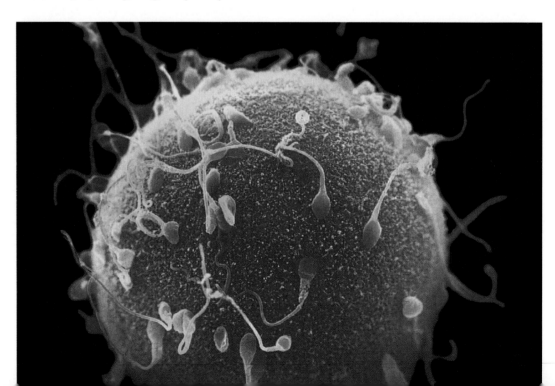

Any person who may have been concussed and who fails to recover fully in the course of the few days following an incident should visit the doctor again.

What you can do

Everyday activities can be just as dangerous as high-risk ones: you are just as likely to be concussed if you have an accident while cycling without a helmet as you are if you take part in violent or dangerous sports. It is sensible to always protect the head by wearing a suitable helmet or other protective headgear if you take part in any activity where head gear is recommended.

OUTLOOK

A single episode of concussion is unlikely to be harmful but repeated hard blows to the skull, such as a boxer might endure, may lead in the long term to impaired concentration, slow thinking and slurred speech.

SEE ALSO **Brain and nervous system; Head and injuries**

Confusion

Confusion is to some degree a part of normal life – for example, a person who is woken suddenly from a deep sleep remains confused until the brain re-orients itself to the outside environment. But a person who is confused for no obvious reason or continues to suffer confusion for longer than a few seconds needs medical attention. The confusion may be a symptom of dementia, poisoning, stroke, seizure, head injury or **concussion**.

SYMPTOMS

The various symptoms of confusion are not always immediately apparent and may not be noted until a range of symptoms occur simultaneously.

■ The confused person's attention meanders or flits from one thing to another.

■ When the person is given something on which to focus attention, such as words to read or a simple puzzle to perform, he or she cannot concentrate.

■ The person fails to react to significant new features in the environment, such as someone entering the room.

■ The person may be unable to follow a train of thought or grasp what is said.

■ The person seems to have forgotten how to carry out routine tasks such as using a telephone.

■ The person continues or repeats an action long after the original stimulus to act has passed – for example, he or she carries on waving away a fly when the fly is no longer nearby or continues wiping a misted window when the need to do so has been removed.

■ The person mutters or speaks in nonsensical or disjointed sentences.

Symptoms of confusion often appear in association with other mental dysfunctions such as hallucinations, amnesia, agitation or apathy, weakness, trembling and emotional instability.

CAUSES

Confusion is essentially a dysfunction of attention. The brain areas that control attention are very widely distributed around the brain, so almost anything that interferes with brain function can cause confusion (see **Brain and nervous system**). The condition may come on suddenly (acute confusion) or creep up over a period of weeks (chronic confusion).

Likely causes of acute confusion include:
■ Inflammation of the brain tissue (encephalitis), resulting from a viral or bacterial infection such as flu.
■ Drunkenness.
■ Taking drugs – for example, barbiturates, tranquillizers, antidepressants, antihistamines or narcotics (drugs derived from opium, including painkillers such as codeine and morphine, as well as heroin).
■ Head injury.
■ Stroke.
■ Seizure.

Causes of chronic confusion may be:
■ Dementia.
■ Alcohol dependence.
■ Metabolic disorders – for example, **kidney** failure, excess blood sugar (**hyperglycaemia**), **acidosis**, **anaemia** or **liver** failure.
■ Temporary disruption of the circulation to part of the brain. These mini-strokes or Transient Ischaemic Attacks (TIAs) may not be noticed when they first occur.
■ **Schizophrenia.**
■ **Depression.**

It should not be assumed that confusion in an elderly person is an indication of dementia. A doctor should carry out a thorough physical examination to check for other possible causes before making a diagnosis.

TREATMENT

The treatment of confusion depends on the underlying condition. If no obvious cause is found, confusion may be treated with tranquillizers if other symptoms include agitation, or with antidepressants if the confusion is associated with apathy.

SEE ALSO **Alcohol and abuse; Amnesia; Brain and nervous system; Dementia; Drugs, medicinal; Encephalitis; Head and injuries; Metabolism and disorders; Poisoning and gassing; Schizophrenia; Seizure; Stroke**

Congenital disorders

In the developed world congenital disorders, also known as birth defects, are one of the commonest causes of death in babies just before, during and shortly after birth. They are often due to genetic (hereditary) abnormalities.

Most congenital disorders take the form of visible abnormalities that are present from birth. Thousands of such disorders are now recognized, including several that are fatal and cause stillbirth. Some spontaneously correct themselves over time.

Congenital defects of the brain and central nervous system and of the heart and blood vessels are the main causes of infant death in developed countries such as the USA and the UK. The majority of deaths from such disorders occur in the first year of life, mostly in the first month.

On average 30 in 1000 babies born worldwide have a congenital disorder.

TYPES OF DISORDER

There are three types of congenital disorder. Disorders caused by the defective or abnormal development of an organ or body part are called malformations. They include congenital heart defects, **spina bifida, cerebral palsy** and biochemical disorders such as **cystic fibrosis, sickle cell anaemia** and **muscular dystrophy.**

Those caused by damage to a part of a fetus that has previously developed normally are called deformations. An example is club foot.

Those caused by the abnormal development of tissues – which may involve skin, bones, nerves, organs or other tissue – are generally described by doctors as dysplasia.

CAUSES

Congenital disorders may be caused in one of several ways. Some are due to the effects of a mutation (change) in a single dominant gene or in a pair of recessive genes (see **Genetics and genetic disorders**). These mutations may be inherited or may arise spontaneously.

Other disorders are caused by abnormalities involving whole chromosomes or sections of chromosomes (see **Chromosomal disorders**). Some are caused by several genes acting together with an environmental factor.

Some are caused by a fetus being exposed to a teratogen, a chemical or drug that has a harmful effect on fetal development, others by abnormal conditions within the womb – as in the case of club foot, which is caused by a normal foot being crowded during its growth in the womb.

DIAGNOSIS, TREATMENT AND SURVIVAL

Congenital disorders may not be discovered until after a baby is born, although new techniques using ultrasound have made certain abnormalities easier to diagnose antenatally (see page 330). Surgical advances, especially the introduction of cardiopulmonary bypass, have dramatically reduced mortality from congenital heart disorders in the developed world since around 1960.

Babies born with **Down's syndrome** now have a much greater life expectancy than used to be the case. About 90 per cent survive beyond five years of age, although respiratory infections and added complications of congenital heart disorders can still cause early death.

Spina bifida – failure of vertebrae to close during development to protect the spinal cord – is often associated with **hydrocephalus**, swelling of the head due to fluid being unable to drain away from the spaces around the brain. Both conditions can be repaired: by plastic surgery to close the vertebrae and fitting a valve to allow fluid to drain from the brain. **Anencephaly**, the absence of most or all of the brain, is untreatable and always fatal.

THE FUTURE

The rate of serious abnormalities such as Down's syndrome and central nervous system disorders has dropped since 1985 in the developed world. This has been attributed to improved and more accessible screening methods. In addition it is now known that if a woman takes folic acid before conception it reduces the chances of central nervous system defects such as spina bifida.

Research suggests that genetic screening will be developed to detect not only mutations but genetic variations that are partially responsible for characteristics such as intelligence or susceptibility to heart disease or mental illnesses. Doctors are united in opposing the development of screening tests for trivial defects and non-life-threatening characteristics, and would be against offering abortion in cases where these defects have been identified. Strict controls will be needed to prevent the misuse of advances in genetics and screening techniques.

In the long term, **cloning** techniques may make it possible to add genes to an egg that will benefit not only the person who grows from the egg but also his or her descendants. As such techniques are developed, there is likely to be pressure to use them to try to improve family genes. Most scientists are opposed to such 'germ line gene therapy', but some believe there are circumstances in which it might be justifiable.

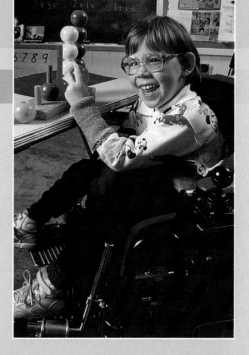

▼ **Enjoying life**
A four-year-old girl with cerebral palsy takes pleasure in educational play. Both at school and at home, a child with special needs should be treated as far as possible as a normal child.

Coping with long-term special needs

Parents who discover that their baby has a long-term health problem that may last for life often feel a sense of great sadness and disappointment. They may also wonder if they are in some way responsible for their infant's condition and suffer irrational feelings of guilt about it.

Coming to terms with a congenital disorder takes up a great deal of time and emotional energy – which means that there is less time and energy available for relationships with other members of the family.

This is normal and natural, and as long as a normal equilibrium is restored it will do no lasting harm. But, once the shock has been absorbed, it is essential for everyone's sake, including that of the child affected, to return to a proper balance. The special needs of a child with a long-term health problem are part of family life rather than its central issue.

Mothers should not try to carry the strain of coping with a child with special medical needs on their own – nor should they be expected to. Close friends and other family members should provide support and be called

upon for it. Both parents, not just the mother, should be involved in discussions with doctors and in key decisions about the future.

It is important for parents to remember that a child with special needs, like any other child, needs encouragement more than protection, and love more than either. As far as possible, a child with special needs should be treated as a normal child, obeying the same household rules as other children (thereby avoiding jealousy) and sharing normal activities and social life with them.

Screening for congenital disorders

A number of screening tests are available that enable the early detection of abnormalities before birth.

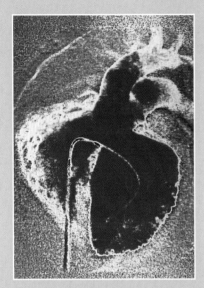

▲ **Heart disease**
A defect called a 'hole in the heart', revealed in this angiogram, causes enlargement of the heart and the pulmonary artery.

Some women are more likely to have babies born with congenital abnormalities, and in such cases doctors will generally offer, in addition to normal blood tests, ultrasound scanning (see below), amniocentesis, chorionic villus sampling (CVS) or fetoscopy to check for abnormalities. Even if a woman has indicated that she would not consider having an abortion if serious genetic abnormalities were identified, the tests may be done to prepare her. Some abnormalities can be corrected in the womb.

ULTRASOUND

Ultrasound scanning uses beams of high-frequency soundwaves directed into the womb from a probe (the transducer) placed on the abdomen. Some of these waves are reflected in an echo effect: bone and gas reflect a lot of sound and show up as white in the scan; the placenta, which does not reflect so well, appears grey; the amniotic fluid does not reflect any sound at all so it appears black. By recording the echoes, a detailed picture can be built up of the fetus's position, size and shape and any abnormalities can be identified.

Recent improvements in image sharpness mean that ultrasound scanning can now be used to detect a growing number of congenital disorders. Scanning can now be carried out early enough for abortion to be offered if the parents so wish. These include **spina bifida, hydrocephalus,** anencephaly, achondroplasia (a growth disorder in which the arm and leg bones fail to grow) and congenital **heart** abnormalities.

The level of risk

Ultrasound scanning is painless and can be used repeatedly with apparently no health risk to the mother or to the fetus she is carrying.

AMNIOCENTESIS

By performing an **amniocentesis** a doctor can take fetal cells for chromosomal analysis without disturbing the fetus itself. In an amniocentesis the cells are taken from the amniotic fluid that surrounds the fetus, in which such cells are always present. The chromosomes in the cells can be examined to reveal chromosomal disorders such as Down's syndrome. The amniotic fluid itself can also be analysed to provide evidence that indicates the presence of some other disorders. Higher-than-normal levels of alphafetoprotein, for example, may indicate a fetus affected by spina bifida.

Using ultrasound scanning to detect abnormalities

Women are given a routine ultrasound in about the 12th week of pregnancy to check progress and confirm the forecast delivery date.

Those at risk of having a baby with congenital abnormalities have a second scan in the 16th or 17th week of pregnancy to check for problems. Water-soluble oil is spread over the mother's abdomen so that the scanning head makes good contact with her skin. The handheld transducer is moved over her abdomen and picks up the reflected signal (see main text) before transmitting it to the analyser, which converts the electrical signal into a picture on the screen (right). The scanner produces 30 pictures a second, so radiographer and mother can see the baby moving. The image is recorded on videotape for doctor and nurses to examine later. Some hospitals offer nuchal transparency scans which measure a layer of fluid between two folds of skin in the back of the baby's neck, and can reveal evidence of Down's syndrome.

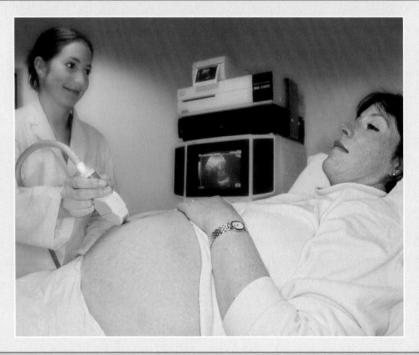

How common are genetic disorders?

Around 2–3 per cent of babies born in the UK have a congenital disorder – 13,000 babies a year. Frequency figures given below are per 10,000 births.

DISORDER	TEST	FREQUENCY
Cardiovascular disorder	Fetoscopy	9.75
Cleft lip and palate	Fetoscopy	7.2
Down's syndrome	Amniocentesis	5.8
Sickle-cell anaemia	Fetoscopy	1
Spina bifida	Amniocentesis	1.1

Pregnant women over the age of 38 are normally offered amniocentesis (or chorionic villus sampling, see below) because they have a higher then normal risk of having a baby affected by Down's syndrome. The test may also be offered to women who have already had a child with Down's syndrome or those who have a close relative with the syndrome.

How it is performed

A local anaesthetic is given and then a hollow needle is inserted through the abdominal wall and uterus into the amniotic sac in order to suck out a small fluid sample. The procedure is painless, although the woman may feel a slight pricking. Amniocentesis is usually performed around the 15th–16th week of pregnancy. Throughout the procedure an ultrasound image is generated as a visual guide to the doctor inserting the needle.

The level of risk

Amniocentesis carries a 0.25–0.5 per cent risk of causing a miscarriage, so is used only when the likelihood of having a baby affected by a serious condition outweighs the risk of abortion. The biggest disadvantage of amniocentesis is that it takes place relatively late in pregnancy, and the wait for results is weeks rather than days. The emotional strain of choosing to abort at the fourth or fifth month can be hard to bear.

CHORIONIC VILLUS SAMPLING

Chorionic villus sampling, or CVS, has been developed in recent years to make it possible to sample fetal cells for suspected genetic abnormalities at a much earlier stage of pregnancy than is possible using amniocentesis. It is carried out around the 10th to 12th week of pregnancy.

How it is performed

Using an ultrasound image for guidance, the doctor inserts a fine hollow needle into the uterus in order to draw off a few cells from the villi at the edge of the placenta. These cells come from the fetus and can be analysed for genetic, chromosomal or biochemical abnormalities. The advantage of chorionic villus sampling over amniocentesis is that it allows earlier and therefore safer abortion.

The level of risk

The test has the disadvantage of a 2 per cent risk of inducing miscarriage – higher than that for amniocentesis. In some teaching hospitals, however, where doctors perform the test several times a day, the risk is far lower.

FETOSCOPY

Fetoscopy is less commonly used than amniocentesis or chorionic villus sampling because it has a much greater risk of causing miscarriage. It is carried out after the 16th week of pregnancy. Fetoscopy is a hi-tech procedure normally only available in larger hospitals.

How it is performed

A thin, flexible hollow tube fitted with a light and a telescopic probe is inserted into the uterus through a small cut through the abdominal wall, made under local anaesthetic. The instrument, called a fetoscope, is used to look at the fetus and to take fetal blood samples from the umbilical cord. Medical staff use ultrasound to guide the fetoscope and avoiding harming the fetus.

Abnormalities of the face, limbs or body can be viewed, and the fetal blood can be tested for disorders such as thalassaemia or sickle-cell anaemia. A camera is often attached to the instrument to take pictures of the fetus for later use in diagnosis.

The level of risk

Fetoscopy carries a 3–5 per cent chance of miscarriage. It is used only when the mother is at high risk of carrying an abnormal fetus.

GENETIC COUNSELLING

Families with a history of genetic disorders or those who already have a child affected by a genetic disorder may want genetic counselling. This can be arranged through a family doctor. A genetic counsellor can explain how a condition caused by a genetic mutation comes about, and the risks of passing on the condition to another child and to future generations.

CONTACT **Association for Spina Bifida and Hydrocephalus** 42 Park Road, Peterborough PE1 2UQ (01733) 555988 (www.asbah.org). **Down's Syndrome Association** Langdon Down Centre, 2a Langdon Park, Teddington TW11 9PS; 0845 230 0372 (www.dsa-uk.com) **Grown Up Congenital Heart Patients Association** 75 Tuddenham Avenue, Ipswich, Suffolk IP4 2HG; helpline 0800 854 759 (www.guch.demon.co.uk)

Conjunctivitis

Conjunctivitis is a very common disorder of the eye. It involves inflammation of the normally transparent membrane called the conjunctiva that covers the white of the eye and the inner surfaces of the eyelids. The redness is caused by the widening of tiny blood vessels in the membrane, and is usually temporary.

Most cases of conjunctivitis are the result of allergy or infection by bacteria or viruses, or by irritation caused by chemicals, cigarette smoke or contact lenses or, for example, hay fever. Both eyes may be affected, often one after the other.

Acute conjunctivitis lasts for anything from a few days to a few weeks, depending on the cause and whether effective treatment is given. Chronic conjunctivitis lasts for months or years, or may be virtually permanent.

SYMPTOMS

Conjunctivitis causes only slight discomfort or irritation, frequently accompanied by a mild gritty sensation or itching. Sharp pain combined with the feeling that there is a foreign body in the eye is not usually a symptom of conjunctivitis. There are several other signs.
- Pinkness or redness in the membrane covering the white of the eye may be localized or may extend over the whole surface.
- There is commonly a discharge, which may result in blurred vision and cause the eyelids to stick together.
- Occasionally there is a small tender swelling in front of the ear on the same side as the affected eye, and a general feeling of malaise; this is typical of viral conjunctivitis.

TREATMENT

Do not try to treat yourself – it is easy to make the problem worse. Seek medical advice.

What a doctor may do

Sometimes a doctor may refer a person with conjunctivitis to an ophthalmologist, especially if the conjunctivitis is particularly virulent – as, for example, may occur in a newborn infant. Before deciding whether a referral is necessary, the doctor will do some or all of the following.
- Examine the eyes with a hand lens and torch.
- Take a swab of the discharge, if any.
- Check that the vision is unimpaired.
- Carry out tests to eliminate more serious conditions such as acute **glaucoma**, corneal ulcer (see **Cornea and disorders**), a foreign body in the eye, or internal eye inflammation.

Depending on the cause, the doctor may prescribe **antibiotics**, antiviral drugs, anti-inflammatory drops or antihistamine drops (see **Allergy**). Lubricants or **decongestant** drops may occasionally be prescribed.

SEE ALSO *Eye and problems*

Connective tissue disorders

Connective tissue disorders affect the tissue that binds together cells in the skin, joints, muscles and blood vessels. Connective tissue is made up of various proteins, of which collagen is the most important (see also **Collagen diseases**).

Disorders affecting connective tissue are persistent and recurring, with periods of remission; their complexity makes them hard to diagnose. For example, Sjogren's syndrome (dryness of the mouth together with dryness of the eyes) is a connective tissue disorder associated with rheumatoid **arthritis**; it occurs in 6–10 people in every 1000 in the UK. Systemic **lupus** erythematosus is another connective tissue disorder.

CONTACT **Arthritis Research Campaign** Copeman House, St Mary's Court, St Mary's Gate, Chesterfield, Derbyshire S41 7TD; helpline 0870 850 5000 (www.arc.org.uk)

Consciousness

In normal consciousness people are aware of their surroundings, their own existence and that of others. When brain activity is interfered with in some way, a person may enter an altered state of consciousness.

Altered states may be pleasurable and self-induced, such as the sensation of being drunk. But an altered state may be an intensely frightening symptom of illness such as the auditory hallucinations experienced by someone with **schizophrenia** or **manic depression**, or the visual hallucinations of someone with **delirium**.

Some altered states – such as lucid dreams and out-of-body experiences – occur spontaneously. These show that the brain is capable of a wider range of conscious awareness than is normally experienced. The following are altered states.
- Out-of-body experience – a feeling of leaving one's body, which may include 'seeing' oneself from another point of view.
- Near-death experience – a phenomenon that can affect people in life-threatening danger; it usually combines an out-of-body experience with the impression of moving along a tunnel towards a bright light, accompanied by a feeling of ecstasy.
- Trance – a state of detachment from one's physical surroundings that is usually combined with a feeling of great relaxation. It may be induced by **meditation, hypnosis,** or by repetitive actions such as ritual dancing.
- Intoxication – this may involve a blunting of the senses and confusion, such as can

occur after consumption of alcohol; intensity of sensation or hallucination following the use of a hallucinogenic drug such as LSD; intensified emotion after taking ecstasy or increased arousal following the use of cocaine.

■ Lucid dreaming – a term used to describe normal waking consciousness experienced while asleep; the dreamer 'wakes up' but continues to experience the dream.

SEE ALSO *Alcohol and abuse; Drugs, misuse of; Epilepsy*

Constipation

Constipation is a condition in which the bowel is emptied infrequently, the faeces are hard or small, or the elimination of faeces is difficult or painful. It can affect people at any age.

Constipation in babies is hard to diagnose. It may be normal for a baby or young child to defecate only every three or four days; dry, hard stools that are difficult to pass are a more reliable indication. Suspected constipation in infants should be treated by giving them extra bottles of water or diluted fruit drinks.

The tendency to constipation usually persists throughout life unless changes to diet and lifestyle are made. If the constipation has an underlying cause, such as **haemorrhoids**, treating the primary problem may help.

CAUSES

The possible causes of constipation include:
■ insufficient intake of dietary fibre;
■ inadequate fluid intake;
■ old age and consequent reduced mobility;
■ **drugs**, commonly **painkillers** and **antidepressants**;
■ dehydration and immobility caused by illness;
■ medical conditions such as **irritable bowel syndrome**, an underactive thyroid gland (see **Myxoedema**), **multiple sclerosis, stroke, lupus** and **Parkinson's disease**;
■ anal fissure – a tear of the skin at the entrance to the back passage, which makes passing faeces very painful (see **Anus and problems**);
■ pain caused by **haemorrhoids**;
■ the consequences of a surgical operation;
■ damage to the colon due to laxative abuse;
■ obstruction, narrowing or cancer of the bowel (see **Bowel and disorders**).

TREATMENT

Lifestyle changes are often the most effective way to treat constipation.

What you can do
■ Drink more fluids.
■ Eat a diet that includes plenty of fibre,

bran, bran cereals, wholemeal bread, fresh fruit and vegetables (see also **Diet**).
■ Apply soothing creams or ointments if the passage of faeces is painful.
■ Seek advice from your pharmacist on using laxatives and bulking agents – but as a short-term measure only.
■ For elderly people, encourage increased mobility and regular trips to the toilet.

When to consult a doctor
Seek medical advice if any of the following circumstances applies.
■ The problem persists for over two weeks.
■ The problem is severe or is not responding to treatment, and if there is any bleeding from the anus.
■ There has been a recent change in bowel habits, particularly if you are over 40.

What a doctor may do
A doctor is likely to advise on increasing fluids, improving diet and incorporating more exercise into the daily routine. Advice may be given on treatment with laxatives and suppositories. In cases where there is a buildup of faeces, an **enema** may be necessary.

A doctor will also investigate and treat any underlying illness. If a problem such as bowel **cancer** is suspected, the patient will be referred to hospital for specialized tests.

Complementary therapies
Herbal medicines and **massage** may help to relieve constipation.

PREVENTION
Adequate fluids and dietary fibre, combined with regular exercise, provide the most effective prevention against constipation.

COMPLICATIONS
Haemorrhoids may result from straining to pass faeces during prolonged constipation.

SEE ALSO *Bowel and disorders*

Consultant

A consultant is a highly trained and experienced specialist in a particular branch of medicine. Hospital consultants take a prominent role in all decisions about the diagnosis and treatment of patients in their care, although other team members assist in investigative tests and treatment procedures. In busy hospitals there may be several consultants at senior and junior level, assisted by a group of junior doctors.

Patients are referred to a consultant by their GP, and remain in the care of the same consultant unless the patient or GP considers it necessary to seek a second opinion about the patient's condition.

SEE ALSO *Medical staff*

Contact lenses and problems

Contact lenses are small, shaped lenses that are placed directly onto the front surface of the eye. They are used to correct optical defects such as short-sightedness, long-sightedness, astigmatism and presbyopia (see **Eye and problems**).

Sometimes contact lenses are fitted for therapeutic purposes – for example, to even out the distortions of vision caused by an irregular cornea or to protect a severely irritated eye.

Most vision defects are correctable with contact lenses, and the majority of people are able to wear them without too much discomfort – although certain environmental conditions, such as a dusty atmosphere, may increase the likelihood of problems such as chronic eye infection, dry eye or an unstable cornea.

In the case of severely short-sighted people, or where there is a large difference between the lens strength needed to correct each eye, contact lenses may provide a more comfortable and less distorting correction than spectacles.

HOW DO I GET CONTACT LENSES?

Contact lenses may be prescribed only by a registered doctor, optometrist or a dispensing optician with appropriate qualifications.

■ At your first appointment you will be given a full eye examination to check the health of your eyes and their suitability for wearing lenses.

■ A trial lens will be inserted to evaluate your response and to establish a good fit. The lens should be comfortable and stable, but not so tight as to restrict tear flow underneath the lens.

■ If you wish to wear lenses full time, you will be advised of a 'building-up' period that will help your eye to adapt to the presence of a lens and to a reduced oxygen supply.

USING CONTACT LENSES

The newer a lens is, and the less it is handled, the lower the risk of infection and the better the quality of image possible through the lens.

Soft lenses are available in a daily disposable form, or may be replaced weekly, fortnightly, monthly or at longer intervals. Rigid lenses tend to require replacement annually. Whatever type of lenses you wear, always keep a spare pair to hand in case of loss or damage.

Storing and cleaning contact lenses

Unless you use daily disposable lenses, you need to establish a routine for cleaning your lenses:

■ never rinse your lenses in tap water;

■ clean them using the recommended solutions;

■ keep the case clean and replace it regularly;

■ for lenses used over longer periods, enzyme tablets may be needed to remove protein.

Types of contact lens

The first 'hard' contact lenses, made of durable perspex, have been largely superceded by rigid gas-permeable lenses that allow the eye to 'breathe'.

Rigid gas-permeable lenses Rigid lenses are made from a variety of materials. Permeability ranges from high to low – the higher the permeability, the more oxygen gets through to the cornea, but the lens can be less durable. Lack of oxygen over an extended period of time can change the shape of the cornea. Rigid lenses can provide excellent vision for people who have pronounced astigmatism. Some people find them easier to handle than soft lenses, but they may initially be less comfortable to wear and require a longer period of adaptation. Rigid lenses need replacing once a year at least.

Soft lenses Soft lenses are made from a number of different materials, often hydroxyethyl methacrylate or silicone hydrogels. The lenses range from those with a lower water content for shorter wearing times to those with a higher water content for longer wearing times. Newer silicone hydrogel materials allow continuous wear for several days at a time. Many, especially low-water content lenses, restrict the flow of oxygen to the cornea. Soft lenses are much more popular than rigid ones because of their initial comfort – they generally cannot be felt by the wearer after they have been in the eyes for a few minutes. But they carry a small risk of increased danger of infection and should be cleaned with extra care. Convention soft lenses usually need to be replaced every few months.

Disposable lenses New manufacturing techniques have made it possible for wearers to have a fresh pair of lenses regularly at reasonable cost. Daily disposable lenses do away with the need for a lens cleaning routine and cut the risk of infections. Alternatively, lenses can be replaced fortnightly, monthly or at longer intervals.

Cosmetic contact lenses Although tinted contact lenses are fashion accessories, they are not intended for personal use and are not to be shared or swapped. Swapping can pose a health risk to young people through cross infection. Further problems can arise when lenses are bought from non-ophthalmic outlets as no assessment of their suitability for wearing contact lenses will have been carried out and it is unlikely that any advice on lens care and hygiene will be received. Lenses should be bought only from a registered optical professional.

Problems associated with wearing contact lenses

If you wear contact lenses and one or both of your eyes becomes red, blurry or persistently uncomfortable, take out the lenses and seek the advice of your eye-care practitioner. If in doubt, take them out. Never rinse your lenses in tap water – it can cause infection.

SYMPTOM	POSSIBLE CAUSE	ACTION
Discomfort on putting lens in eye.	▪ Foreign body in eye. ▪ Damaged lens. ▪ Corneal abrasion (see **Cornea and disorders**).	▪ Remove, rinse and re-insert lens. ▪ Replace lens with a new one. ▪ Remove lens until eye is better. The eye will usually need a 24-hour break. Ask your practitioner for advice.
Discomfort after wearing lens for a short while.	▪ Deposits on lens. ▪ Allergic response to lens or to cleaning solution.	▪ Remove lenses more frequently for cleaning. Clean them even more carefully. Perhaps try another cleaning solution. ▪ Replace lens with a new one.
Discomfort even after removing lens.	▪ Possible corneal infection.	▪ Seek immediate medical advice.
Discomfort from time to time.	▪ Environmental factors such as smoke or dry air. ▪ Lens has moved to side of eye.	▪ Avoid known irritants, or ask for advice about a lubricant for the eye. ▪ Gently lift eyelid and, using other hand, move lens back into position with tip of finger.
Blurred vision.	▪ Wearing a right eye lens in a left eye and vice versa. ▪ Lens may be scratched or have a deposit on it. ▪ Lens does not fit properly.	▪ Remove lenses and re-insert them into the correct eye. ▪ Replace lens. ▪ Change in prescription needed.
Red eye.	▪ Infection. ▪ Allergic response to solution or lens.	▪ Remove lens and seek medical advice. ▪ Change solutions or lens material – ask your practitioner for advice – or change to daily disposable lenses.

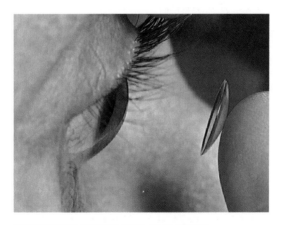

▶ **Inserting a lens**
Place the lens, concave side uppermost, on the inside tip of an index finger. Using a finger from the other hand, gently lift the top eyelid. Looking straight ahead, place the lens on the centre of the eye.

CONTACT LENSES AND CHILDREN

The high level of care needed to keep lenses clean and safe means that they are not suitable for young children. Older children may wear lenses, but they and their parents need to be aware of the hygienic measures to avoid infections and other problems. Children who wear lenses must have frequent checkups to monitor the health of their eyes.

FOLLOW-UP CARE

▪ Eye health and vision should be regularly checked if you wear contact lenses. It is vital to be diligent about attending your aftercare appointments.

▪ At each checkup your practitioner will look for changes in the cornea, such as the growth of new blood vessels at the edge of the cornea or localized areas of clouding – these indicate that insufficient oxygen is getting through. You may have to reduce the amount of time you wear lenses or change to a different lens material.

Contagious diseases

Contagious diseases are diseases that are spread from one person to another by direct or social contact person-to-person. All contagious diseases – measles, chickenpox or the common cold, for example – are infectious, but many infectious diseases – typhoid, syphilis or AIDS, for example – are not contagious because they are spread by means other than person-to-person direct or social contact. Infectious diseases that are not contagious can be spread in many ways, including through contaminated food or water, sexual contact or contaminated blood.

Contraception

Contraception methods and advice are provided free of charge by the National Health Service and can be obtained from GPs, family planning clinics and many genito-urinary clinics.

The ideal method of contraception does not exist – for most people there is some inconvenience involved. The factors that influence the choice of method include its failure rate, ease of use, side effects, reversibility and the extent of interference with sexual spontaneity. There are also medical factors such as age, history and lifestyle risks, as well as religious beliefs that oppose artificial contraception.

BARRIER METHODS

These form a physical barrier that prevents sperm from reaching an egg. Male and female condoms, the diaphragm and the cervical cap are all barrier methods. Condoms are readily available, simple to use and help to prevent the spread of sexually transmitted infections (STIs) and **HIV**.

Polyurethane male condoms can prevent the loss of sensation sometimes felt with latex ones. The outer ring of female condoms may inhibit foreplay. Diaphragms and caps block or cover the cervix and require specialist fitting and annual checks. Poor-fitting diaphragms may increase the risk of cystitis. Both reduce the risk of cervical cancer and some STIs, but not HIV.

Latex condoms, caps and diaphragms can be damaged by oil-based lubricants and some vaginal medications. If one splits or slips during intercourse, seek emergency contraception.

CHEMICAL METHODS

These are contraceptive products containing chemical substances that kill sperm. They come in the form of pessaries, creams, jellies, foaming tablets, aerosols and vaginal sponges. They can be messy and may rarely cause irritation.

HORMONAL METHODS

Pregnancy can be prevented by altering a woman's hormonal balance. Introducing an increased level of hormones interferes with phases of her menstrual cycle, particularly ovulation.

The Pill

The most commonly used hormonal method is the Pill. There are two types: the combined oral contraceptive (COC) and the progestogen-only pill (POP), which used to be known as the 'mini-pill'. The combined oral contraceptive contains oestrogen and progestogen and prevents ovulation. It is the most commonly used form of contraception among women under 35. It reduces the risk of ovarian and endometrial cancer, but can cause temporary side effects such as weight changes, mood swings and nausea. The pill may also increase blood pressure. Periods on COCs may be shorter and lighter.

The progestogen-only pill thickens cervical mucus to prevent sperm reaching an egg and makes the lining of the uterus unfavourable for implanting an egg. It must be taken at the same time each day. This pill is useful for women who can not take the COC for health reasons such as an increased risk of a blood clot. A doctor should be consulted for further advice.

A woman should use an extra method of contraception if she takes the combined oral contraceptive more than 12 hours late or the progestogen-only pill more than three hours late.

Implants, injections and intrauterine system

These are slow-release methods of delivering progestogen, which work in the same way as the POP and provides contraception for three years. Implants consist of a tiny tube inserted into the

Contraceptive devices: reliability rates

The reliability of contraceptive methods (when they are used correctly) is usually expressed as a percentage of effectiveness.

FEMALE

Female sterilization	over 99%	Female condom	95%
Pill (COC)	over 99%	Diaphragm	92–96%
Implants/injections	over 99%	Cervical cap	92–96%
Pill (POP)	99%	Natural family planning	94%
IUS	98%	Vaginal sponge	90%
IUDs (depending on type)	98%		

MALE

Male sterilization	over 99%	Male condom	98%

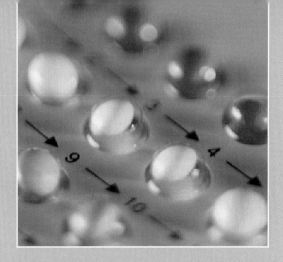

▶ **The Pill**
It is important to take the tablets as directed. Missing a dose, vomiting, diarrhoea and certain antibiotics may lose or reduce protection against pregnancy.

upper arm under local anaesthetic; fertility returns after they are removed.

Injections are given at 8- or 12-week intervals, depending on the type, and cannot be removed once given. Side effects include weight gain, and as with all hormonal methods effectiveness may be reduced by some prescription medicines.

The intrauterine system is a hormonal IUD releasing progestogen. It is an effective method and works for five years. Rarely, there is a risk that the device will perforate the uterus or that the body may expel it.

INTRAUTERINE DEVICES
An intrauterine device (IUD) is a plastic and copper device inserted into the womb via the cervix. It stops sperm from meeting the egg or the egg settling in the lining of the womb. The device works for three to ten years, depending on the type fitted. An IUD does not protect against sexually transmitted infections, so a condom may also have to be used. Disadvantages may include heavier or painful periods and the risk that the device may be spontaneously expelled. There may be slight bleeding between the first two or three periods after it has been fitted. Rarely, IUDs increase the risk of pelvic inflammatory disease and ectopic pregnancy.

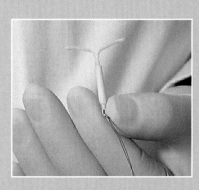

▲ **Intrauterine system (IUS)**
An IUS is fitted in the womb by a trained doctor. It slowly releases the progestogen hormone and works effectively for up to five years.

STERILIZATION
Sterilization is a surgical procedure that may be difficult to reverse and should only be considered if no more children are wanted. In women, the Fallopian tubes, along which the egg travels to the uterus, are cut or blocked by rings or clips. Men have a vasectomy, a minor operation in which the tubes that carry sperm from the testes to the penis are cut.

NATURAL FAMILY PLANNING
Different techniques can be used to predict fertile periods in a woman's cycle, allowing couples to abstain from sex at these times. This may be the only acceptable method for couples who do not want to use 'artificial' contraception. In a 28-day cycle, the fertile time is around 8–9 days.

Pregnancy is unlikely in the early and late phases of the cycle. However, individual cycles vary and sperm can survive for up to seven days, so infertile times can be difficult to predict. Natural family planning can take up to six cycles to learn effectively, and illness, stress and travel may make fertility indicators more difficult to interpret. Natural methods should be taught by a trained Natural Family Planning teacher.

New methods include predictive tests such as Persona, which interpret urine samples, and the temperature method, which relies on the fact that body temperature rises slightly around ovulation.

EMERGENCY CONTRACEPTION
Emergency hormonal contraception (sometimes known as the 'morning-after pill') should be taken within 72 hours of unprotected sex and is available from family planning clinics, NHS walk-in centres and pharmacies. Two pills are taken 12 hours apart. They are more effective the sooner the first pill is taken after sex. The second pill should be taken no later than 16 hours after the first. Hormonal methods work by preventing or delaying ovulation or from preventing implantation of the fertilized egg. A second choice of postcoital contraception is the insertion of an IUD up to five days after unprotected sex. This may stop an egg being fertilized or implanting in your womb and can be used as ongoing method of contraception.

CONTACT fpa (Family Planning Association)
2–12 Pentonville Road, London, N1 9FP; helpline 0845 310 1334 (www.fpa.org.uk)
Brook Advisory Centres Helpline 0800 0185 023 (www.brook.org.uk)

Contra-indication

A contra-indication is a symptom, condition or circumstance that makes it unwise to use an otherwise appropriate treatment. Drug manufacturers list the particular conditions that are contra-indications for a drug in the drug's patient information leaflet. This serves as a usage warning – 'if you have this condition, do not use this drug'. For example, if a liver disorder is a contra-indication for a drug, it means that if you have a liver disorder you risk adverse side effects if you take the drug.

In some cases, known as absolute contra-indications, the adverse effects can be very serious. **Allergy** to a drug or drug group such as penicillins, is an absolute contra-indication. If a drug, taken by a pregnant or breastfeeding mother, can cause damage to a baby, then pregnancy and breastfeeding will be listed as absolute contra-indications for the drug.

SEE ALSO *Drugs, medicinal*

Convulsions

Convulsions are the external physical signs of a **seizure**. People suffering convulsions may fall to the ground and writhe or jerk uncontrollably, or they may tremble all over while remaining standing. They may also lose bladder control and drool at the mouth, their eyes may flicker or roll upwards. They are generally not in control of their bodily actions.

Convulsions in young children

It can be frightening to witness a child having a convulsion but it is important to keep calm.

Babies and children under five can have fits if the brain becomes inflamed during the feverish stage of an infectious illness. Children suffering convulsions may twitch violently, clench their fists, arch their backs, hold their breath and go very red in the face and neck. Although frightening, isolated fits do not usually have any serious implication for a child's health. At least one in 30 children have them at some time. There is a slightly increased chance of a convulsion in the three months following the MMR (measles, mumps and rubella) vaccination.

If a fit occurs, call an ambulance – a child who has a convulsion should be seen by a doctor as soon as possible. Help the child to cool down by removing clothes and bedding but do not let him or her get cold. Put pillows around the child to stop bangs and bruising. If the child vomits, gently turn his or her head to one side to prevent choking.

CAUSES

Convulsions are caused by a temporary disturbance in normal brain activity. Neurons in one part of the brain suddenly start to fire (turn on and off) very rapidly and this abnormal activity may spread to the entire brain. The convulsions are the result of the uncontrolled firing of cells in the areas of the brain that produce physical movements. These movements are not under conscious control and a person having convulsions is usually entirely unaware of what is happening.

TREATMENT

Remove anything that could cause injury from around the person who is convulsing – knives, furniture with hard edges and hot drinks, for example. Do not attempt to interfere with people suffering convulsions unless they are in immediate danger – in the middle of the road, for example.

Biting the tongue is rare, and you do not need to try and wedge anything in the mouth of a convulsing person to prevent it. If you do so, you may cut the mouth and tongue or break the person's teeth while trying to insert the object, or cause them to choke.

If the convulsion continues for more than five minutes, call an ambulance. Otherwise, once the convulsions have stopped, the person should be placed in the **recovery position**.

Someone coming round from a convulsion will probably be confused and dazed for a few minutes and should be encouraged to lie quietly. The seizure may be followed by intense fatigue, and the person should be allowed to sleep it off.

Corn

A corn is a thickening of the skin on the toes and feet, usually caused by tight or badly fitted shoes. Soft corns may develop between the toes when they rub together. In hard corns, the skin's outer layer thickens when there is pressure on a bony part of the foot. The corn consists of a central core surrounded by thick layers of skin that become hard and inflexible.

You can buy corn plasters (small rings of sponge) over the counter in chemists. These help to relieve pressure on a corn. A chiropodist or your GP can pare down excess skin using a scalpel. Stubborn corns can be frozen off with liquid nitrogen – a chiropodist or the community nurse at your GP surgery can perform this treatment.

Corns can become infected, especially in diabetics. If you have diabetes and develop corns, have them treated promptly.

SEE ALSO *Chiropody; Foot and problems*

Cornea and disorders

The cornea is a thin transparent area at the front of the eyeball. It acts as the eye's main focusing structure, bending light through the eye's internal lens to a point of focus upon the **retina** (see diagram, **Eye and problems**).

DISEASES OF THE CORNEA

The cornea's transparency depends upon the collagen fibres in the stroma (see The layers of the cornea, right) being separated in a regular way that makes reflected light rays cancel one another out. Swelling of the cornea will disrupt this regular arrangement and make the cornea lose its transparency. Any of the following symptoms should be discussed with a doctor or ophthalmologist.

Keratitis

Keratitis is inflammation of the cornea. Contact lens wearers have an increased risk of keratitis: they must stop wearing lenses if keratitis is suspected (see **Contact lenses and problems**). There are four main types of keratitis. All require immediate medical attention.

■ Bacterial keratitis – usually following a wound or weakness that allows bacteria into the otherwise well-protected cornea. A sufferer will often feel severe eye pain, and may have redness in the areas adjacent to the cornea. Bacterial infection can lead to scarring of the cornea within hours. Corneal scarring can make you blind or severely reduce vision.

■ Viral keratitis – often caused by the **herpes** virus or an adenovirus (see **Viral infections**). A sufferer from viral keratitis will feel eye pain and may also feel unwell, possibly with a sore throat and swollen glands. If you think you may have viral keratitis, avoid using steroid eye drops as they may make the infection worse.

■ Amoebal keratitis – for example, from acanthamoeba found in dirty water in undeveloped countries. The main symptom is severe eye pain.

■ Allergic or non-infective keratitis – symptoms are often mild pain and redness of the eye.

Degenerations of the cornea

The cornea tends to degenerate as you grow older. The most commonly seen degeneration is the build-up of lipid material (see **Cholesterol**) in the periphery of the cornea. It builds up in a ring pattern known as an arcus. The more peripheral the degeneration, the less impact it will have upon your vision.

Abnormal growth

Any of the five major layers of the cornea may grow abnormally, causing the cornea to lose its transparency. Many cases have a hereditary component. Most are painless and progress slowly over years. In keratoconus, for example,

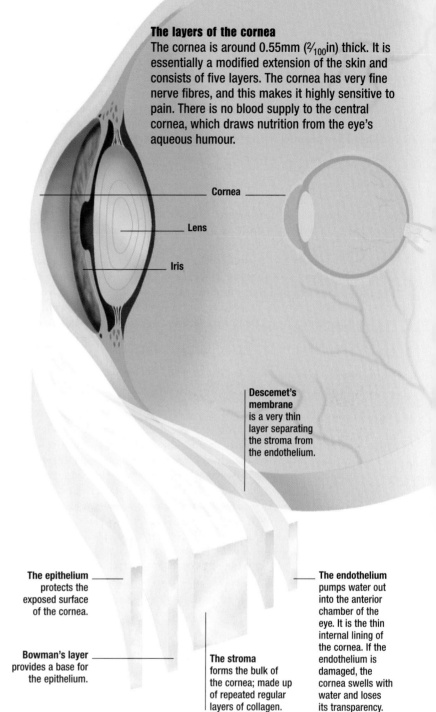

The layers of the cornea

The cornea is around 0.55mm ($^2/_{100}$in) thick. It is essentially a modified extension of the skin and consists of five layers. The cornea has very fine nerve fibres, and this makes it highly sensitive to pain. There is no blood supply to the central cornea, which draws nutrition from the eye's aqueous humour.

Cornea

Lens

Iris

Descemet's membrane is a very thin layer separating the stroma from the endothelium.

The epithelium protects the exposed surface of the cornea.

Bowman's layer provides a base for the epithelium.

The stroma forms the bulk of the cornea; made up of repeated regular layers of collagen.

The endothelium pumps water out into the anterior chamber of the eye. It is the thin internal lining of the cornea. If the endothelium is damaged, the cornea swells with water and loses its transparency.

the cornea becomes gradually thinner. Some cases eventually require a corneal graft. A cornea from a recently deceased person is sewn into the gap left when a diseased cornea is removed. Because the cornea has no blood vessels in it, rejection is less likely than with other body organs.

OUTLOOK

Diseases of the cornea are often sight-threatening, but technical advances are making **refractive surgery** far more effective. Timed delivery of anti-inflammatory/anti-infective agents is delivering better care of keratitis.

Coronary angioplasty

A coronary angioplasty is a procedure in which a blockage of one or two coronary arteries is relieved using a balloon catheter (the narrowed artery is expanded by means of a sausage-shaped balloon attached to the tip of a flexible tube) under X-ray control. This procedure cannot be used if there are many areas of narrowing of the arteries.

People are given this procedure when they have **angina** that is not responding to medicine. Half of those who have a coronary angioplasty feel short-term chest pain during the procedure.

In 95 per cent of cases, the operation is a success – the symptoms of angina grow less or disappear altogether for at least two years. Blockage of the coronary arteries recurs after two years in 30 per cent of cases.

SEE ALSO *Angioplasty; Heart and circulatory system*

Coronary artery disease

The left and right coronary arteries supply blood to the heart muscles. The coronary arteries branch off from the aorta (main artery) just after it leaves the heart, and then divide to deliver oxygen to every area of the heart. Coronary artery disease is a condition in which the coronary arteries become narrowed or blocked by fatty or fibrous deposits (atheroma), restricting the supply of oxygen to the heart's muscles. Coronary artery narrowing may produce chest pain (**angina**), especially on exertion. It can also lead to heart failure, although even in severe narrowing there may be no symptoms. Sudden complete blockage of one or more artery branches results in muscle death – a heart attack or **myocardial infarction**.

A tendency to coronary artery disease often runs in families, but it may be brought on by risk factors such as smoking, excess alcohol, raised blood pressure, diabetes, high cholesterol levels, a high-fat diet, or lack of exercise.

SEE ALSO *Heart and circulatory system*

Coronary bypass

In a coronary bypass operation, diseased coronary arteries are usually replaced with veins taken from the leg or chest. This is also known as coronary artery or vein bypass grafting.

There are several cases where a coronary bypass is recommended. It can help people with **angina** whose activities are limited even though they are taking the maximum allowed drug

doses. It may be recommended for those who are at high risk of dying because two or three coronary arteries are severely affected or the heart is not working efficiently, or for people who are not suitable for balloon **angioplasty**. The operation carries a risk of stroke or heart attack, but it can improve the symptoms and outlook for angina. It does not remove the need for treatment for high blood cholesterol levels, hypertension, blood thinning or diabetes.

SEE ALSO *Heart and circulatory system*

Coronary thrombosis

Coronary thrombosis is a condition in which a branch of the coronary arteries becomes significantly or totally blocked by a blood clot. This cuts off the oxygen supply to part of the heart muscle, leading to permanent damage or even death (see **Myocardial infarction**).

Corticosteroids

Corticosteroids are **steroid** drugs that resemble natural hormones produced by the adrenal glands. As drugs, corticosteroids are widely used for their anti-inflammatory effect. They are prescribed for skin disorders, chronic illnesses such as rheumatoid arthritis, lupus, Crohn's disease and ulcerative colitis, and to prevent asthma attacks. Eczema and hay fever can improve with corticosteroid treatment. An injection of corticosteroids into an inflamed joint, such as tennis elbow, can relieve pain.

GENERAL ADVICE

■ Long-term use of high doses can cause side effects, such as mood changes, muscle wasting and a susceptibility to infection.

■ You may be advised to carry a medical card if taking corticosteroids. This warns that their use should not be stopped suddenly.

■ Gradual withdrawal of treatment is needed to allow the body to readjust.

SEE ALSO *Addison's disease; Drugs, medicinal*

Cortisone

Cortisone is a **corticosteroid** drug, resembling one of several **hormones** secreted by the cortex (outer part) of the adrenal glands. It used to be prescribed as hormone replacement therapy in **Addison's disease**, a disorder in which the adrenal cortex no longer secretes hormones. It has now largely been superseded by other drugs, such as hydrocortisone.

SEE ALSO *Drugs, medicinal*

Cosmetic and plastic surgery

Cosmetic surgery is designed to improve appearance – for example, to reshape the nose or flatten the stomach. It is only one element of plastic surgery, which is used largely to reconstruct parts of the body damaged by injuries, growths and defects.

On average plastic surgeons in the UK spend only 15 per cent of their time on cosmetic work. Most of their time is spent on medically necessary plastic surgery.

Plastic surgery encompasses operations to help both patients with congenital or birth deformities and those with acquired deformities resulting from accident, disease or infection. In the first category are people with congenital defects of the breasts, chest, hands and skin, **cleft lip and palate** and other congenital facial deformities (see **Face and problems**) and urogenital defects (see **Urinary system**). In the second are those who have had benign or cancerous growths removed from the breast, head, neck, skin or soft tissue (see **Cancer**), for example, and those who have suffered hand injuries such as **burns** and **scars**.

CLEFT LIP AND PALATE
A child born with a cleft lip (a separation in the upper lip) or cleft palate (a separation in the roof of the mouth) will be offered an operation to close the separation and improve appearance. He or she may also have difficulty hearing, speaking and eating normally and the operation will only be one part of the package of medical care.

In modifying a cleft lip, a plastic surgeon will normally make a cut on either side of the cleft, turn the cleft's pink outer side inward and draw the muscle and skin on the two sides of the cut and on the lip together. The operation, which leaves a scar that gradually fades, is normally performed when a baby is around 10 weeks old.

In rebuilding a cleft palate the surgeon will normally make a cut either side of the separation and move tissue into the cleft to build the area up. The operation is normally carried out when a child is 9–18 months old.

WOUNDS, GROWTHS AND BLEMISHES
Skin and tissue grafting (see page 343) is used to disguise wounds arising from accidents and to reconstruct areas from which a growth or tumour has been cut.

Various procedures carried out under local anaesthetic remove blemishes such as birthmarks and improve the appearance of scars that are red, raised and itchy or **keloids** – hard raised areas where an overgrowth of thick tissue develops at the site of a healing scar. For example, laser surgery is used to treat children born with pinkish birthmarks known as port-wine stains. A particular laser light beam that is absorbed by haemoglobin (the red pigment in blood) is used to destroy the abnormal blood vessels in the birthmark. The treatment can lighten the birthmark so effectively that it disappears almost completely. Lasers can also be used to remove skin growths and warts, to blur the edges of a scar, and to improve moles, wrinkles, rough areas and freckles.

RESTORING HAND MOVEMENT
If a person has webbed fingers (syndactyly), the surgeon may be able to make a zigzag cut in the abnormal tissue that joins the fingers, then remove or re-form the tissue there to give a normal hand shape. Surgeons can restore

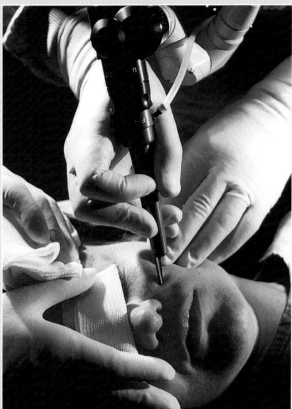

◀ **Laser**
A single laser treatment might be enough to remove 'spider veins' on the face. A large, disfiguring birthmark might need ten treatments.

Nose reshaping

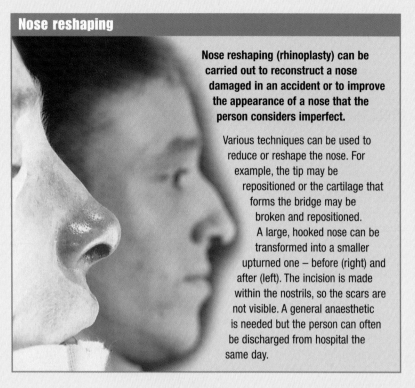

Nose reshaping (rhinoplasty) can be carried out to reconstruct a nose damaged in an accident or to improve the appearance of a nose that the person considers imperfect.

Various techniques can be used to reduce or reshape the nose. For example, the tip may be repositioned or the cartilage that forms the bridge may be broken and repositioned. A large, hooked nose can be transformed into a smaller upturned one – before (right) and after (left). The incision is made within the nostrils, so the scars are not visible. A general anaesthetic is needed but the person can often be discharged from hospital the same day.

near-normal hand use to children born with more than four fingers on each hand (polydactyly) by removing the extra fingers and rebalancing the hand tendons and joints. Plastic surgeons can also help with developmental hand problems such as **carpal tunnel syndrome** (in which pressure on the nerve in the wrist can cause numbness, aches and problems using the hand), trigger finger and ganglia (see **Hand and problems**) or rebuild a finger or thumb lost in an accident.

In treating carpal tunnel syndrome, for example, the surgeon may cut from the mid-palm to the wrist and remove the tissue that is pressing on the nerve and causing the pain. Keyhole surgery may also be used. Patients wear a splint after the operation to restrict movement.

THE PURSUIT OF BEAUTY

Cosmetic surgery may represent a small proportion of plastic surgeons' work, but its use is growing dramatically in the West. In the USA the number of cosmetic procedures such as liposuction and tummy tucks has risen eightfold since 1990, a rise mirrored in the UK. Cosmetic surgery is increasingly used as a means of remaking the body in pursuit of an ideal concept of beauty.

Facelift and forehead lift

Facelifts produce the best results in people whose skin still has some elasticity; they are usually performed, under general anaesthetic, on people in the 40–60 age group.

A common method is to make an incision above the hairline at the temples, following the natural line to the front of the ear, around the earlobe

and behind the ear into the scalp. The skin, and sometimes the underlying muscle, is then freed from the underlying bone, stretched tightly and stitched to the solid structures in front of and behind the ear.

In a forehead lift, an incision is made in the hairline or a few centimetres back from the scalp, extending from one side to the other. The skin is then pulled up and tightened, as in a facelift. This can also be carried out with the aid of an **endoscope** and smaller incisions just beyond the hairline, which avoids the need for an ear to ear incision. Sagging eyebrows can also be lifted in this way.

Eyelid reduction

Eyelid reduction, known medically as a blepharoplasty, is carried out under general anaesthetic. An incision is made, following the natural lines of the upper eyelids, in the creases of the upper lids and just below the lashes in the lower lids, then excess fat, skin or sagging muscle is removed. An incision on the inner surface can be used for some lower-eyelid procedures.

Collagen and botox injections

Injections of collagen (from animals or the patient) are commonly given, under local anaesthetic, to smooth out wrinkles and frown lines and to enhance the appearance of the lips. A test dose of collagen is given in the arm first and checked after a month for allergic sensitivity. Collagen breaks down in the body, so the treatment may need repeating. Although very fine needles are used, they can leave a small mark for up to a day.

Botox (an abbreviation of botulinum toxin) can be used to treat forehead lines, lines around the nose and mouth, and neck wrinkles. Botox works by paralysing or weakening facial muscles, smoothing out the contours. Re-injection will be needed initially every four to five months to keep the muscles paralysed, then less frequently.

Body sculpturing

Surgery to resculpt the body is increasingly popular – breast enlargement is the most common form of plastic surgery undergone by women in the UK.

Breasts can be reduced surgically or enlarged by the insertion of implants (see **Mammoplasty**). Another form of breast surgery is a mastopexy, in which drooping breasts are improved by removing excess skin from under the breast, remodelling the breast tissue into a tighter cone, and re-siting the nipples at a higher level. Further drooping is possible with ageing and pregnancy, but a good support bra minimizes this possibility.

Another common procedure is the 'tummy tuck' (abdominoplasty). Under general anaesthetic, a long, curved incision is made across the lower part of the abdominal wall at the level of the pubic hair. Excess skin and fat is removed, leaving the belly button in place. A similar procedure called an apronectomy is used for people who have a large fold (or apron) of skin and fat hanging over the pubic area. Most abdominal surgery will require a short stay in hospital, from one to three days.

Liposuction

Liposuction is used to remove fat from certain areas of the body, such as the hips, neck, arms, stomach and thighs. It is usually done under general anaesthetic. A small tube called a cannula, which is attached to a powerful suction machine, is inserted at various points on the body through puncture wounds. It is thought that fat cells do not grow back, so the change in contour is likely to be permanent provided the person does not put on weight. Painful bruising may develop after the operation, and discoloration can last for about a month.

COMPLICATIONS OF PLASTIC SURGERY

If you are treated by a qualified plastic surgeon complications are very unlikely and generally minor. However, they cannot be ruled out entirely and should they occur, a further procedure may be needed. Possible problems include:

- general anaesthetic complications, such as chest infections or vein thrombosis;
- infection of the site of the surgery, leading to delay in healing and increased scarring;
- minor infections. These may need treatment with antibiotics;
- bleeding from a broken blood vessel. The leaking vessel will need to be stitched in cases of severe bleeding;

- blood clots (haematomas) forming beneath the wound. These may be treated with antibiotics or a drainage procedure may be necessary;
- scar problems, such as contraction, widening or thickening of the scar;
- damage to the nerves causing numbness around the scar area.

Skin grafting

Skin grafting is the most widely used form of plastic surgery and is used to cover areas where skin has been lost due to burns, injury or surgery. It is sometimes done using a local anaesthetic, but more complex procedures require a general anaesthetic. The skin is usually taken from some other area of the body (known as the donor site) and stitched to the underlying tissue in the area to be covered (the recipient site).

Patients usually provide their own skin for grafting, but skin from an identical twin has been used. The skin grows back at the donor site, but sometimes the new layer is a slightly lighter colour than the original. Apart from improving

◀ **Laboratory skin**
Human skin grown from living tissues in culture can be used in place of transplanted skin in graft operations.

Artificial skin is also being developed – it is used as both a protective covering and a structure onto which the patient's own cells can regenerate the lower layer of skin that may have been lost in the trauma.

appearance, skin grafts to cover large areas of exposed underlying tissue prevent extensive fluid loss and protect wounds from bacterial infection. They can, in some cases, be life-saving.

Skin grafts can be temporary or permanent. Temporary grafts are used in an emergency – when someone has severe burns, for example, surgeons may use skin donated by other people who have died (known as allograft, homograft or cadaver skin) as a temporary cover for the cleaned burn. Alternatively, animal skin (xenograft or heterograft), usually from a pig,

---

Cosmetic surgery – Dos and Don'ts

Opting to go 'under the knife' is a big decision, and the results may not be all that you hope for.

Do

✔ Discuss your cosmetic surgery wishes with your family and with your GP.

✔ Check whether the surgeon is registered with the British Association of Aesthetic Plastic Surgeons.

✔ Insist on speaking to the surgeon before the operation and ask to see 'before' and 'after' photographs of the surgeon's work.

Don't

✗ Rush into any decision without talking it over.

✗ Be pressurized by 'consultants' who may be keener on your money than on your well-being.

✗ Expect miracles.

may be used. Temporary skin grafts adhere to the wound but are removed when the wound is ready for a permanent graft. In a permanent graft, the patient's own skin is usually used (an autograft).

SKIN GRAFT TECHNIQUES

Various methods of removing and transplanting the skin are used. In pinch grafting, small pieces of skin are placed all over the wound. This technique is very useful where there is poor blood supply or the possibility of infection. In split-thickness grafting, the donor skin is taken from the top layer. This method is useful for large areas, but cannot be used for weight-bearing areas or those exposed to friction, such as the hands and feet.

Full-thickness grafting uses all the layers of the skin – being harder-wearing than split-thickness grafting, it can be used for the hands and feet.

In skin flaps, the skin remains attached to the donor site with its blood supply intact. It is not cut loose until the blood supply at the recipient end has fully developed. It is useful for grafts on the face, neck and hands.

Mesh grafting is used when the donor skin is in short supply. Using a meshing machine, small slits are made in the donor material so that it can be expanded like a fish net. Although it means that a larger area can be covered, this method is only used when no other option is suitable because it often leaves small, diamond-shaped scars.

AFTER THE GRAFT

A graft takes about 72 hours to establish its own blood supply. A diet high in protein and carbohydrate will help this process. Infection and trauma may prevent a successful graft, so good

nursing is essential, and strict sterile techniques should be used for dressings. Antibiotics may be needed to prevent infection.

Once the wound has healed, regular gentle massage of the scar can help to reduce it. Areas of skin that are usually exposed may need to be protected from sunlight for the first 12 months to prevent excessive formation of pigment.

Someone who has had a skin graft will always have to take care to avoid excessive exposure of the graft to sunlight. Camouflage make-up used in exposed areas may be used to help a person to resume a normal social and working life.

HOW THE GRAFT WILL LOOK

While some grafts may eventually become virtually invisible, others will remain visible, particularly where infection or blood clotting under the graft has complicated recovery. The transplanted skin will retain the characteristics of the donor site. It may therefore not match the colour and texture precisely of the adjacent skin, and may be less or more sensitive than the surrounding skin.

It is thought that scar maturation can be speeded up using silicone gel sheets. These are waterproof flexible sheets that can be applied to soften the scars and reduce inflammation. The degree of improvement depends on the size of the scar, the nature of the skin, and the quality of wound care after the operation. Many patients retain visible marks of surgery at both donor and recipient sites, and it may be a year or more before the final results can be seen.

Scars are always visible to some extent but are most obvious if the excess scar tissue causes the area to be raised. Various techniques can be used to improve scarring. These include laser surgery, in which a high-energy light beam is used to cut away the upper surface of the skin, and dermabrasion, which involves 'sandpapering' the skin using specialist equipment. Dermabrasion is quite painful and it is usually carried out under general anaesthetic.

COMPLICATIONS

Shrinkage or contracture of the graft may occur, with the graft pulling away at the edges. A feeling of tightness or a distorted appearance can result. Grafts do not have sensation and many are less able to withstand damage such as the rubbing of belts and shoes.

Tissue expansion

The body can be encouraged to grow the right sort of skin to cover a wound.

Tissue expansion is a skin repair technique that can help to minimize scarring. The surgeon inserts an expander – a device like a balloon – beneath the skin in the area that needs new skin growth. Over a few days the expander is gradually filled with salt water, which stretches the tissue in the area around the recipient site and makes the skin there stretch and grow. The new skin's colour is an almost perfect match for that of the surrounding skin.

Tissue expansion is ideal for repairing the scalp, because the newly grown skin will grow hair in the same way as normal scalp skin – whereas with skin and tissue transplanted from other parts of the body hair growth can be erratic or non-existent.

CONTACT **British Association of Aesthetic Plastic Surgeons** and **British Association of Plastic Surgeons** Royal College of Surgeons of England, 35–43 Lincoln's Inn Fields, London WC2A 3PE; BAAPS adviceline (020) 7405 2234 (www.baaps.org.uk; www.baps.co.uk)

Costochondritis

Costochondritis is a swelling of the joint between the ribs and breastbone, causing pain in the chest region, especially during coughing or deep breathing. One or more lumps may develop on the wall of the chest. In older people, costochondritis can sometimes be confused with **angina pectoris**.

The cause of costochondritis is unknown. Sometimes the condition resolves without any treatment; more often, the swelling persists, but eventually becomes painless. Painkillers and nonsteroidal anti-inflammatory **drugs** (NSAIDs) may be helpful in the interim. Costochondritis is also known as 'Tietze's syndrome'.

Cot death

The sudden and unexpected death of a baby for no obvious reason is called a 'cot death'. However, the term is misleading because a baby can also die suddenly or unexpectedly in a pram, a car or in someone's arms.

Cot deaths are very rare, and the risk may be reduced by following some simple guidelines – for example, do not lay babies down to sleep on their fronts, do not wrap them up too warmly in their cots – babies overheat very quickly – and do not allow anyone to smoke near them (see **Sudden infant death syndrome**).

Cough

The cough is part of the body's respiratory defence, a forceful blast of air out of the lungs and airways to clear excess mucus or inhaled irritants. Coughs are often a symptom of an underlying disease and can spread infection. Occasionally a violent cough will fracture a rib.

CAUSES

The most common cause of an acute cough (one lasting up to two weeks) is a cold.

Causes of a chronic cough (one lasting more than two weeks) include:
- smoking, which irritates the lungs and airways, causing a constant production of mucus that leads to 'smoker's cough';
- asthma;
- allergic rhinitis;
- sinus problems;
- oesophageal reflux (heartburn);
- bronchitis;
- drugs – in particular ACE inhibitors, which are prescribed for raised blood pressure and heart problems (10 per cent of people using them develop a cough as a side effect).

TREATMENT

Seek medical advice if you have any of the following symptoms (especially if the cough lasts for longer than two weeks):
- thick yellow or greenish phlegm;
- high temperature;
- you are coughing up blood;
- losing weight;
- shortness of breath or wheezing (especially when sleeping or exercising);
- chest pains;
- swelling in the legs.

Treatment depends on the underlying cause and the effect the cough is having on you. Some treatments are designed to stop the cough, others to make it more effective in clearing mucus. If you have a bacterial infection, the doctor is likely to prescribe **antibiotics**. If you smoke, stop.

Counselling

Counselling is a form of psychological therapy in which the counsellor and the client focus on the problems that an individual is experiencing so that the client can work towards living more resourcefully and successfully.

The counsellor's role is to listen and to help the client clarify and organize his or her thoughts – not to suggest solutions. Counsellors work principally with everyday problems, such as relationship difficulties or **bereavement**, or in a specific area, such as with people who are HIV-positive. Counselling is not recommended for complex mental health or personality problems unless offered as part of a package of psychological treatments.

SEE ALSO *Psychology; Relationship counselling*

Crab lice

Crab lice are harmless insects found in the pubic or other coarse body hair. Symptoms include itching and visible brown eggs (nits) on hair shafts. They are usually contracted during intimate body contact with someone who already has them. Less often, they can be caught from linen and bedclothes. To treat them you can buy over-the-counter products from a pharmacist, or see your doctor for a prescription. Clothing and bedding must be disposed of, or washed at a temperature higher than 60°C (140°F) to prevent re-infection.

▼ **Crab lice**
The lice crawl from hair to hair and cannot jump or fly. A person infected with crab lice should avoid sex until the infestation has been dealt with.

Cradle cap

Cradle cap is a condition in which crusty white or greasy brown or yellow scales form on the scalp and sometimes the forehead of a young baby. It is probably caused by overactivity in the baby's sebaceous (oil) glands, and does not usually occur after 12 to 18 months of age.

Cradle cap does not itch or upset a baby, and eventually clears of its own accord. Gentle daily shampooing with a baby shampoo or washing with aqueous cream helps to loosen the scales, as does massaging aqueous cream or warm oil into the scalp.

Sometimes cradle cap spreads to other areas of the body, in which case it is called seborrhoeic eczema or seborrhoeic dermatitis. If this occurs, your doctor may prescribe a mild hydrocortisone cream. Complementary preparations that might help include calendula (marigold) ointment.

Cramp

Cramp is a strong localized contraction of muscle that results in sharp pain and lasts for several minutes. Cramp is common during exercise, but tired and overworked muscles are also susceptible. It may occur where a muscle is held in a certain position – **writer's cramp** is an example – or at night during sleep.

The causes of cramp are not known. One theory is that it is caused by exercise-induced **dehydration** and an imbalance of sodium, potassium, calcium and magnesium, the minerals that help to regulate muscle contraction and relaxation. Another theory is that damage to muscle fibres allows too much calcium to leak into the muscle membranes with the result that the fibres become locked. Cramp occasionally results from a lack of salt.

TREATMENT

For almost immediate relief from pain, stretch the muscle and gently massage the area or have it done for you (see **Relieving cramps**). The following can help to prevent cramps.
- Practise a daily routine of stretching.
- Drink plenty of water before, during and after prolonged exercise. Thirst is a poor indicator of fluid requirements: by the time you are thirsty, you are already dehydrated.
- Herbal remedies such as cramp bark, black haw and valerian may help to prevent cramp. Consult a herbalist for the correct treatment.

When to consult a doctor

Seek medical advice if you experience regular and persistent cramps. These may be caused by poor circulation resulting from other conditions such as **diabetes**. The doctor might carry out

Self-help
Relieving cramps

What you can do to assist someone suffering from cramp depends on where in the body the pain occurs.

- **Lower leg** The sufferer should lie down on his or her back. Take the affected leg and straighten it while pressing down on the knee with your other hand. Hold the foot under the heel and use your other hand to push the toes gently upwards. When the spasm eases, gently massage the affected muscles until the area feels relaxed.

- **Foot** The person with cramp should place the affected foot firmly on the floor. If the toes are in severe spasm, pull the foot upwards slightly to lift the toes off the floor and gently try to straighten them. In cold weather, the sufferer should put on some warm socks.

- **Hand** Ask the sufferer to straighten and massage the affected fingers until the muscles relax. Warmth can be comforting when the spasm eases, especially in cold weather.

tests for diabetes and for cardiovascular and neurological disorders.

SEE ALSO *Muscular system*

Creative visualization

Creative visualization is the process of picturing a scene clearly in the mind and using this image therapeutically. To assist the process, the person is encouraged to describe sights, sounds, smells and textures. This technique may be used in systematic desensitization (see **Behaviour therapy**) or **relaxation** training.

Cretinism

Now known as congenital hypothyroidism, this is a condition caused by a deficiency of iodine due to thyroid dysfunction, usually dating from birth or before. Signs include slow growth and mental development, a large tongue and a hoarse cry. Affected children tend to have coarse facial features and large foreheads. If left untreated, cretinism can cause brain damage leading to permanent mental retardation.

SEE ALSO *Thyroid and disorders*

Crohn's disease

Crohn's disease, also known as regional enteritis, is a chronic inflammatory disease that usually affects the ileum, the lower part of the small intestine (see **Bowel and disorders**). It can, however, involve any part of the digestive tract; in elderly people it often affects the rectum and anus. The intestinal wall thickens in the affected area and **ulcers** form.

Cases of the disease appear to be increasing, especially in children. The condition is most often diagnosed during adolescence and early adulthood, but may appear at any age.

SYMPTOMS

The symptoms are extremely variable, and depend on the area affected and the severity of the condition. Generally, they include:
- diarrhoea, with foul-smelling stools;
- abdominal pain;
- loss of appetite and weight loss;
- fever;
- tiredness;
- anal **abscesses** and sores.
  Additional symptoms may include:
- joint pain;
- mouth ulcers;
- inflamed eyes;
- painful red lumps on the skin.

TREATMENT

Tests are needed to confirm Crohn's disease and distinguish it from **ulcerative colitis**. They include fibre-optic or video investigations, **barium investigations** and blood tests. Common forms of treatment include:
- anti-inflammatories;
- **antibiotics**, in the case of abscesses;
- dietary measures – although these vary from person to person, in general, a high-protein, high-calorie, vitamin-rich diet is needed;
- surgery – which may be needed to remove severely affected parts of the bowel;
- stopping smoking, which may help.

PREVENTION

The cause of Crohn's disease is unknown and there are no known preventive measures. The condition has a genetic component.

COMPLICATIONS

The complications of Crohn's disease include intestinal blockage, nutritional deficiencies and an anal fistula – an opening between the anal canal and the surface of the skin that can develop if an abscess in the rectum bursts.

OUTLOOK

Symptom-free periods of remission alternate with relapses, which are more likely to occur at times of emotional stress and after surgery. In some cases, symptoms gradually disappear.

Most people who develop Crohn's disease in the UK do so before they reach the age of 30. The peak age is between 14 and 24.

CONTACT **National Association for Colitis and Crohn's Disease** 4 Beaumont House, Sutton Road, St Albans, Herts AL1 5HH (01727) 844296 (www.nacc.org.uk). Support and information for sufferers and their families.

Croup

Croup is an infection of the voice box (larynx), the main airway (trachea) and the bronchi, the two narrow tubes leading from the trachea into the lungs. In the UK, between 80,000 and 100,000 children aged six months to four years suffer from croup each year.

The cause is usually a viral infection. Croup is more common in winter and can be alarming for parents, especially when a child wakes during the night with a distressing, barking cough.

SYMPTOMS

The symptoms of croup include:
- similar symptoms to those of a common **cold**, with a slight fever;
- a hoarse, barking cough;
- noisy breathing.

TREATMENT

Croup should be treated as for a cold.

When to consult a doctor

See a doctor urgently if:
- your child has a high fever;
- there is a marked indrawing of the chest wall with each breath.

Call an ambulance if:
- breathing is rapid and difficult;
- the child is restless and struggling to get air;
- the child turns pale, grey or blueish.

What a doctor may do
- Prescribe **steroids**, either as a tablet or inhaled mist, to ease breathing.
- Give oxygen, intravenous fluids and plain mist to assist breathing.
- Recommend hospital admission.

What you can do

To relieve the symptoms sit with the child in a bathroom full of steam. Give plenty of fluids.

COMPLICATIONS

Inflammation and swelling of the narrow airway may result in a life-threatening difficulty in breathing.

OUTLOOK

Croup generally resolves itself without the child becoming severely ill. About 6 per cent of children develop croup repeatedly and suddenly at night without signs of infection. This is known as spasmodic or recurrent croup and often ceases within two hours. The condition is more common in children who suffer from an **allergy**.

Cruciate ligaments

Ligaments are bands of fibrous tissue that link two bones together at a joint. The pair of cruciate ligaments within each knee joint attach the thigh bone (femur) to the large shin bone (tibia). The cruciate ligaments form a cross within the knee, running diagonally from front to back. They prevent the knee joint from twisting and keep the knee bones in place.

Damage to these ligaments is a common injury among footballers – especially when they twist on a foot that has sunk into soft ground.
SEE ALSO *Ligaments and problems*

Cryopreservation

Cryopreservation is the preservation of tissues in the cold with or without freezing. The technique of storing blood at low temperatures has been used for many years. More recently, other tissues have been stored for other medical purposes such as **infertility** and **transplantation**.
WHY IT IS DONE
■ **Infertility** Eggs (ova) and sperm can be frozen. This helps the timing of a test-tube fertilization. Embryos themselves can be frozen, and then implanted singly in the womb. This avoids having to implant several fertilized eggs in the womb, which can result in multiple pregnancies.
■ **Transplantation** The kidneys, heart, liver and lungs, when cooled, can be stored for short periods of time to enable transport from the donor to the recipient.
■ **Sperm and egg banks** Sperm and eggs are sometimes frozen as an 'insurance' before operations or treatment likely to affect fertility.
OUTLOOK
Recent research has focused on the efficacy of freezing pancreatic cells for transplant into people with diabetes and long-term storage of organs for transplantation.

Cryosurgery

Cryosurgery is a surgical technique in which liquid nitrogen is used to freeze and hence destroy an unwanted area on the skin such as a warts, verrucas and skin blemishes.

Many GPs carry out cryosurgery in their clinics, since it is quick and relatively easy to perform. The area treated may feel sore for a day or two after treatment, and sometimes a blister can form before healing starts.

Depending on the condition, a person may need several cryosurgical sessions, at intervals of three or four weeks.

Cryptorchidism

Cryptorchidism – more commonly known as an undescended testicle – is a condition affecting baby boys in which only one of the two testicles appears in the scrotum. In normal development both testicles descend into the scrotum during the seventh month of pregnancy.

Cryptorchidism affects 3–4 per cent of full-term baby boys worldwide and the risk increases considerably with premature birth.

In most cases, undescended testes drop of their own accord in the first nine months of life; they rarely descend later.
SYMPTOMS
Usually, although not always, the absence of a testicle from the scrotum will be detected at birth or in early infancy. This absence could be caused by:
■ the total lack of a testicle;
■ a muscle reflex whereby the testicle overreacts to cold or touch and retracts – this is known as a retractile testis and usually corrects itself naturally by puberty;
■ the testicle descending to the wrong place, usually into the groin or the base of the penis, a condition known as an ectopic testis;
■ the failure of the testicle to descend at all.
CAUSES
In normal development, hormones from the mother and hormones released by the testes cause the spermatic cord to which each testicle is attached to lengthen and the testes to descend into the scrotum. Insufficient hormones or a blockage may prevent this from happening.
TREATMENT
If you are concerned about an undescended testes, see your GP or midwife.
■ Hormone injections may be given to stimulate descent. If this does not work, the testicle can be fixed in the right position with a surgical procedure known as an orchidopexy. This should be performed before the child is three.
■ Where the other testicle is developing normally, an underdeveloped undescended testicle may be removed. An orchidopexy can also be performed on an ectopic testicle.
OUTLOOK
Cryptorchidism increases the risk of infertility, because the testicle is too hot inside the body. It also increases the risk of testicular cancer.

If the testicle remains undescended into adulthood, the risk of cancer is even higher. Since the testicle is undescended, the cancer is also that much harder to detect. For this reason, an undescended testis in an adult is always completely removed.
SEE ALSO *Testicles and disorders*

CT scan

Computer tomography (CT) is a highly sophisticated form of **X-ray** scan that allows doctors to have very detailed pictures of the inside of the body without having to operate or perform invasive examinations.

Sensors in the scanner detect the X-rays passing through a person's body and the information is then processed in a computer. The images are stored as 'slices' of the body; these can be as thin as 1mm and provide far more information than a conventional X-ray.

CT scanners can also capture images of the brain, kidneys, liver and other organs that cannot be seen on routine X-rays.

WHAT'S INVOLVED

Before the scan, a special dye may be drunk or injected into the veins. This dye makes it easier to see certain organs or important areas of the body on the scan pictures.

The patient lies on a table, which moves into the scanner. The table then moves slowly backwards and forwards so that pictures can be taken of different areas of the body.

A scan usually takes 15–30 minutes; the length of the test depends upon the number of pictures taken. A newer type of CT scanner, known as the spiral CT scanner, can take detailed pictures very quickly.

■ It is important to lie still when the pictures are taken; patients are likely to be asked to hold their breath for a few seconds.

■ While a scan is taking place, the patient is alone in the room. This is to protect staff from exposure to X-rays. But the radiographer (the medical technician who carries out the scan) can talk to patients through a microphone and see them through a window. The patient can ask for the scan to be stopped at any time.

■ Having a CT scan does not hurt, but some people find it uncomfortable to lie on the table for a period of time. Others do not like being in the scanner, especially if they suffer from claustrophobia; usually, the radiographer will try to help the person to feel as relaxed as possible.

Preparing for a CT scan

Different instructions are given, depending upon the part of the body to be scanned – it is important to follow them carefully. For a scan of the abdomen, for example, patients are usually asked not to eat or drink anything for six hours before the test.

AFTER THE TEST

Results are not available immediately. The images need to be interpreted by a specialist, who will write a report and send it to the patient's doctor. This can take up to two weeks.

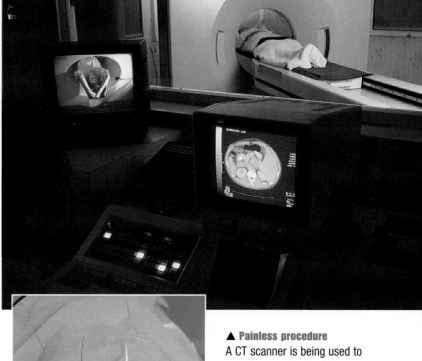

▲ **Painless procedure**
A CT scanner is being used to examine a patient's abdomen. The radiographer operates the scanner from behind a protective glass screen.

◄ **Precise art**
White crosslights are used to position a patient's head so that specific areas of the brain can be scanned.

COMPLICATIONS

Complications are extremely rare. Because X-rays are involved, the person is exposed to radiation, but the dose is carefully monitored. Very occasionally, there may be allergic reactions to the dye injected into the veins. Patients should let the doctor or radiographer know if they have any allergies.

Cushing's syndrome

Cushing's syndrome is a disorder caused by extensive levels of the hormone cortisol in the body. It can result from overproduction of cortisol by the adrenal glands, or be a side effect of glucocorticoid medications prescribed for inflammatory illnesses such as rheumatoid arthritis. It may also result from overproduction of **adrenocorticotropic hormone** by the pituitary gland, caused by lung cancer or other tumours.

SEE ALSO *Adrenal glands and disorders; Drugs, medicinal*

Cuts

A cut is a slit in the skin, and is usually the result of an accidental wound. Cuts are extremely common. They are usually minor injuries, but since they involve a break in the skin there is always a risk of infection.

TREATMENT

Most cuts are easily treated at home.

■ If the cut is bleeding, allow blood to flow for a few seconds to help clean out the wound.

■ Wash the cut gently with cooled boiled water to remove any dirt and debris.

■ If you wish, apply an **antiseptic** spray or cream to the area of the cut.

■ Cover the cut with a plaster or dressing – but leave minor cuts on the face uncovered.

■ If bleeding is difficult to control, press a clean pad of gauze or non-adhesive material over the site for a few minutes.

When to consult a doctor

If there are any of the following signs of infection, seek medical advice.

■ Redness around the cut.

■ Increasing pain or tenderness.

■ Pus oozing out.

■ High body temperature.

It is also advisable to see your doctor if any of the following apply.

■ The edges of the cut will not come together.

■ The cut is still bleeding after you have applied direct pressure to the wound for 15 minutes.

■ Bleeding recurs after more than 15 minutes.

■ The cut was made with a rusty or dirty object.

■ There is something embedded in the cut.

■ A deep cut is over a joint, on the face or extends into a moist area such as the mouth.

SEE ALSO **FIRST AID**

CVS

CVS, or chorionic villus sampling, is an antenatal test to detect fetal abnormalities. In the first three months of pregnancy the fetus is surrounded by a membrane called the chorion. It contains fetal cells; a small sample of these can be taken and checked for abnormalities.

CVS can detect chromosomal disorders, including **Down's syndrome**, some gender-linked single-gene and blood disorders, including **cystic fibrosis** and **haemophilia**, and certain metabolic diseases. It is done earlier than **amniocentesis** and has a marginally higher risk of miscarriage.

CVS is usually carried out between 10 and 12 weeks of pregnancy. Some of the fronds, or villi, that cover the chorion are drawn off, either by passing a needle through the mother's abdomen and into the uterus, or, more rarely, by introducing a flexible tube through the cervix. **Ultrasound** is used for guidance, and a local **anaesthetic** administered before the needle is inserted. Initial results may be available in 48 hours and full results within five days. The accuracy rate is over 97 per cent.

SEE ALSO **Congenital disorders; Pregnancy and problems**

Cyanosis

Cyanosis is a blueish discoloration of the skin, lips or tongue that is caused by a lack of oxygen. This is what causes someone to turn 'blue with cold' when low temperatures slow down blood flow. It can indicate more serious problems. For example, fingers that look blue even in warm conditions may be due to a blood circulation problem, while a blueish tongue can be symptomatic of heart disease.

Cyst

A cyst is an abnormal cavity, lined with tissue and filled with fluid. Most cysts are harmless, occurring as lumps anywhere in the body.

COMMON TYPES OF CYST

In general, consult your doctor if you discover any sort of lump. Cysts most often appear on the skin or in the reproductive organs.

Skin

Cysts on the skin, called sebaceous cysts, occur when the grease glands in the skin become blocked. These painless lumps gradually grow bigger, filling with a semi-solid substance. They have to be removed if they become large enough to be a nuisance or risk becoming infected.

Ovaries

Most ovarian cysts are benign (non-cancerous), and many disappear without any treatment. Sometimes, however, a cyst grows very large, and is surgically removed. There are few symptoms associated with ovarian cysts, but they can affect a woman's periods, making them more painful or heavier, or stopping them altogether. A large cyst may also cause pain during intercourse and abdominal discomfort.

Occasionally, ovarian cysts are associated with **endometriosis**. They fill with brown fluid and are known as chocolate cysts.

Testicles

Cysts on the testicles, or epididymal cysts, are common, especially in men over 40. They occur in the epididymis, the tissue around one side and on top of each testicle. They do not need treatment unless they become uncomfortable, when they may be removed surgically.

Cystic fibrosis

Cystic fibrosis is an inherited genetic disorder. It affects a number of organs in the body, particularly the lungs and pancreas, by clogging them with thick, sticky mucus. There is no cure, but treatment gives children with the disease a higher quality and length of life.

One in 25 people in the UK carries the cystic fibrosis gene, usually without knowing it. If a baby is born with the disease, it means that both parents carry the faulty gene. But even if both parents carry the faulty gene, the child has only a one in four chance of being born with the disease.

Gene therapy – in which the correct version of the defective gene is transported into the lungs – offers hope for the future, but trials are still at an early stage.

SYMPTOMS

Symptoms vary from one person to another, but usually include difficulty with breathing including wheezing and coughing, and susceptibility to chest infections.

A deficiency of the digestive enzymes normally secreted into the gut by the pancreas leads to severe digestive disorders. People with cystic fibrosis are unable to digest fats and proteins properly, so that more undigested food than normal is passed out in unusually bulky stools.

DIAGNOSIS

Cystic fibrosis is not always obvious at birth, but there are early clues to the condition. All affected children overproduce salt in their sweat, so that salt crystals sometimes appear on the skin, which tastes very salty when kissed.

Other signs include:
- a persistent cough that worsens with chest infections;
- frequent chest infections;
- stools that are persistently bulky and smell unusually nasty;
- poor weight gain.

If a child has some of these symptoms a doctor may recommend that the child's sweat is tested for unusually high levels of salt. Further tests may be needed to confirm diagnosis.

TREATMENT

Depending on symptoms, treatment may involve **drugs** and **physiotherapy** to clear mucus from the lungs and reduce secretions. A nebulizer may be used to moisten mucus and make it easier to cough. Chest infections need prompt treatment with **antibiotics**. Nutrition can be greatly helped by a high-calorie diet and the use of vitamins and enzymes. In very severe cases, a lung transplant may be considered.

LIVING WITH CYSTIC FIBROSIS

Exercise and good nutrition can both do much to help people with cystic fibrosis since a healthy, well-nourished body can deal more effectively with the chest infections and weight loss caused by the disease. An exercise regime devised by a physiotherapist can prevent deterioration of the lungs (see **Physiotherapy**).

Children with cystic fibrosis need to eat more calories and protein than normal to compensate for the loss of fat and protein caused by the disease. For adults with the disease, protein intake should be double the usual recommended amount. Fatty foods, sugary foods, starchy foods, milk and dairy products, and foods rich in vitamins and minerals should also be eaten in abundance.

SEE ALSO *Congenital disorders; Diet*

CONTACT **Cystic Fibrosis Trust** 11 London Road, Bromley, Kent BR1 1BY; helpline 0845 859 1000 (www.cftrust.org.uk)

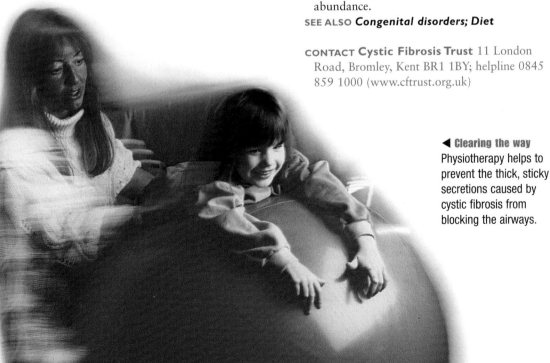

◄ **Clearing the way**
Physiotherapy helps to prevent the thick, sticky secretions caused by cystic fibrosis from blocking the airways.

Cystitis

Cystitis is an inflammation or infection of the bladder lining. Cystitis is more common in women than in men because of the difference in anatomy: the urethra (the duct that drains the bladder) is much shorter in women, making it easier for infection to reach the bladder.

SYMPTOMS

The symptoms of cystitis depend on the severity of the infection. In mild cases, only one or two symptoms may occur, but in severe cases a sufferer may develop them all, including:

- burning, stinging or discomfort on passing urine (dysuria);
- a need to rush to the toilet;
- passing frequent, small amounts of urine;
- low abdominal pain or tenderness;
- backache;
- smelly, cloudy or bloodstained urine.

An untreated bladder infection can spread upwards to infect the kidneys, resulting in the more serious condition of **pyelonephritis**.

CAUSES

There are two main causes of cystitis:

- infection of the bladder;
- friction or chemical irritation of the urethra (see **Urethritis**).

Infection is usually due to bacteria, such as *Escherichia coli* (*E. coli*), which normally live in the large intestine. Sexual intercourse is one of the commonest triggers of cystitis since it can push bacteria up into the urethra. This is sometimes referred to as 'honeymoon cystitis'.

Irritation of the urethral opening from friction can also cause symptoms of urgency, frequency and discomfort on passing urine.

TREATMENT

Preparations of potassium citrate such as Cystopurin, which make the urine less acid, may be helpful. Cystopurin, taken as an oral powder, is available from pharmacies without a doctor's prescription.

What you can do

As soon as symptoms start, drink a pint of water. Then drink half a pint every twenty minutes for the next three hours if you can. Drinking plenty of water helps to flush out bacteria and to dilute your urine so that it does not sting as much when you urinate.

Unless you suffer from high blood pressure or heart trouble, take a teaspoon of sodium bicarbonate dissolved in water every hour for three hours. This makes the urine less acid, relieves discomfort and helps to stop bacterial growth.

Drinking 300ml (10fl oz) of cranberry juice a day or taking cranberry extracts helps to stop bacteria from sticking to the bladder wall.

When to consult a doctor

Seek medical advice if:

- symptoms last longer than a day or keep recurring;
- you are pregnant;
- your urine is cloudy or stained with blood;
- you develop a fever or uncontrollable shakes.

What a doctor may do

A doctor who suspects a bacterial urinary tract infection may do one or more of the following:

- test your urine using a dipstick test to look for signs of white blood cells, blood, protein and substances produced by bacteria (nitrites);
- send a urine sample to a laboratory to culture and identify any bacteria present, and find out what **antibiotics** will kill them;
- prescribe antibiotics.

If you suffer from recurrent cystitis, you may be investigated for conditions such as **diabetes**, or anatomical abnormalities of the urinary system using **X-ray**, **ultrasound** or **endoscopy**.

Complementary therapies

Supplements containing natural extracts of the herbs dandelion, bearberry and peppermint can help to prevent recurrent cystitis.

PREVENTION

There are several things you can do to help to prevent recurrent attacks of cystitis.

- When sitting on the toilet, tilt your pelvis up so that your anus is lower than the urethra.
- After passing water, lean forward to squeeze out the last few drops of urine.
- Wipe your bottom from front to back only.
- Wash with warm, unperfumed soapy water after every bowel movement and sexual intercourse.
- Urinate immediately after intercourse, whenever possible, and, if using a diaphragm, consider another method of contraception.
- Avoid using bubble bath, vaginal deodorants, perfumed soap and talcum powder.
- Drink 2 litres (3.5 pints) of fluid daily.

SEE ALSO *Urinary system*

Cytomegalovirus infection

Cytomegalovirus is a common viral infection belonging to the **herpes** family. It usually remains symptomless or causes a mild flu-like illness. It is passed on by close personal contact with an infected person, via sexual intercourse or blood transfusion. The virus can also pass through the placenta and in rare cases can affect the unborn child. Although the symptoms of cytomegalovirus are milder than those of a common cold, infection may be serious in people suffering from reduced immunity.

D & C

D & C is an abbreviation for dilation and curettage, a gynaecological procedure used to remove tissue from the lining of the womb (endometrium).

D & C has traditionally been an in-patient procedure carried out under general **anaesthetic**. The operation itself takes only a few minutes. As long as all goes well, the woman is able to go home on the same day as the operation or soon afterwards. Convalescence is usually about a week. During this time lifting or moving heavy objects should be avoided, as well as any activities that place a strain on the abdominal muscles. This includes using upright vacuum cleaners and carrying heavy grocery shopping.

D & Cs have now largely been replaced by out-patient procedures that can be performed without a general anaesthetic, such as Vabra curettage, which uses a fine scraping instrument attached to a suction device.

WHY IT IS DONE

D & Cs have been performed to investigate the cause of and treat heavy menstrual bleeding. The procedure is also used in cases where an incomplete miscarriage or abortion is suspected. The process of D & C will make sure that nothing is left in the womb that might cause infection or further bleeding. A D & C is also sometimes used to abort a fetus in the very early stages of pregnancy.

The other common reasons why a D & C might be performed are as follows.
■ To check the lining of the womb for precancerous cells.
■ To remove precancerous or cancerous cells.
■ To investigate and remove **fibroids**.
■ To investigate **infertility**.

WHAT'S INVOLVED

After the woman has been given a general anaesthetic, the surgeon uses steel tubes called dilators to stretch open the channel through her cervix. A small spoon-shaped instrument called a curette is then passed through the channel and used to scrape away the lining of the womb.

If the procedure is an investigative one, a sample of the uterine tissue will then be sent to a laboratory for testing.

COMPLICATIONS

There is a slight risk of infection from the D & C procedure. The symptoms of an infection include high temperature, increased abdominal tenderness, and bleeding or pain when passing urine.

SEE ALSO *Abortion; Gynaecology and tests; Menstruation; Pregnancy and problems; Reproductive system*

Dandruff

Dandruff is a common condition in which there is excessive flakiness of the skin on the scalp but no redness or inflammation.

If the scales causing the flakiness are greasy, stick to the scalp and cause severe irritation, the problem may be a form of **eczema** called seborrhoeic dermatitis. In this case, itchy, flaking skin may also appear on the eyebrows, the beard, on the chest or back and in the creases of the arms and legs.

SYMPTOMS

Dandruff is a harmless condition but it can be itchy or irritating. The white flakes of skin it causes to be shed into the hair and then onto collars and shoulders of clothes can cause self-consciousness and embarrassment.

Dandruff may be more pronounced in people suffering from chronic illnesses, including **AIDS**.

CAUSES

The condition is thought to be linked to an overproduction of yeasts (*Pityrosporum ovale*) that normally live on the human skin.

TREATMENT

Dandruff can be cured quickly and easily by the repeated application of an antidandruff shampoo containing an **antifungal** agent such as ketoconazole. Regular hair brushing removes dead skin and promotes circulation in the scalp. It is advisable to restrict your intake of sugar which increases the productions of yeast.

When to consult a doctor

Seek medical advice if:
■ scratching leads to a scalp infection;
■ the dandruff does not respond to several weeks of home treatment;
■ your scalp is uncomfortably irritated despite home treatment.

What a doctor may do

■ Check that the dandruff is not caused by infection or a skin disorder, such as eczema or **psoriasis**.
■ Give further advice on how to treat the dandruff.
■ Possibly prescribe antifungal or **steroid** preparations.

Complementary therapies

■ Scalp massage may help to improve circulation.
■ Aromatherapy oils such as tea tree can be diluted in a carrier oil and applied overnight.
■ Homeopathic remedies may help. Which remedy depends on specific symptoms: some of the most common include graphites, sepia and sulphur.

COMPLICATIONS

Scratching may cause the scalp to bleed or become infected.

Deafness

Deafness is the partial or total loss of hearing in one or both ears. It can be caused by a mechanical problem that blocks the conduction of sound in the ear canal or the middle ear. This is called conductive deafness. Damage to the inner ear, auditory nerve or auditory nerve pathways in the brain is defined as sensorineural deafness. The two types of deafness can be distinguished by comparing how well a person hears sounds conducted by air with how well a person hears sounds conducted through the bones (see Diagnosis).

Loss of hearing
The problems that cause hearing loss can be very varied and originate in different parts of the ear.

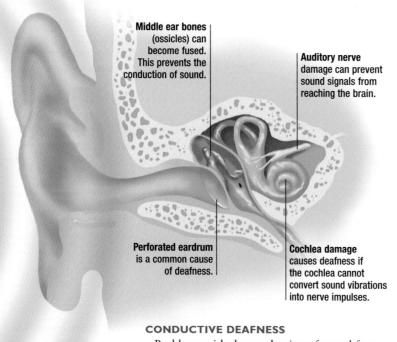

Middle ear bones (ossicles) can become fused. This prevents the conduction of sound.

Auditory nerve damage can prevent sound signals from reaching the brain.

Perforated eardrum is a common cause of deafness.

Cochlea damage causes deafness if the cochlea cannot convert sound vibrations into nerve impulses.

CONDUCTIVE DEAFNESS
Problems with the conduction of sound from the external ear to the inner ear can be traced to several sites. It can originate in the external ear canal, where it can be caused by:
■ a build-up of wax;
■ a benign outgrowth of cartilage from a bone (meatal exostoses);
■ a build-up of skin cells, often seen mixed with wax, in the ear canal (epithelial debris);
■ a developmental abnormality, with the result that the ear canal has not developed (congenital atresia).

In the middle ear, deafness can be caused by:
■ perforation of the eardrum (the tympanic membrane);
■ fluid in the ear (glue ear) or inflammation in the middle ear (otitis media);
■ otosclerosis, a condition in which the small

bones that conduct sound in the middle ear (the ossicles) become fused together;
■ damage or trauma to the eardrum or the ossicles, caused by direct force or sudden explosive noises.

In general, conductive deafness responds to treatment and hearing may be recoverable.

SENSORINEURAL DEAFNESS
Sensorineural deafness, also called perceptive deafness, can be of two types: sensory, when the inner ear is affected, and neural when the auditory nerve or its pathways in the brain are affected.

Causes of sensory hearing loss
■ Age: the gradual and progressive loss of hearing that is common with advancing age, also known as presbyacusis.
■ Noise damage: prolonged exposure to loud noises causes hearing loss at certain frequencies, particularly those of the human voice.
■ Congenital defects, such as the damage caused to the inner ear when a pregnant mother contracts German measles (rubella).
■ Meniere's disease (endolymphatic hydrops), a condition caused by a build-up of fluid in the inner ear, resulting in deafness, buzzing in the ear (tinnitus) and vertigo.
■ Fractured base of skull, generally caused by a blow to the face or head.

Causes of neural hearing loss
■ Brain tumours, causing damage to nearby nerves and the brainstem – the point where the brain meets the spinal cord.
■ Infections, particularly in childhood, when the auditory nerve can be damaged by mumps, German measles (rubella), meningitis or inner ear infections.
■ Auditory nerve pathways in the brain can be damaged by diseases that destroy the nerve covering such as **multiple sclerosis**.
■ Acoustic neuroma, a tumour of the part of the auditory nerve that lies in the inner ear.

In general, sensorineural deafness is hard to treat, and it is very rare for an affected person to recover any hearing.

DIAGNOSIS
A doctor will look in your ears and may use a tuning fork held near your ear and then against your head to establish whether hearing loss is due to conductive defects or sensorineural problems.

For a full assessment of your hearing your GP may refer you to the hospital ear, nose and throat (ENT) clinic or audiology department for an audiometry test. The patient sits in a soundproof room, and is asked to indicate when they hear sounds emitted at specific pitches and volumes from an electronic device called an audiometer.

A precise diagnosis

As well as audiometry, there are several other tests available, that may be used for a precise diagnosis of hearing problems.

TEST	PROCEDURE
Tympanometry	This tests if the middle ear is working properly. A device blows tiny amounts of air into the ear canal, and measures sound reflected back by the eardrum.
Auditory brain stem response	This test distinguishes between sensory and neural hearing loss by measuring how the nerve impulses in the brain respond to sound.
Electrocochleography	This measures the activity of the cochlea and the auditory nerve and is used in young children with profound hearing loss.
Oto-acoustic emissions	This test measures the 'echo' produced by the cochlea in response to sound. It shows if the cochlea is working properly and is used as a screening test for newborn babies.

Hearing by air conduction is tested by asking the patient to listen to the sounds through headphones, so that sound has to travel through the air to reach the eardrum. The faintest sound that can be heard is recorded, to discover whether the ear is less sensitive than it should be. Any hearing loss indicates a problem in the auditory pathway. This could be in the ear canal, the middle ear, the inner ear, the auditory nerve or the auditory nerve pathways in the brain.

Hearing by bone conduction is tested by placing a vibrating pad against the head behind the ear and delivering the sounds from the audiometer by vibration. The vibrations spread through the bone to the cochlea in the inner ear. Specialized hair cells in the cochlea convert vibrations into nerve impulses that travel along the auditory nerve to the brain.

If hearing by air conduction is reduced, but hearing by bone conduction is normal, then there is a conductive hearing loss. If the hearing is reduced by both bone and air conduction then there is a sensorineural hearing loss.

TREATMENT

The treatment of deafness depends on the cause. The most common cause of conductive deafness is wax or skin debris in the external ear canal. Olive oil or sodium bicarbonate eardrops can be used to soften the wax. Sometimes this is sufficient to clear the problem. The skin grows outwards from the eardrum and will carry wax and debris out of the ear canal as long as it is soft enough. If the wax remains in the ear it can be removed by gentle syringing with warm water. This must be carried out by a doctor.

To treat conductive deafness caused by fluid in the middle ear, an ear, nose and throat (ENT) surgeon uses an operating microscope that cuts through the eardrum and sucks out the fluid. A small tube called a grommet may be placed through the eardrum to allow the fluid to drain. The grommet is eventually pushed out as the eardrum heals. Surgery is also effective for conductive deafness caused by **otosclerosis**.

COMPENSATING FOR HEARING LOSS

For many people with deafness there is no cure. Treatment involves compensating for the hearing loss as much as possible. Lipreading, hearing aids and sign language can all help greatly with communication. For some people, a cochlear implant can greatly improve hearing.

▶ **Loud and clear**
This young girl, who has just received a cochlear implant, is hearing for the first time in her life. She may need time to adjust to hearing the different sounds around her.

▶ **Word pictures**
Students of sign language learn a combination of hand shapes, movements, facial expressions and shoulder movements that enable them to communicate with fellow 'signers'.

Lipreading and sign language

Many local authorities in the UK provide classes to learn, or to learn to teach, lipreading or sign language. Those whose hearing is badly affected, or who are likely to become deaf, should consider attending such classes.

Hearing aids

Sound amplification with a hearing aid will help people with either conductive or sensorineural hearing loss, particularly if they have trouble hearing the sound frequencies of normal speech. The initial experience may be disappointing for some people but hearing improves as they become accustomed to the device, so it is worth persevering with a new aid for a least two months. Modern hearing aids have proved especially helpful in teaching deaf children.

Cochlear implants

A person who is profoundly deaf and cannot hear sounds even with a hearing aid may benefit from a cochlear implant which gives a sensation of hearing to severely or profoundly deaf adults and children. A cochlear implant is an electronic device made up of external and internal parts. The external part is worn like a hearing aid, either on the head or clipped to clothes. This contains a sound processor that translates sounds into signals that are sent to the internal part surgically implanted in the ear. Electrodes fitted inside the cochlea, in the inner ear, transmit the electrical signals from the sound processor to the hearing (auditory) nerve. The brain recognises these signals as sounds.

A cochlear implant can help deaf people to hear sounds such as doorbells, telephones and alarms. It helps some people with lipreading and allows people to use the telephone. It is more likely to be effective in someone whose hearing loss is recent or who was successfully using a hearing aid before the implant.

CONTACT RNID (Royal National Institute for Deaf people) 19-23 Featherstone Street, London EC1Y 8SL; helpline 0808 808 0123; textphone 0808 808 9000 (www.rnid.org.uk) **British Deaf Association** 1-3 Worship Street, London EC2A 2AB; helpline 0800 6522 965; textphone 0870 770 3300; videophone (020) 7496 9539 (www.bda.org.uk) **National Deaf Children's Society** 15 Dufferin Street, London EC1Y 8UR; helpline 0808 800 8880 (www.ndcs.org.uk)

Types of hearing aids

Some aids are worn on the body, others in or behind the ear, and they vary greatly in quality and cost. The NHS is beginning to supply digital aids, which generally provide a much better sound quality than analogue aids.

▶ **Remote-control aids**
The aid (right) fits in the outer ear, while a remote control device allows the wearer to tune to particular frequencies, cutting down, for example, on background noise.

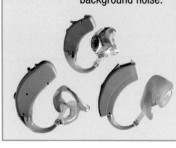

◀ **Behind-the-ear aids**
These widely used aids are available on the NHS or privately, and are suitable for various degrees of hearing loss. The more expensive privately bought aids are more effective.

▶ **In-the-ear aids**
These aids fit entirely into the ear and have an easy-to-use volume control. They are suitable for people with mild to moderate deafness.

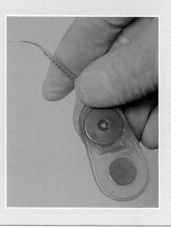

◀ **Cochlear implant**
Profoundly deaf people may be able to have a cochlear implant. A small receiver is implanted under the skin on the scalp; this transmits sound impulses via a processor, which the user wears externally. Implants are expensive, but the NHS may pay the costs in some cases.

Death and dying

We all live with the knowledge of our own mortality. Our attitude to dying can make a huge difference – to the way we treat terminally ill people, to the way we grieve and to the way we prepare for our own death.

Dying and bereavement are among the most difficult experiences we will face. Coping with death can be easier if we have some idea of what to expect – in terms both of emotions and of the basic practicalities of arranging funerals.

In 1900 most people in the UK died at home; by 1960 only about half did so. By 2000 it was less than one in five.

CARE OF THE TERMINALLY ILL
Terminal care aims to help dying people to make the most of the time they have left and to retain the maximum level of independence. Hospices and homes for the terminally ill provide caring environments where people can spend their remaining time, and help them to control their symptoms to the utmost. They offer nursing and social care, as well as providing family support, including help in dealing with bereavement.

FACING DEATH
Discussing death and making provision for what will happen afterwards are important aspects of facing death, both for the dying person and their loved ones.

Talking about dying
Open communication can be a vital comfort for both dying people and their loved ones, offering a chance to face fears, search for meaning, make plans and say goodbyes. The following may help:
- encouraging the person to talk honestly – don't have any taboo areas;
- listening sensitively and acknowledging feelings;
- being open about your own feelings;
- expecting that you will each experience a range of emotions – anger, guilt, blame, fear and sadness are all usual;
- not offering advice unless asked;
- accepting laughter and humour when it appears;
- allowing the person to reminisce.

Planning for dying
There are many constructive things you can do faced with impending death. They may help you come to terms with what is happening. These are some areas to consider.
- A will – to allocate property and provide for children.
- Financial planning – a solicitor can draw up an Enduring Power of Attorney so that someone else can take decisions if you are no longer able to.
- Terminal care – including choosing where to die (home, hospice, hospital), and exploring what facilities are available, such as home nursing.
- Treatment choices – talking to relatives and doctors about what treatment you would like to have and what you want to refuse, making an advance directive or appointing a health care proxy.
- Planning a funeral or commemorative service – including deciding whether you want to be buried (and where) or cremated.
- Advance directive – also known as a 'living will', can be prepared by yourself or a solicitor.

Dealing with death

People may experience a range of very common emotional responses to the prospect of death.

EMOTION	TYPICAL REACTION
Shock and disbelief	'This can't be happening to me.'
Denial	'I'm not ill – the doctors have got it wrong.'
Anger	'This is so unfair. I don't want to die.' Anger might be directed at medical staff, family members or God.
Bargaining	'If I take the treatment/stop smoking/go to church I'll be all right.'
Sadness	'I feel so desperate; I want to cry all the time.' This is natural, but prolonged depression may require medical help.
Acceptance	'I am ready to face death, and want to live what is left of my life as fully as I can.' Many people forge closer and more meaningful relationships, and some report that this is the most rewarding time of their lives.

It is most usually a statement that a person does not want their life to be prolonged artificially when it becomes critical. Your living will needs to be available at the crucial time, so make sure relatives or friends know about its existence, and consider lodging a copy with your GP.

Dealing with pain

When it becomes clear that recovery is unlikely, the emphasis of treatment shifts to palliation – that is, the relief of symptoms. Effective pain relief relies on regular doses of **analgesic** drugs. Other problems such as nausea, constipation, shortness of breath, lack of appetite or weakness and wasting can also be greatly alleviated.

AFTER A DEATH

If death occurs at home, and was expected, contact the person's GP, who will usually issue a certificate and a formal notice for the registrar. If a death is sudden, unexplained, accidental, violent, due to an industrial disease or to surgery, or if no doctor had seen the deceased person in the 14 days before death, the GP will usually inform the coroner. If this is the case, you will need the coroner's authorization before registering the death. If the death occurred in hospital, arrange to collect the person's belongings and for the body to be collected from the mortuary. You can take the body home until the funeral if you wish (the funeral director can arrange this for you), or it can lie in the funeral director's chapel of rest.

Plan the funeral, and if not yourself, contact the deceased's personal representative – this is the executor if there is a will, or the administrator if not, this is usually a close family member. The representative is responsible for dealing with all financial and legal arrangements relating to the estate. Consider putting a notice in the local paper.

Alternative burials

Should you feel that a religious service with a conventional burial or cremation is not for you, there are other options that can be considered.

If you are considering a non-religious ceremony, the British Humanist Association can put you in touch with a local secular officiant. You can still opt for burial or cremation, but the service will not be religious.

A 'green' burial is now possible and there are a number of sites offering burials either in nature reserves or woodlands, using biodegradable coffins; a tree may be planted on the site of the grave.

Sea burials are permitted at two British sites. You need to obtain a form from the coroner and a licence from the Marine Consents and Environment Unit.

Factfile
Who is involved after a death

When a death has taken place there are several professional people involved in the legal administration and funeral arrangements.

■ The **GP** or **hospital doctor**: where the death was expected or occurs in hospital, the doctor authorizes registration of the death with the local registrar.

■ The **coroner**: decides whether an inquest or post-mortem is required.

■ The **funeral director**: arranges the burial or cremation. Make sure you ask for a detailed quote, in writing, of the services the firm will provide. Contact the Funeral Standards Council (details below) if you require further information.

■ The **registrar**: issues a certificate of death, enabling burial or cremation to take place.

Planning a funeral

Most people opt to use a funeral director. Local firms provide various packages, and the cost is usually met from the dead person's estate. If the person was religious, his or her minister will advise on arranging a service, and a burial plot if required. For cremation, the crematorium will explain what forms are needed. Ensure you tell them if you wish to have the ashes afterwards – you may want to keep them, or scatter them in a favourite spot.

If the deceased person was not religious you may wish to consider a non-religious service conducted by secular officiant.

SEE ALSO *Autopsy; Bereavement; Euthanasia; Hospice; Hospital; Organ donation*

CONTACT **The British Humanist Association** 1 Gower Street, London WC1E 6HD (020) 7079 3580 (www.humanism.org.uk) **CRUSE Bereavement Care** 126 Sheen Road, Richmond, Surrey TW9 1UR (www.crusebereavementcare.org.uk) **The Funeral Standards Council** 30 North Road, Cardiff CF1 3DY (029) 2038 2046 (www.funeral-standards-council.co.uk) 'Green' burials: further information from (www.uk-funerals.co.uk/greenburials) **The Marine Consents and Environment Unit** Room 309 Eastbury House, 30-34 Albert Embankment, London SE1 7TL (020) 7238 6617 **The Natural Death Centre** 6 Blackstock Mews, Blackstock Road, London N4 2BT 0871 288 2098 (www.naturaldeath.org.uk) **Hospice Information** Help the Hospices, Hospice House, 34-44 Britannia Street, London WC1X 9JG; helpline 0870 9033 903

Decompression sickness

Decompression sickness is a condition that occurs during a rapid decrease in atmospheric pressure – for example, when divers surface too quickly. As they surface, water pressure falls and the body tissues release gases such as nitrogen and oxygen, disolved in the body fluids during the descent. During a slow ascent they are expelled through breathing; but if a diver's speed exceeds the rate at which nitrogen can be carried to the lungs and exhaled, bubbles may form in the tissues. These may block blood vessels, causing pain, especially in the joints (see **Bends**). Bubbles may lodge in the lungs, the ear, the spinal cord and the brain, affecting breathing and nerve function and possibly causing paralysis and death.

Decompression sickness is also called caisson disease because it affects construction workers in caissons (watertight containers used to carry out construction work under water).

SYMPTOMS

These may appear up to 24 hours after a dive.
- Itching and mottled skin.
- Severe pains around shoulder and knee joints.
- Breathlessness or chest pain.
- Pins and needles or numbness.
- Visual disturbances.
- Dizziness, staggering and weakness.
- Nausea, vomiting.
- Severe headache.

Treatment involves sitting in a hyperbaric (decompression) chamber while air pressure is first increased to the level to which the sufferer was exposed, then reduced at a safe rate to sea-level pressure. Divers can prevent decompression sickness by using the correct air mixture, and surfacing at the rate recommended in a reliable manual for the duration and depth of the dive.

Decongestants

Decongestants relieve congestion of the nose and sinuses caused by inflammation of the mucous membranes lining these passages. The inflammation is often due to infection (eg common **cold**) or an allergy (eg **hay fever**). Most decongestants are vasoconstrictor drugs that narrow blood vessels, reducing the thickness and swelling of the nasal lining and improving drainage and decreasing secretions. The vasoconstrictors used (called sympathomimetics) include ephedrine, pseudoephedrine, phenylephrine and oxymetazoline. They are best taken as nose drops or nasal sprays rather than by mouth to reduce the risk of side effects, such as raised blood pressure. They should never be taken by mouth if you have a heart condition or high blood pressure.

GENERAL ADVICE
- Decongestants should be used for a few days only as they will eventually stop working or may even cause increased ('rebound') constriction.
- They must not be taken with MAOI **antidepressants** because severe hypertension may result.

SEE ALSO *Drugs, medicinal*

Deep vein thrombosis

Deep vein thrombosis (DVT) is a condition in which the blood clots in a deep vein, causing a blockage, usually in the leg or pelvis. Part of the blood clot may detach and travel to the lungs, resulting in a life-threatening **pulmonary embolism**.

CAUSES

Deep vein thrombosis occurs when blood is more prone to clotting, due to:
- thrombotic blood disorders;
- raised oestrogen levels (during pregnancy, or when taking the contraceptive pill or hormone replacement therapy);
- dehydration;
- immobilization during prolonged bed rest, air travel or after an operation.

DVT may also be triggered by vein damage caused by **thrombophlebitis**.

SYMPTOMS

Deep vein thrombosis may have no visible signs, but it usually produces deep, boring pain, tenderness, warmth, swelling and redness. Walking may be painful if the calf is affected.

Diagnosis is confirmed using various methods: a blood test; an ultrasound to show blood flow; or venography, in which dye is injected into a vein and tracked using X-rays (similar to **angiography**). More than one test for blood disorders and underlying causes may be needed.

A blocked vein may lead to dilated skin veins, long-term swelling (oedema). A firm elastic stocking is a helpful preventative measure but may not be suitable for people with peripheral arterial disease.

TREATMENT

Treatment consists of injections of an anticoagulant drug such as heparin, to thin the blood, followed by anticoagulant tablets such as warfarin. Treatment lasts for at least three months, depending on the cause of the DVT and the likelihood of recurrence. Women should not take oestrogens again. A chest X-ray and ECG are required to exclude the presence of a pulmonary embolism.

Air-travellers should avoid dehydration, move the legs frequently, and take medical advice about aspirin and compression stockings.

Degenerative diseases

Dramatic increases in life expectancy over the past 50 years mean that a growing number of people are suffering from age-related degenerative problems, ranging from arthritis to Alzheimer's disease.

Degenerative disease is a term used by doctors to describe any progressive breakdown in the structure or working of a body organ or system. The breakdown may be due to ageing, have a genetic or environmental cause, or result from wear and tear – repeated physical strain, for example. Strictly, the term excludes damage caused by injury or cancer, but it is often broadly interpreted. As life expectancy in the developed world increases with each new generation – more than 1600 people now reach the age of 100 each year in the UK, compared with 200 each year around 50 years ago – so does the number of people with degenerative diseases.

The most common types of degenerative disease are cardiovascular disease, **arthritis**, **osteoporosis** and **Alzheimer's disease** (see **Heart and circulatory system**).

One in three people in the UK over the age of 80 are disabled by a degenerative disease.

Diseases not linked to age

Some degenerative diseases are not confined to old age. For example, muscular dystrophy, a severe muscle-wasting disease, affects infants and children as well as adults.

Motor neurone disease – a group of degenerative disorders that affect nerves in the upper or lower parts of the body – often strike in middle age; symptoms may include difficulty in swallowing, limb or facial weakness, slurred speech, muscle cramps, impaired mobility and, in the later stages, respiratory problems. Other degenerative disorders not strongly linked to old age are **multiple sclerosis**, **Huntingdon's disease** and **CJD**. The cause is often unknown, although genetic factors may be involved. CJD, which usually affects young people, is believed to be caused by eating the meat of cattle affected by BSE.

◀ On the move again
Some people whose walking ability has been severely impaired by a degenerative disease can regain a measure of independence with a pavement buggy or similar mobility aid.

PROTECTING YOURSELF AGAINST DEGENERATIVE DISEASES

Although degenerative diseases are closely associated with age, they are not an inevitable consequence of it. Many conditions are now being linked to chronic infections, toxins and immune system disorders that – if recognized early enough – can be treated before they start to cause damage.

For example, eating sensibly can protect your heart and perhaps prevent late-onset diabetes. A diet high in antioxidants and low in saturated fats can arrest, and perhaps reverse, the gradual clogging of arteries that limits the supply of blood and strains the heart. A diet low in refined sugar may prevent the exhaustion of insulin-producing cells that leads to late-onset diabetes, which in turn can cause degeneration of the kidneys and eyes. (See **Diet**.)

Osteoarthritis – the erosion of bone in joints – can be caused either by physical wear and tear or by untreated rheumatoid arthritis, which eats away the protective cartilage, leaving the bones exposed. Wear and tear may be minimized by avoiding the sort of physical exercise that stresses the joints, while rheumatoid arthritis can be treated with anti-inflammatory drugs.

Osteoporosis – the weakening of bone mass – can be limited by weight-bearing exercise that encourages new bone growth. Even the brain degeneration that causes dementias such as Alzheimer's disease may be limited by ensuring that the brain is kept active.

Degenerative diseases tend to be progressive, but there are few symptoms that cannot be relieved by good medical care.

SEE ALSO *Age and ageing; Brain and nervous system; Immune system and disorders*

Dehydration

Dehydration is a condition resulting from loss or lack of water in body tissues. Excessive water loss is frequently combined with a loss of sodium and potassium, which may cause body organs to malfunction.

Dehydration is a consequence of inadequate water intake or water loss through diarrhoea, vomiting or excessive sweating during a fever. It may also be caused by uncontrolled **diabetes** or some types of kidney failure.

Babies dehydrate much faster than adults because any substantial water loss represents a higher percentage of their bodies' water content.

If you fear that a baby in your care may be dehydrated, gently pinch the skin on the baby's forearm and pull it up, then release. If the skin at once resumes its normal appearance, the baby is probably not dehydrated, but if the skin remains puckered, seek medical advice urgently.

SYMPTOMS

Typical symptoms of dehydration include:
- concentrated (dark-coloured) urine;
- dry skin and mouth;
- swollen tongue;
- rapid pulse and rapid breathing;
- cold feet and hands;
- loss of skin elasticity;
- in severe cases, lightheadedness, irritability, confusion and loss of consciousness.

TREATMENT

It is necessary to rehydrate the body with rehydration fluids as quickly as possible.

What you can do

- Drink rehydration fluids. These contain essential salts and glucose and can be bought in pharmacies in powder or tablet form to dissolve in water. Sports drinks are not advised.
- Prepare a home-made rehydration drink by mixing one teaspoon of table salt with eight teaspoons of sugar in one litre of tap water.

When to consult a doctor

Consult a doctor immediately if a baby shows any symptoms of dehydration, or if an adult shows severe signs.

Severe dehydration requires hospitalization so that fluids can be replaced through a drip.

COMPLICATIONS

If dehydration is untreated, blood pressure will fall to dangerously low levels, causing shock and damage to the kidneys, liver and brain.

PREVENTION

Drink plenty of water, especially during hot weather, before and after strenuous exercise and during a fever. Drink rehydration fluids when suffering from diarrhoea or vomiting.

OUTLOOK

Recovery is good if fluids are replaced quickly.

Delirium

A delirious person is confused, disoriented and agitated, and is likely to suffer hallucinations or delusions. In delirium tremens – a symptom of withdrawal from chronic alcoholism – a person has the symptoms of delirium and may also shake uncontrollably.

SYMPTOMS

People who are delirious typically mutter or shout incoherently, and may be convinced that other people are out to harm them.

CAUSES

Delirium may be caused by anything that disturbs the normal functioning of the brain. This includes head injury, brain inflammation from infectious illness, drug abuse and adverse reaction to medicinal drugs. It is commonly seen after surgery (especially in children and elderly people), as a reaction to anaesthesia.

TREATMENT

Treatment depends on the cause. If delirium occurs after a head injury or as a reaction to a drug, the affected person should be seen urgently by a doctor. If the delirium is linked with fever, the person should be soothed, kept cool and watched carefully, in consultation with a doctor. If a delirious person lapses suddenly into unconsciousness, or starts convulsing, a doctor should be called.

A person suffering from delirium should be encouraged to lie down in a fairly light, cool room (darkness increases the likelihood of hallucination). Other people can help by providing soothing talk aimed at calming and allaying fear, and gentle distraction during periods of lucidity.

Delirium tremens

Delirium tremens is a type of delirium linked almost exclusively with a sudden withdrawal from alcohol after very heavy (and usually long-term) over-consumption

The condition comes on hours or days after the person has stopped drinking, and its start is marked by irritability, restlessness, lack of concentration and insomnia or disturbed sleep with nightmares. There is a characteristic shaking (tremor), most noticeable in the hands but sometimes extending to the entire body. About one in four people with delirium tremens has a seizure.

Delirium tremens usually lasts for several days, during which time the affected person shows increasing distress and confusion. He or she may experience terrifying hallucinations – of foul smells, threatening voices and the sensation of being pushed or hit. Sometimes the affected person sweats profusely and becomes dehydrated. Recovery is usually quite sudden, but in about one in 10 per cases the person dies from physical disorders caused by long-term abuse of alcohol.

A person suffering from delirium tremens should be taken to hospital, where doctors may prescribe sedative drugs and vitamin B injections.

Delusions

Delusions are mistaken or false beliefs that cannot be altered by rational argument. People who are mentally ill may have a false belief that they are all-powerful or that they are victims of persecution or an external force that is taking over their bodies or minds. Some people who believe that their body has changed in some way react by trying to do harm to themselves.

Delusions are a common feature of mental distress, particularly **paranoia** and **dementia**, and may be a symptom of **schizophrenia** or **manic depression**.

TREATMENT

Trying to empathize with the feelings of fear, confusion and isolation experienced by the person suffering from delusions may help to alleviate the problem; trying to reason with the person about the delusions does not. A doctor may prescribe drug treatment – generally **tranquillizers**.

SEE ALSO *Mental health and problems; Psychosis*

Dementia

Dementia is a gradual, long-term deterioration of a person's ability to think clearly and to remember everyday events. Eventually it leaves the person unable to live independently.

The most common form of dementia is **Alzheimer's disease** but other causes include **Huntingdon's disease**, impaired blood supply to the brain, **CJD** and **AIDS**. Dementia may also be caused by drug or alcohol abuse.

Although dementia most commonly affects people later in life, it is not the same as poor memory or forgetfulness, which some people complain of as they grow older.

SYMPTOMS

In the early stages, people affected by dementia may become confused and forgetful and find it difficult to make decisions.

As the disease progresses, the affected person can develop feelings of anxiety, fear and aggression. Delusions and paranoia are common – for example, patients may believe that their relatives are stealing from them or trying to harm them.

In the later stages, people with dementia may lose long-term memory and fail to recognize even their close family members.

TREATMENT

Treatment of dementia is geared to enabling people with the condition to lead lives that are as near normal as possible for as long as possible. It may include practical assistance in the home, such as the provision of meals or help with personal and domestic hygiene, as well as emotional support for both the person with dementia and that person's carers.

When Alzheimer's disease is in its early stages, drugs may help to preserve the affected person's mental faculties for several months and may also alleviate symptoms such as aggression, irritability, restlessness and depression.

Residential care is likely to be needed in the later stages of dementia.

Complementary therapies

Complementary therapies cannot provide a cure for dementia but **relaxation techniques** and **aromatherapy** may be soothing.

Some essential oils such as rosemary, herbs such as gingko biloba, and the nutrient lecithin – which occurs naturally in egg yolks and is also available as a supplement – peanuts and green leafy vegetables, may help to improve the powers of memory.

COMPLICATIONS

As dementia progresses, an affected person will no longer be able to manage his or her own affairs. It is important to seek legal advice before major problems arise.

PREVENTION

Dementia related to poor blood supply to the brain may be prevented by reducing risk factors such as smoking and high blood pressure. But, since the causes of most forms of dementia are not fully understood, there are limited opportunities for prevention.

OUTLOOK

Dementia usually becomes progressively worse until death occurs, often from respiratory infection or other chronic illness. But the person's emotional health and general well-being can be improved by sensitive care and good support services.

SEE ALSO *Alzheimer's disease; Brain and nervous system; Huntington's disease*

CONTACT **Alzheimer's Society** Gordon House, 10 Greencoat Place, London SW1P 1PH 0845 300 0336 (www.alzheimers.org.uk) The society offers help and support for people affected by Alzheimer's disease.
MIND 15–19 Broadway, London E15 4BQ Mind*in*foline 0845 766 0163 (www.mind.org.uk) Mind publishes a range of helpful books and and leaflets; it has a network of 200 local branches, some of which also provide mental health services.
Carers UK Ruth Pitter House, 20–25 Glasshouse Yard, London EC1A 4JT 0808 808 7777 (Wed & Thurs, 10-12 & 2-4pm) (www.carersuk.demon.co.uk) Carers UK offers advice, information and support for carers.

In the UK, dementia affects one in 20 people over the age of 65 and one in five over the age of 80.

Dentists and dentistry

Regular visits to your dentist from an early age will help to maintain healthy teeth and gums. A dentist will also check for problems involving the tongue or soft tissues of the mouth and provide advice on how to prevent disease.

Dental checks every six months used to be standard, but the recommended interval between visits now varies, depending on the state of your teeth and the advice of your dentist. Most dentists advocate preventive care to keep treatments to a minimum. Patients are shown how to care for their teeth and given oral health advice to help to keep their mouth free from disease. As well as attending checkups, consult a dentist if you suffer from toothache, chip or lose a tooth, or have problems with dentures. Your dentist can also advise on how to deal with bad breath and jaw problems. Anaesthetics and new techniques have taken much of the pain out of dentistry, and a focus on prevention means that drastic treatments have become rarer.

FINDING THE RIGHT DENTIST

Before registering with a dentist, decide exactly what kind of service you want.
■ NHS treatment provides routine care at fixed prices. But it is not always easy to find an NHS dentist, and not all treatments are covered.
■ Private care offers longer sessions with a dentist and a greater choice of treatment options, but it is usually more expensive than NHS care.
■ Some practices provide both NHS and private treatment and allow you to choose between them depending on your treatment needs.

You may also want to consider registering with one of the following types of dental practice:
■ a practice with a hygienist who will advise on brushing and flossing to improve preventive care;
■ a family practice geared to treating children;
■ a practice with expertise in treating nervous patients that offers sedation;
■ a practice that has late or unusual opening hours to fit in with your working life;
■ a practice that provides cosmetic dentistry treatments such as bleaching;
■ a practice that offers a dental scheme whereby you pay a set amount annually for dentistry.

NHS Direct can provide details of NHS dentists in your area, many of whom offer private care.

THE DENTAL CHECKUP

After enquiring about any problems since your last visit, the dentist will examine your mouth under a bright light, often using a mirror and a probe. The dentist will check that any new teeth such as wisdom teeth are emerging correctly and will look for any signs of decay or gum or mouth disease. Water and air from a syringe may be used to clean off any debris; air blown onto the teeth may also indicate any sensitivity. After every dental session, the tray of instruments used is sterilized and the gloves are thrown away.

The dentist works with a nurse, who will use a suction device to remove excess saliva from your mouth, prepare instruments and fill in records. If your last dental checkup was some time ago, X-rays may be taken to see whether there are any hidden problems such as decay between your teeth or problems in the roots. Bite-wing X-ray films are placed between your teeth, one for each side, and an X-ray machine placed by your cheek. Panoramic X-rays, or OPG (orthopantomograph) machines, may be used to provide an image of the whole jaw as well as sectional images of teeth, roots and sinuses. Some practices have intra-oral cameras linked to a monitor so that the dentist

▶ **Computer dentistry**
A colour-enhanced dental X-ray will help a surgeon identify problems such as impacted teeth and bone loss.

can use images of the patient's mouth to explain problems and treatment options.

If you require treatment, you will usually need to make another appointment. If you are unclear about what is being recommended, ask for a treatment plan and an estimate of the cost.

Your dentist or a hygienist may also scale and polish your teeth to remove plaque and calculus. Plaque is a sticky film containing bacteria that can build up in the mouth; the bacteria can produce acids that attack the teeth, penetrating the enamel and causing decay. Calculus is plaque that has hardened on the teeth.

HAVING A TOOTH EXTRACTED

If you are having a tooth extracted, eat before you go to the dentist – you will not be able to eat for some hours afterwards. Your blood sugar level can drop after an extraction, making you feel faint or weak. If this happens, have a drink of squash or juice to restore your blood glucose levels. Avoid drinking anything very hot or cold, and do not touch the area where the tooth has been extracted or you may hinder the healing process. Wrap a clean handkerchief around cotton wool, lay it across the socket and bite onto it to stop any bleeding. Go back to the dentist if this fails to stop the bleeding.

REPLACING MISSING TEETH

If one or two teeth are extracted or lost, they may be replaced with a bridge whereby an artificial tooth is attached to adjoining teeth. Crowns (see next page) are made to fit the natural teeth either side of the gap. They are fixed onto the plate and cemented over the natural teeth. Several treatment sessions may be needed to have a bridge fitted. Dentures may be used where more than two teeth are lost (see page 366).

A permanent dental implant can be used to replace one or more missing teeth. A hole is drilled in the jaw and a small titanium rod inserted, usually under local anaesthetic. The screw is left to heal for several months before an artificial tooth is placed over the top although, increasingly, teeth are being placed on the implants immediately. Implants can be an alternative to dentures, but inserting them can be a long and expensive process.

MAJOR DENTAL TREATMENT

If decay invades the pulp of the tooth, after an abscess has caused infection there, root canal treatment may be necessary. In this procedure, the remaining pulp and nerve are removed, the roots and abscess are drained, and antiseptic is used to sterilize the cavity. The root canals are shaped with a series of files and the roots and interior of the tooth are then filled; in some cases the tooth

Materials for fillings

Various materials are used for fillings, the cheapest of which is amalgam. Fillings rarely last a lifetime and usually need replacing after several years.

Amalgam A mixture of mercury, tin and silver, amalgam is often used to fill back teeth because of its strength and durability. Although mercury is toxic, there is no evidence that it is harmful in the tiny amounts used in fillings. But, as a precaution, pregnant women are advised not to have an amalgam filling placed or removed.

Composite A filling, usually made from a blend of resin and silica, composite is bonded to the tooth, then set with a blue light source. It is used to fill teeth near the front of the mouth because it is less noticeable than amalgam.

Inlay Made from gold, porcelain or composite, an inlay or a filling is produced from an impression taken of the cavity. Inlays are generally used for large cavities in the back teeth.

Glass ionomer A coloured filling material that contains fluoride. Once placed in the tooth it may prevent further decay, so it is often used for children's first teeth or to fill a cavity in the base of a tooth (see picture, right). It is set in the same way as a composite filling.

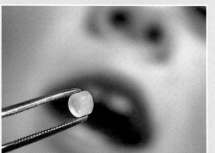

is covered with a crown to strengthen it. The procedure may require several sessions.

If root canal treatment does not successfully remove all the infected pulp from a tooth, an apicectomy may be necessary. This is a surgical procedure in which an incision is made in the gum and the end of the root is cleaned and trimmed. This is usually carried out in the practice under a local anaesthetic.

Difficult extractions – such as removing a wisdom tooth that has become stuck (impacted) because of lack of space in the mouth – are usually done in the practice under a general anaesthetic. Antibiotics may be prescribed for any infection.

NUMBING THE PAIN

Most dental treatments are carried out under local anaesthetic. An anaesthetic such as Lignocaine is injected into the gum near the tooth to be treated. An anaesthetic gel can be applied before the injection to numb the area and reduce discomfort. Injections are a very effective way of numbing the nerves in the mouth so that no pain is experienced during treatment. But people who are very anxious about treatment can have it carried out under sedation. This usually takes the form of inhaling gas and air (nitrous oxide and

Avoiding tooth problems

To maintain good oral health, take your dentist's advice:

- brush twice a day with a toothpaste containing fluoride;
- avoid sugary snacks and drinks;
- have regular dental checkups;
- chew sugar-free gum;
- don't smoke;
- limit fizzy or acidic drinks.

oxygen), but a sedative can also be injected into a vein. Not all dentists offer sedation.

Some dentists offer relaxation techniques, including hypnotherapy, which can induce a state of altered consciousness to make the patient relaxed and immune to discomfort.

DENTAL SPECIALISTS

Most dental care and treatment is carried out by general dental practitioners in their surgeries, but complex work may require specialist treatment. Dental specialists include:

■ endodontists, who specialize in root canal treatment and apicetomies;

■ orthodontists, who deal with irregularities and overcrowding of teeth and correction of the bite;

■ periodontists, who treat advanced gum disease;

■ oral surgeons, who carry out extractions, jaw surgery and may insert implants;

■ restorative dentists, who provide crowns, bridges and fillings;

■ prosthodontists, who specialize in dentures.

ORTHODONTICS

Orthodontic treatment is used to straighten or realign crooked or crowded teeth, but it is not simply a cosmetic procedure – it prevents decay by enabling the teeth to be cleaned properly. Orthodontics can also improve your bite in cases where teeth do not meet correctly – a bad bite makes it harder to chew food thoroughly and strains the jaw muscles. Most orthodontic patients are children or teenagers, but adults can also benefit.

Simple treatment may require the person to wear a removable brace that exerts gentle sustained pressure to move the teeth into the correct position.

A fixed brace is necessary for more complex treatment, and some patients need to wear additional headgear at night, to increase the pressure. This process usually takes a minimum of between 18 months and two years, with visits to the dentist every four to six weeks. Once the teeth are in the correct position, a retainer may have to be worn for a further six months to maintain the position of the teeth.

Orthodontic work on children's teeth may be available on the NHS; some adults may also be entitled to NHS treatment. Private orthodontists offer tooth-coloured brackets, which make the brace less visible.

Only healthy teeth are regarded as suitable for orthodontic treatment, and while wearing braces it is important to clean your teeth properly.

ROUTINE AND COSMETIC TREATMENT

Almost everyone has at least one filling at some point in their lives. Fillings are used to replace a

decayed area of a tooth and to prevent the decay from spreading. The decayed area is removed, usually by drilling. Other methods include air abrasion, which is precise and virtually pain-free, or use of laser or a gel such as carisolv, that dissolves soft tissue. But these methods may not be suitable and are not widely available.

Chipped or cracked teeth can be repaired. A tooth may be given a replacement surface in the form of thin porcelain veneer. This is often used to improve the appearance of teeth that are irregular or stained. Discoloured teeth can also be lightened with hydrogen peroxide (bleach).

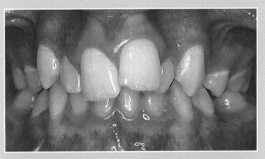

◄ **Crooked correction**
In cases where teeth need radical realignment, a fixed brace is used. The first step is to fix a small bracket to each tooth.

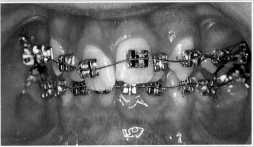

◄ **Straightening up**
The brackets are joined by a flexible wire, which allows the teeth to be guided accurately and gently into place.

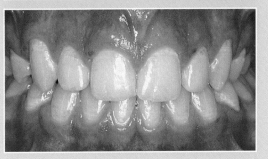

◄ **Raising a smile**
Even though the process may take several months or more to complete, the end result should be a straight set of teeth set off by a radiant smile.

A protective cover, or crown, can be fitted over a tooth that is broken down through decay, badly discoloured or misshapen. Crowns are made of porcelain or porcelain bonded to metal. The tooth is ground down and shaped into a peg. An impression of the peg is made and a temporary cover is fitted while the crown is made in a laboratory to the dentist's prescription. The crown, which should match the shade of existing teeth, is cemented into place. Fitting a crown may require two or three appointments. Teeth may need to be extracted if they are badly decayed or loosened due to gum disease. Extractions can also be performed to make room in the mouth for orthodontic work. They are usually done in the dentist's surgery under a local anaesthetic, but more complex procedures may need to be carried out in hospital.

TREATMENT FOR GUM DISEASE

Gum problems are usually treated by a dentist. Inflammation of the gums, or gingivitis, is very common and is caused by bacteria in plaque. The dentist or a hygienist will use a scaler to remove plaque and calculus from the teeth and advise you on preventive care.

Gingivitis can develop into periodontal disease, which causes the gums to recede followed by eventual tooth loosening and loss. Treatment can involve root planing, a special cleaning of the roots of the teeth, antibiotics, mouthwashes, or surgery to remove the diseased area of the gum. A periodontist may be consulted about how to prevent periodontal disease.

Gum disease can be prevented by careful home care including brushing and flossing, as well as having regular visits to your dentist or hygienist.

TREATMENT FOR JAW PROBLEMS

Aches around the face and head may be caused by the teeth meeting incorrectly and abnormal clenching or grinding; a dentist can treat this problem or give you advice about how to deal with it. If you grind your teeth at night, you may wake up with a dull headache. A dentist can advise wearing a special mouthguard or recommend an orthodontist to correct your bite.

If you lose a tooth, a dentist may be able to re-implant it. Placing the tooth in milk improves the chances of saving it.

TREATMENT WITHIN THE NHS

Fees for specific dental health treatments within the NHS are set by the Department of Health, limited by a maximum amount payable for any course of treatment. The patient pays the dentist 80 per cent of the cost of the treatment and the remainder is paid to the dentist by the NHS. The dentist will need to obtain official approval for any course of dental work costing more than the set maximum.

Children and young adults under the age of 18, expectant mothers, mothers of children under 12 months and some benefit claimants are exempt from fees. There are restrictions on the types of treatment you can have on the NHS – for example, you may be offered only amalgam fillings in certain teeth.

By law, Primary Care Trusts must ensure that there is enough NHS dental provision in the area, and some provide dental centres staffed by salaried dentists. These clinics deal mostly with patients who are in pain and need emergency treatment care.

PRIVATE TREATMENT

Private patients pay for all their dental treatment and the cost varies greatly between practices. If you are considering private treatment, it is advisable to follow up recommendations and visit several practices before choosing one. Some dentists provide both NHS and private care. Dentists sometimes offer payment plans, whereby an annual or monthly sum covers a range of basic

Dentures

Dentures can be fitted to replace missing teeth. They may be partial, replacing one or more teeth, or complete, replacing all teeth in both jaws. Unlike crowns and bridges, dentures are removable.

Dentures are artificial teeth attached to a plastic or metal plate that rests on the ridges of the gums or clasps onto any natural teeth. Suction and muscle control keep them in place; lower dentures have no suction and tend to move more.

Dentures are made specially for each individual, but they often become uncomfortable or loose because the gums and supporting bones shrink after natural teeth have been extracted; the shrinkage occurs rapidly for the first six months, then more slowly.

An annual checkup will allow early detection of any problems such as mouth cancer. All dentures should be checked if they become uncomfortable.

Dentures should be removed at night and left in a denture cleaner. If they are left in place, the roof of the mouth becomes soft and spongy and a yeast infection may develop. Denture wearers should brush their gums and palate twice a day to keep them healthy. Some wearers use dental fixative to keep dentures in place but this is not recommended for regular use; your dentist can adjust your dentures to make a better fit if they have become loose.

Ill-fitting dentures may make the mouth sag at the corners, causing a buildup of saliva, which can lead to infection (see **Cheilosis**). The wearer may stop eating foods that need chewing, and there is a danger of serious weight loss and health problems linked with poor diet, such as vitamin deficiency. Another unpleasant side effect is mouth ulcers.

As people age, the soft tissue of the mouth thins and dentures can become painful, rubbing the inside of the mouth. A dry mouth – a common side effect of some medications such as antidepressants and of some cancer treatments – exacerbates the problem, and may also cause dentures to fit less well.

treatments. Laboratory fees for crowns, veneers, dentures, mouth guards and other technical work are additional. Certain dentists belong to a national scheme such as Denplan or Cigna; others have their own plan.

DENTAL STANDARDS

There are more than 30,000 dentists and some 11,000 dental practices in the UK. All practising dentists are obliged to register with the General Dental Council (GDC) and to conform to the council's ethical code. Those who fail to do so and whose practice or behaviour falls below acceptable standards may be struck off.

HOMEOPATHIC DENTISTRY

Complementary therapies such as homeopathy cannot offer an alternative to dental treatment but can provide a useful adjunct to it. Some dentists are trained in homeopathy and may offer remedies such as arnica to reduce swelling and pain after extractions. Few homeopathic dentists use mercury in their fillings.

DENTISTRY FOR CHILDREN

Teaching children to reduce how often they consume sweets and fizzy drinks and to look after their teeth correctly can lay the foundation for a lifetime of healthy teeth.

It is never too early to start instilling healthy practices. Introduce your baby to a trainer mug for drinking as soon as you can; sucking on a bottle should be discouraged as soon as an infant is old enough to drink from a mug or glass. Infants should never be allowed to go to sleep with a bottle in their mouth, especially one that contains sweet drinks.

When children are very small, plaque can be removed from their teeth with a cotton bud. Later on, this may be replaced by a child's toothbrush and toothpaste, which has a lower level of fluoride than ordinary toothpaste.

Parents should oversee a child's toothbrushing until the child is about seven years old. Before this age, it is advisable to make sure that the child does not use too much toothpaste as this may cause mottling of the teeth (fluorosis). A pea-sized smear of toothpaste is recommended.

Children can start visiting the dentist when their first teeth appear, and all children should have seen a dentist by the time they are two years old. Regular checkups help to ensure that the teeth are coming through correctly and allow the child to get used to seeing a dentist.

Practices specializing in children's dentistry help make visits enjoyable; for example, stickers may be given to reward children for good behaviour.

As your child's permanent teeth appear, plastic sealants may be recommended to protect the

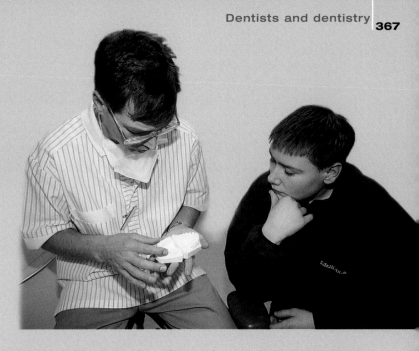

biting surface of the first molars. These teeth have tiny cracks (fissures) between them that are particularly susceptible to decay. However, covering the cracks with sealant helps to keep decay at bay. The process is pain-free and is recommended when the permanent molars have just come through, between the ages of six and thirteen.

When children need fillings in their first teeth, the dentist may insert glass ionomers, which leach fluoride into the teeth to strengthen them. Baby teeth provide the spaces for the second teeth to grow into, so it is worth taking care of them. If a child loses some first teeth, the permanent teeth may be overcrowded when they come through and extractions may be necessary. Children's teeth may become discoloured from swallowing toothpaste or taking antibiotics, particularly tetracycline. White filling material or veneers can be used to conceal small stains when the child is older.

SEE ALSO *Gums and gum disease; Halitosis; Teeth and problems*

▲ **Children's dentistry**
Fear of going to the dentist often begins in childhood, but it can be avoided or overcome. It is important to find a sympathetic dentist who is accustomed to dealing with anxious people.

CONTACT **British Dental Health Foundation**, Smile House, 2 East Union Street, Rugby, Warwickshire CV22 6AJ; helpline 0845 063 1188 (www.dentalhealth.org.uk) **British Dental Association** provides an online directory of dentists at www.bda-findadentist.org.uk **NHS Direct** will provide details of NHS dentists on 0845 4647 (www.nhsdirect.nhs.uk) To find a dentist offering a dental plan, see www.denplan.co.uk or www.cigna.co.uk Dentists skilled in relaxation techniques are listed at www.nofeardentistry.co.uk **British Homeopathic Dental Association** provides contact details of dentists who work homeopathically (www.bhda.co.uk)

Depression

Depression is a common illness that affects most people at some point in their lives. When it grips someone, activities that were previously fulfilling seem to become a waste of time.

In its mildest form, depression means feeling miserable and dissatisfied. If you have mild depression, you can carry on with a normal life, but everything seems more of a struggle. Severe depression can stop you living your life the way you want to. You may feel helpless and even suicidal. When negative thoughts dominate a person's life and continue for a long time, the depression is described as 'clinical'.

Depression occurs as often in men as in women, but in the UK twice as many women as men seek medical help. Depression is common in older people, but it can be mistaken for an early sign of dementia or overlooked as 'just getting old'. Depression is not limited to adults – children and young people can also become depressed.

COMMON CAUSES

The causes of depression are many and various. You may know why you are depressed – it may be a natural reaction to something happening in your life, such as divorce – or there may be no apparent cause. Depression sometimes runs in families, but how much this is due to genetics and how much to environment or upbringing is not clear. Negative life experiences are more likely to lead to depression if your feelings about the negative event are not expressed or explored.

Common causes of depression include recent life events, such as a **bereavement**; financial or relationship problems; **disability**; childhood experiences that have affected the way you feel about yourself and the world; and traumatic experiences such as a physical attack. Other possible triggers of depression are recent life changes, such as moving house or having a baby. Poor diet, lack of exercise and physical illness sometimes lie behind bouts of depression.

SYMPTOMS

Depression affects different people in different ways and there is a wide range of emotional and physical symptoms. These include sadness, low mood, constant irritability, seeing the worst

▼ **A common affliction** Depression is nothing to be ashamed of – one person in five will be affected at some point in life. In the UK, 2.9 million people are diagnosed as depressed at any one time.

in everything, feeling worthless, guilty and despairing, and losing interest in things you used to enjoy such as reading, sport, social activities, music or sex. Depressed people are also often preoccupied with thoughts of death or suicide.

Other symptoms include eating problems – for example, having no appetite and losing weight, or overeating and gaining weight – and sleep problems such as waking early, having difficulty getting to sleep, or being unable to get up.

Depression may be an underlying cause if you have serious problems involving concentration, thinking or making decisions, or if you feel agitated, anxious and unable to relax (see **Anxiety**). Likewise, if you feel tired all the time or as though you have no energy, or if you suffer from headaches, aches and digestive pain, depression may be at the root of your problems.

TREATMENT

It can be very difficult to seek help when you feel depressed and listless, but deciding to do something about your depression is the first step to putting things right. See a doctor if you have had five or more of the symptoms described above for at least two weeks.

The sooner you obtain treatment for severe depression, the sooner you will start to get better. If you feel unable to help yourself, or feel desperate or suicidal, see a doctor, telephone the Samaritans or tell someone you trust.

A doctor may talk to you about your feelings and symptoms and may also want to talk to family members or a close friend. The doctor will also want to eliminate physical causes. Depression may be a symptom of an underlying condition, or may even be a side effect of medication.

The doctor will discuss options for treatment, or possible combinations of treatments, and may prescribe antidepressants or other drugs. You may be referred to another practitioner for talking therapies such as counselling, cognitive behaviour therapy or psychotherapy.

If you are severely depressed, you may be admitted to the psychiatric ward of a hospital.

Depression may disappear without treatment, especially if it is a normal reaction to a life event. But if it persists it can disrupt your life and relationships. Your treatment should depend on the severity of the depression, how long you have had it and how much it is disrupting your life.

Medication

Antidepressant drugs are the most common drug treatment for depression. They do not cure depression but can reduce the symptoms and help you through a crisis to the point where you can help yourself. Antidepressants aim to restore chemicals in the brain to a healthy level. This involves increasing levels of noradrenaline and seratonin, two chemicals in the brain that affect mood. Antidepressants fall into three main groups: tricyclics, monoamine oxidase inhibitors (MAOIs) and seratonin-specific reuptake inhibitors (SSRIs) (see **Drugs**).

Antidepressants do not offer instant relief – they often take between two and four weeks to have an effect. They do not work for everyone, and can cause unpleasant side effects. Tricyclics can cause drowsiness, blurred vision, a dry mouth and constipation. MAOIs can interact with other drugs and foods containing tyramine (such as cheese), causing a sudden rise in blood pressure. SSRIs may cause agitation and nausea.

Electroconvulsive therapy (ECT)

Electroconvulsive therapy may be given to severely depressed people when antidepressant drugs have failed to work. The depressed person is put to sleep with an anaesthetic, then a small electric current is passed through the brain. The electric shock gives the brain a seizure. This stimulates the release of the neurotransmitter chemicals that carry messages between brain cells, which appears to improve the mood of the depressed individual.

ECT is a controversial treatment that can have side effects such as short-term memory loss. Doctors will recommend it only as a last resort.

Talking therapies

Therapies such as counselling, cognitive behaviour therapy and psychotherapy can help people who want to explore and understand themselves and their depression. These talking therapies can be beneficial used alongside antidepressants or instead of them.

Counselling examines your feelings at the time of the depression and can help you to adjust to life events, illnesses or losses. Cognitive behaviour therapy aims to encourage you to replace negative thought patterns with positive ones. Psychotherapy helps you to find and explore the root causes of your depression.

Some people find it unhelpful to focus on their problems. What seems to matter most in talking therapies is the relationship between individual and therapist. Continue treatment only if you feel comfortable with the counsellor or therapist.

Talking therapies are available within the NHS in some areas, both in GPs' surgeries and in hospitals. Many voluntary organizations and self-help groups offer counselling and support at low cost or free of charge or you may choose a fee-charging therapist privately.

What you can do

There are no instant solutions to depression. What you can do for yourself depends on how low you are feeling. You may feel paralysed and unable to act. If so, you may need professional help or drugs to get you to a point where you

> For many people, a combination of talking treatments and antidepressants is the best way of coping with depression.

Postnatal depression

Many women feel exhausted, helpless or even frightened for several days or weeks after giving birth. In a few mothers, this reaction is stronger and longer-lasting, and may develop into a mental disorder known as postnatal depression.

Women with postnatal depression may suffer mood swings and feel angry and negative towards their baby and their partner. They often feel anxious and have panic attacks. Some also have physical symptoms such as digestive problems and stomach or chest pains.

Try to make time for yourself – a night out or even just a visit to the salon for a haircut may help you to move on from the depression. If you can, take daily exercise – it helps to ease tension. Make sure you eat regularly, because you may feel worse if you go for long periods without food. Most women have good spells when postnatal depression eases and bad ones when it is worse, and the proportion of good spells gradually increases.

can take action to help yourself. Depression feeds on itself – you get depressed, then you become more depressed about being depressed. If you can break the cycle of negative thoughts, you can begin to break the hold that depression has on you. Joining a support group can help to ease isolation and boost self-esteem.

Complementary therapies

Many people find complementary therapies useful for emotional problems. Therapies that can be helpful for depression include **aromatherapy,** **massage, acupuncture** and **meditation.** Many therapies and treatments can be used alongside orthodox medical treatment, but always consult your GP first.

OUTLOOK

Depression can be treated, and most people recover from it, whatever the cause. You may have to try several treatments before finding the one or the combination that is best for you.

LIVING WITH A DEPRESSED PERSON

If relatives or friends are depressed, show that you care by listening sympathetically and being affectionate. Encourage them to talk about how they feel and help them to decide what they can do to deal with the depression. Get some support for yourself – from other family members, depression support groups or carers' groups.

SEE ALSO *Chronic fatigue syndrome; Insomnia; Manic depression; Postnatal depression; Seasonal affective disorder*

CONTACT **Depression Alliance** (020) 7633 0557. Self-help, support groups, information. **Fellowship of Depressives Anonymous** (01702) 433838. Self-help and support. **British Association for Counselling and Psychotherapy (BACP)** 0870 443 5252 (www.counselling.co.uk) for lists of UK counsellors and psychotherapists. **The Samaritans** 08457 90 90 90 (www.samaritans.org.uk) offers confidential telephone support.

Staying well

There are many things that you can do to help you to stay well once your depression has lifted.

■ Join a support group to meet others who suffer from depression. It can alleviate feelings of isolation and helplessness.

■ Look after yourself physically and reduce the stress in your life. Take regular exercise, eat well and practise relaxation techniques.

■ You may need to stay on medication or persist with talking therapy for a time to avoid a relapse.

■ Know your triggers. Be aware of the kinds of things that make you depressed and avoid them if possible.

■ Notice early-warning signs. You may be able to avoid a crisis and get help quickly. It helps if people around you are aware of these signs, too.

Dermatitis

Dermatitis, or eczema, is an inflammatory skin condition. The term 'contact dermatitis' refers to two types of eczema – irritant and allergic. Irritant eczema is triggered by substances that directly damage the skin, while allergic eczema occurs when someone becomes sensitized to something in the environment. Atopic eczema (atopic dermatitis) is a pink scaly rash that is very itchy. It may appear only on wrists and ankles, knee and elbow creases, or it can be much more extensive. There are a number of other types (see box below).

SYMPTOMS

Symptoms of dermatitis vary from mild to severe and can include:

- a patch of dry, scaly, thickened skin;
- redness;
- itching;
- blisters;
- weeping sores that may become infected;
- crusting
- severe inflammation with blisters on hands and feet (pompholyx, see box below).

TREATMENT

Treatment for dermatitis depends on the cause.

- Avoid contact with the substance that triggers the reaction.
- Regularly apply emollients, non-cosmetic moisturizers available from pharmacies and on prescription. A twice daily application of steroid cream may be prescribed, the strength of which depends on the body part affected and the age of the person concerned. Hydrocortisone cream is available from pharmacies without a prescription.

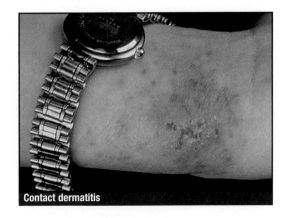

Contact dermatitis

▲ **Contact dermatitis** People who are allergic to the nickel used in some metal watchstraps develop a painful dermatitis rash on their wrist.

- Occasionally, in cases of severe dermatitis, an oral corticosteroid may be prescribed.
- Antihistamines, which can help to reduce itching and swelling, may be prescribed.
- In the case of pompholyx, patch-testing for specific common allergies may be carried out. One in ten people shows a consistent positive result, allowing easy resolution of the problem.

Complementary therapies

Aloe vera and evening primose may be helpful.

COMPLICATIONS

Chronic actinic dermatitis can spread to cause redness over the whole body (erythroderma). This can result in serious loss of body heat and fluids, and in extreme cases heart failure.

PREVENTION

To prevent dermatitis, avoid known allergens and use emollients and soap substitutes daily.

The types and causes of dermatitis

Most types of dermatitis are triggered by contact with an external irritant, but allergy to gluten and the presence of particular antibodies in the blood are among the internal causes.

Allergic contact dermatitis A reaction that occurs in people allergic to substances such as nickel. An estimated one in four people in the UK is affected by nickel-induced contact dermatitis. Common irritants include perfume, chromium and some plants, especially cacti and varieties of the primula family.

Irritant dermatitis This may occur in anyone whose skin comes into contact with chemical irritants such as acids, alkalis, solvents and detergents.

Chronic actinic dermatitis A relatively rare form of allergy to sunlight. Severe cases can also be triggered by exposure to artificial lighting.

Pompholyx Blisters form on the hands and feet in this acute form of dermatitis. It may be caused by wearing powdered natural rubber latex gloves. Using powder-free, non-latex gloves usually solves the problem.

Dermatitis herpetiformis This is an itching, blistering, symmetrical rash that usually appears on the knees, elbows, buttocks or shoulders, and is associated with sensitivity to gluten, which is found in bread and other grain products. Sufferers are advised to adopt a gluten-free diet.

Atopic dermatitis Also known as eczema, atopic dermatitis is an inherited tendency that affects people with a family history of disorders such as asthma, eczema and hay fever. It causes very dry, intensely itchy skin and in severe cases eruptions and crusting of the skin. Atopic dermatitis is associated with the presence of certain antibodies in the blood.

Detached retina

The retina is the light-sensitive membrane at the back of the eye. When it becomes partially separated from its underlying bed, the condition is called a detached retina. It usually occurs because a hole or tear in the retina has allowed fluid to accumulate behind it, and the pressure of the fluid forces the retina away from its bed.

SYMPTOMS

Symptoms include seeing:
- unusual flashing lights;
- a shower of dark floating spots;
- a large floating ring;
- a black curtain with a sharp, curved edge that appears to move inwards from the periphery of vision, obscuring all vision beyond its edge.

If you have the condition and it is not treated, you will lose all useful vision in the affected eye. The more quickly you have an eye operation, the better the prognosis.

CAUSES

The development of a detached retina is often preceded by degenerative changes in the retina that result in holes or tears. The main causes are:
- severe short-sightedness (myopia);
- a penetrating injury to the eyeball;
- abnormalities in the eye's vitreous humour, the transparent, jelly-like substance contained in the vitreous cavity behind the eye's lens;
- a **tumour** in the eye;
- **eclampsia** (convulsions in pregnancy);
- diabetic retinopathy (see **Diabetes**).

In some cases, eye injury that results in a detached retina can be caused by a heavy blow to the head.

TREATMENT

Treatment usually involves an operation to seal off holes in the retina. This may be carried out using a freezing probe or a laser.

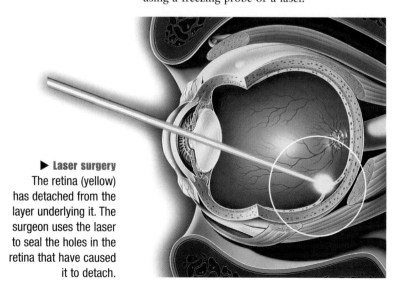

▶ **Laser surgery**
The retina (yellow) has detached from the layer underlying it. The surgeon uses the laser to seal the holes in the retina that have caused it to detach.

> ## ⚠ Warning
>
> About one person in 10,000 in the UK will develop a detached retina. It is entirely painless, but it is an emergency condition. If you have any of the symptoms listed, seek medical advice immediately.
>
> Try to keep your head as still as possible. This may help to reduce the movement of fluid under the detaching retina, which will make the condition worse.

PREVENTION

Anyone at risk should have regular eye examinations with an optometrist.

OUTLOOK

With effective surgery, the recovery prospects are excellent.

SEE ALSO *Eye and problems*

Detoxification

Detoxification is the removal or neutralization of toxic or poisonous substances from the body. This is a natural function carried out by the liver to counteract the effects of potentially harmful substances – including drugs and alcohol. The term is also used to mean a process of withdrawal from alcohol or drugs under medical supervision. Its meaning has further expanded from there to include various minimal dietary regimes used in complementary medicine and **nutritional therapy** and aimed at cleansing the body internally.

Medically supervised detoxification is used for drug addiction where unpleasant symptoms of withdrawal such as **delirium** are likely to occur once drug intake is stopped. It is used particularly for addiction to alcohol – the process is colloquially known as 'drying out'.
- The supervised detoxification process usually involves a stay as an in-patient at a psychiatric hospital or special treatment unit.
- The body is weaned off the substance in a controlled environment in which the addicted person is isolated from any temptations to relapse, and doctors can help to control distressing symptoms.
- Once the substance has been removed from the body, longer-term treatment and counselling will usually be needed to ensure continued abstinence.

SEE ALSO *Addictions; Alcohol and abuse; Behaviour therapy; Cognitive behaviour therapy; Diet; Drugs, misuse of; Liver and disorders*

Diabetes

Diabetes is the name given to two metabolic disorders, the most common form is diabetes mellitus. Diabetes insipidus is much rarer but both are characterized by excessive thirst and increased urination.

In the UK, around 1.4 million people are known to have diabetes mellitus, and it is thought at least a million more people have the condition without being aware of it. This is because the most common form of the condition (known as Type 2 diabetes) may produce only mild symptoms, so it can easily be overlooked.

Diabetes mellitus

Diabetes mellitus is the most common disorder affecting the glands of the **endocrine system**. It is caused by a shortage or lack of the hormone **insulin** produced by the pancreas. The body uses insulin to absorb glucose into cells, and a deficiency leads to abnormally high levels of glucose in the blood and the urine. This causes problems and defects in various parts of the body. There are two main types of diabetes mellitus: Type 1 and Type 2.

■ **Type 1** This is also known as insulin-dependent or juvenile diabetes. In most cases it first appears under the age of 40, and it is commonly discovered in teenagers. The onset is usually sudden – the production of insulin completely halts due to the destruction of pancreatic cells.

■ **Type 2** Non insulin-dependent diabetes is also known as late-onset diabetes as it once commonly affected people over the age of 40, but increasing numbers of children are developing it. It occurs when the insulin produced is not sufficient for the body's needs. The body may be insulin-resistant, in which case the cells are unable to respond to normal levels of insulin. At first the pancreas tries to right the situation by producing more insulin, but it is unable to keep this up over time, and eventually it is unable to release enough to keep the blood glucose levels stable.

CAUSES AND RISK FACTORS

Genes play a part in both types of diabetes mellitus, but environmental factors are thought to be the triggers. Of the people who inherit the genes for Type 1 diabetes, only a small proportion actually develop the condition. Many people newly diagnosed with Type 1 diabetes have antibodies to a protein found in cow's milk, leading some researchers to suggest that feeding babies with formula milk may trigger the immune system to destroy pancreatic cells. It is thought more likely that Type 1 diabetes occurs as a result of a viral infection that damages the pancreas.

Type 2 is by far the most common form of diabetes mellitus. Risk factors include a family history of diabetes, increasing age and being of Asian or Afro-Caribbean origin. Being overweight, particularly if you store fat around the waist, is another risk factor as **obesity** is known to increase insulin resistance. Weight loss and keeping active reduce insulin resistance.

Globally, the number of people who have this form of diabetes is rising. This is attributed to the fact that people in the developed world are increasingly inactive and overweight.

SYMPTOMS

The following symptoms are associated with uncontrolled Type 1 and Type 2 diabetes due to excessive levels of glucose in the blood (**hyperglycaemia**). People with Type 2 diabetes

▲ **Insulin injection**
Diabetic children quickly learn how to inject insulin painlessly into the fat beneath the skin, from where it is absorbed into the bloodstream.

Hypoglycaemic fits

If blood glucose levels fall abnormally low, diabetics may lapse into unconsciousness.

People with Type 1 diabetes may inadvertently take too much insulin, eat too little or exercise too much. The glucose level in their blood may then drop to an abnormally low level (hypoglycaemia). Signs of oncoming hypoglycaemia include faintness, palpitations, sweating, breathlessness and confused or violent behaviour. Sugary food or drink remedies the situation and should be followed by a starchy snack such as a sandwich, or a meal if it is due. Type 1 diabetics should always carry a sugary snack in case of emergency. If the person falls into unconsciousness, seek medical help immediately.

In the UK, diabetes mellitus is up to five times more common among people of Afro-Caribbean and Asian origin than it is among the European population.

may experience only some of the symptoms, or only in a mild form, leading many to be unaware that they have the condition. The symptoms include increased urination (polyuria), excessive thirst (polydipsia), fatigue, unexplained weight loss, genital itching or thrush, blurred vision and tingling in the hands and feet.

DIAGNOSIS AND MANAGEMENT

Diabetes is diagnosed by a blood test to check for glucose. A urine sample may be taken and a glucose-tolerance test may also be performed. Type 1 diabetes is more easily identified than Type 2, which may go undetected for between nine and twelve years.

People with Type 1 diabetes always need to inject insulin because their body is unable to make the hormone. They inject up to five times a day, depending on their lifestyle. They also need to follow a balanced diet to ensure that their blood sugar levels do not fluctuate too widely.

Initially, people with Type 2 diabetes are often able to control their symptoms with regular injections of insulin. Diet, regular exercise, weight loss (if necessary) and oral medication to help the body utilize insulin more efficiently all play a part in managing the condition. As the condition progresses, people may have to rely on insulin injections to balance their blood sugar. Possible future alternatives to injected insulin include nasal and oral sprays, patches, tablets and inhalers.

COMPLICATIONS AND OUTLOOK

Most people with diabetes lead a healthy life. However, there is a risk of serious complications if the condition is not tightly controlled. A short-term risk in Type 1 diabetes is ketoacidotic coma. This is the result of the body breaking down fat and muscle to create energy normally provided by glucose.

Both types of diabetes can lead to complications from the effects of persistently raised levels of blood glucose on the body's blood vessels and nerves. These include coronary heart disease, **stroke** and kidney disease, as well as nerve damage and lack of blood supply to the feet, which in severe cases can result in amputation. Diabetic retinopathy, a disease of the retina, can lead to **blindness**. It is the most common cause of blindness in people aged 20–65 in the UK.

Pregnancy and diabetes

Gestational diabetes mellitus (GDM) affects a small number of pregnant women. It usually develops during the second or third trimester as a result of the body's failure to produce enough insulin to meet the extra demands of pregnancy. Although blood glucose levels usually return to normal after delivery, women who have had GDM have a higher risk of developing Type 2 diabetes in later life.

Pregnant women with diabetes must control their blood glucose level prior to conception and throughout pregnancy to avoid the risk of complications. Too much glucose in the bloodstream increases the risk of malformation. In addition, the baby may grow too big and need to be delivered by **Caesarean** section.

Diabetes insipidus

Diabetes insipidus is a completely separate disorder from diabetes mellitus. The similar names derive from the fact that excessive urination is a symptom of both (diabetes means overflow). Thirst is the other main symptom. In diabetes insipidus these symptoms are caused by an imbalance of antidiuretic hormone (ADH), or vasopressin, which is stored in the pituitary gland and maintains the fluid balance within the body.

There are four types. Neurogenic diabetes insipidus is caused by a deficiency of ADH, while the nephrogenic form is caused by an inability of the kidneys to respond to ADH. The third type, gestagenic, appears during pregnancy and the fourth, called dipsogenic, is caused by abnormal thirst and excessive intake of fluids.

The treatment depends on the cause. In some types, a synthetic form of ADH is taken in a nasal spray or tablet. For sufferers of the dipsogenic form of the disease, the only treatment is limitation of fluid intake with, occasionally, a small dose of synthetic ADH at night.

Diet and exercise to control diabetes

People with diabetes should pay careful attention to diet and activity levels.

The diet should be the same as is recommended for general health, with plenty of fresh fruit and vegetables, wholegrain cereals and pulses, some low-fat protein, less saturated fat (choose poly-unsaturated and monounsaturated varieties), and a minimum of fatty, sugary foods and salt. Eating regularly helps to maintain stable blood glucose levels, and regular exercise is important for managing the diabetes. It can also help to control blood glucose and blood pressure, strengthen the heart and lungs and aid weight control.

CONTACT Diabetes UK Central Office 10 Parkway, London NW1 7AA (020) 7424 1000 (www.diabetes.org.uk)

The Pituitary Foundation PO Box 1944, Bristol BS99 2UB 0845 450 0375 (www.pituitary.org.uk; helpline@pituitary.org.uk)

Diagnosis

A diagnosis is a doctor's analysis of a patient's health problem. Before making a diagnosis, your doctor may ask for a description of your symptoms, check your medical history and perform an examination.

If you complain of a sore throat, for example, the doctor will usually ask about the duration and nature of your symptoms and examine your throat. In some cases, the doctor can confidently diagnose tonsillitis in the consulting room. If, however, you have many symptoms and a complicated medical history, the doctor may not be able to make a diagnosis at once. Blood tests or **X-rays** may have to be performed or the doctor may refer you to a specialist.

A MEDICAL HISTORY

Doctors and nurses are trained to take a medical history, which involves asking questions about your past health and the health of your family. People are often surprised at how many diverse questions doctors ask them; some may seem completely unrelated to their problem or illness. However, a pain in one area may be an indication of a problem somewhere else in the body. For example, if you have a headache you may be suffering from **depression** or high **blood pressure**. Some diseases, such as **angina** and **asthma**, can run in families, which is why doctors often ask about relatives' health.

TESTS

The most common tests used to aid diagnosis are blood tests, urine tests and X-rays.

Blood tests

When a blood sample is taken, it is not automatically tested for a range of conditions. For example, if a doctor has requested a full blood count to ensure that you are not anaemic, no other tests will be run on that blood sample. Ask your doctor which tests are being done and the reasons for doing them so that you are aware of what diagnoses are being considered.

Urine tests

The simplest method of testing a urine sample is with a 'dipstick': a piece of card placed in the sample changes colour if abnormal substances such as protein, blood or glucose are present in the urine. The sample of urine can also be sent to the laboratory in the local hospital for more sophisticated tests. These include testing for the presence of infection and determining the amount of protein or blood in the sample. It is not possible to test for diabetes by a urine test – a blood test is required. But you can confirm a pregnancy with a dipstick or a laboratory test.

X-rays

X-rays can be performed on any part of the body. The most common type of X-ray performed is a chest X-ray, which looks at the size and shape of the heart, the lungs and also the ribs. Certain areas of the body, such as the brain and liver, do not show up well on a standard X-ray and may require a specialized form, such as a **CT scan**. A radiologist interprets the X-rays and sends a written report to your doctor.

IF YOU THINK A DIAGNOSIS IS WRONG

If you think a doctor has made a mistake in diagnosing you, the first step is to discuss the matter with your GP. It may be that the doctor has simply not explained his or her reasoning adequately. The GP may refer you to a specialist for further consultation or refer you for further tests directly.

All patients are entitled to ask for a second opinion and usually the doctor will arrange this. It may mean seeing a different GP in the same practice or being referred to another consultant in the same specialty.

Self-diagnosis

It may seem an attractive option to make your own diagnosis of your health problems on the basis of reading books and articles in newspapers or on the Internet. But this is rarely advisable. Doctors and nurses are highly qualified and able to use both knowledge and experience in making an expert diagnosis.

If used with care, the Internet can be an excellent source of medical information. However, it has been estimated that half of all medical websites have not been reviewed by a healthcare professional – therefore much of the content may be inaccurate or misleading. Many American websites refer to treatment that is unavailable in the UK.

SEE ALSO *Biopsy; Internet: medical information online; Self-examination; Urine tests; X-rays*

The most common blood tests

Blood tests are quick and easy to perform, and provide detailed evidence of the effects of disease on the body. They are an invaluable aid to diagnosis.

TEST	WHAT IT DOES
Full blood count	Indicates anaemia.
Kidney function	Measures levels of salts in the body and checks that the kidneys are working normally.
Liver function	Measures the levels of liver enzymes in the blood to check the liver is working properly.
Glucose	Indicates diabetes.
Thyroid function	Checks the levels of thyroid hormones in the blood to ascertain how well the thyroid is functioning.

Dialysis

Dialysis is a medical procedure that artificially cleans the blood of people whose kidneys have stopped functioning. Normally, the kidneys filter poisonous waste products such as urea, together with excess salts, minerals and water from the blood to form urine. The urine is then excreted from the body. When the kidneys fail, these waste products accumulate in the blood and, if not treated, this can be fatal.

Kidney failure usually develops slowly, and in its early stages can be treated with drugs and by controlling your diet and daily liquid intake. You may be prescribed drugs to to control blood pressure and balance blood acidity. A dietician may advise you to reduce your salt intake or to eat fewer protein-rich foods such as fish, meat, cheese, milk and eggs. People in the early stages of kidney failure are advised to drink around 3 litres (5 pints) of liquid daily.

Dialysis is given in severe cases of kidney failure, either until the kidneys recover or until a donor kidney becomes available for transplantation.

HOW DIALYSIS WORKS

Dialysis works by passing the patient's blood over one side of a semi-porous membrane while the other side of the membrane is washed with a purifying solution known as dialysate. The pores in the membrane allow the molecules of waste products into the dialysate while holding back the larger blood cells and proteins. The dialysate and waste products are then drained and discarded.

There are two main types of dialysis: peritoneal dialysis and haemodialysis (see box). For the first type, a catheter must be inserted through the abdominal wall into your abdominal cavity. This is done in a short operation in hospital under general anaesthetic. You will usually be allowed to return home within two days of the operation. Around two weeks later you will begin a week-long training programme in how to perform peritoneal dialysis..

Most patients undergoing haemodialysis have a short operation to have a sterile, closeable opening (fistula) made in their arm through which a good flow of blood can exit to the dialysis machine. The operation is performed in hospital under local or general anaesthetic. Dialysis centres in hospitals are staffed by specialist nurses, and which type of dialysis is used depends on their assessment of your condition. The nurses may visit you at home to explain the practicalities of your treatment and how to fit it into your routine with the least disruption. Family members and close friends can attend these sessions with you if you wish.

Perintoneal dialysis

Once you have learned how to do it, peritoneal dialysis can usually be self administered and carried out at home or during breaks at work.

Continuous ambulatory peritoneal dialysis (CAPD) uses the membrane that surrounds the abdominal organs (the peritoneum) to filter blood, the task usually carried out by the kidneys.

A catheter is passed through an opening in the abdominal wall. Three or four times a day, a bag of dialysate is attached to the catheter by means of a plastic tube. It is then held aloft so that the fluid can run into the abdominal cavity.

The emptied bag is detached, and waste products and excess water in the blood are left to pass across the membrane and into the dialysate fluid.

After 3–4 hours, the fluid containing these toxins is drained back into the bag and discarded. The process lasts 30–40 minutes.

A variant of this process is called automated peritoneal dialysis (APD). It is done at night over 8–9 hours; most people learn to sleep while their blood is being filtered.

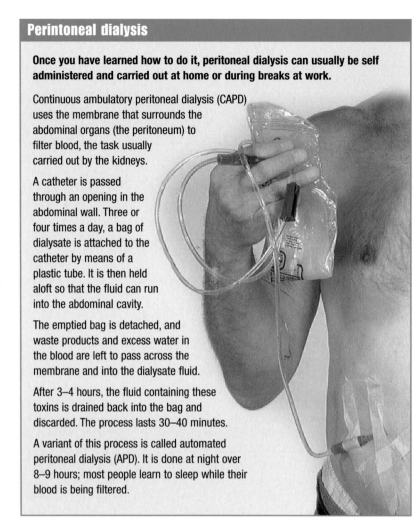

LIVING WITH DIALYSIS

Beginning dialysis treatment does not mean you have to give up your usual occupation. Nurses and doctors encourage dialysis patients to continue their normal activities as before and many employers will agree to adjust your schedule so that you can perform CAPD (continuous ambulatory peritoneal dialysis) or attend a dialysis centre for haemodialysis. However, heavy physical labour is not advised and some people with very demanding jobs – such as building labourers or packers – may need to leave the job on medical grounds.

You should be able to continue driving, although doctors will advise you not to drive immediately after haemodialysis during the first two months of treatment. The medical team will encourage you to exercise and maintain fitness for the general benefit of your health but contact sports such as football or rugby are not recommended for dialysis patients with a fistula because of the risk of damaging it. If you smoke, you will be strongly advised to stop because of the damage the habit does to your lungs and heart.

Haemodialysis

Haemodialysis treatment requires the patient to be connected to a dialysis machine.

It is usually carried out in a dialysis centre, but some people treat themselves at home.

In haemodialysis, an artificial membrane made of celloluse is used to cleanse the blood. An initial operation is necessary to make an opening in the arm, giving access to the vein. During haemodialysis, blood flows from the vein, via tubing, into one side of the artificial membrane, which is attached to a machine.

Dialysate fluid flows into the other side of the membrane. Toxins and excess water from the blood can then pass across the membrane into the dialysate fluid. Once the blood has been filtered, it is returned to the body. The dialysate fluid is discarded.

The whole process takes about 3–4 hours. It usually needs to be done three times a week.

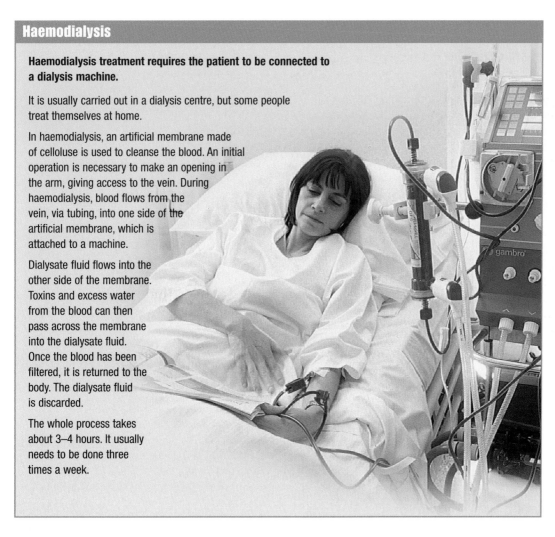

The role of diet

If you are undergoing haemodialysis, you will be on the kidney machine for an average of 12 hours a week. For the rest of the time your kidneys will not be efficiently filtering waste products from your blood. You need to follow a limited diet to control production of waste and fluid. You can eat normal amounts of protein, but must restrict potassium (found in chocolate, fruit and potatoes) and salt. You will be prescribed drugs to prevent excretion of phophates (phosphate binders). The amount of liquid you can drink depends on the amount of urine you produce each day – this varies between individuals and may change after you start treatment. During your training period on the treatment your urine production will be monitored. You will then be given a liquid allowance – 500ml (⅘ pint) daily plus a volume equal to the amount of urine produced.

If you are undergoing peritoneal dialysis, you must be careful to eat enough protein, as each time you drain the dialysate you lose protein. Eat plenty of high-protein foods such as chicken, eggs and fish. There are no limits on potassium-rich foods, and there is usually no need for phosphate binders. You will be given a daily liquid limit. Too much liquid necessitates a stronger mixture of dialysate, which damages the peritoneum over time. Dialysis patients are allowed to drink alcohol in moderation, but it must be counted as part of your diet and fluid allowance.

OUTLOOK

Your kidney function may improve, but if it does not you will have to continue dialysis for life unless you have a kidney transplant. Your medical team will discuss with you whether you are suitable for a transplant. This is usually considered the best option because it can restore your health to its level before you developed kidney disease. The general health of long-term dialysis patients will be closely monitored. Long-term haemodialysis can lead to high blood pressure (hypertension), anaemia and cardiovascular problems. Some people taking peritoneal dialysis in the long term develop an inflamed peritoneum (peritonitis).

SEE ALSO *Blood and disorders; Kidneys and disorders; Transplants*

In the UK over 180,000 people of all ages are affected by kidney disease. Each year almost 6,000 people are newly diagnosed.

Diaphragm and disorders

The purpose of the diaphragm is to work the lungs in the breathing process. As the diaphragm contracts, its shape becomes flatter increasing the volume of the chest cavity. Atmospheric pressure then forces air into the lungs, which expand to fill the space. The diaphragm then relaxes and pushes upwards, deflating the lungs and causing the person to breathe out.

WHAT CAN GO WRONG

Problems arise when the stomach or other abdominal organs push up through the abdomen.

Hiatus hernia

When part of the stomach juts up through the diaphragm into the chest cavity, the condition is known as a hiatus hernia. The cause is not known, but risk factors seem to be increasing age, obesity and smoking, all of which may weaken the diaphragm.

Often a hiatus hernia has no symptoms. Where there are symptoms, these include:
- chest pain;
- heartburn;
- difficulty in swallowing;
- belching.

You may be able to reduce heartburn by losing weight if you are overweight, refraining from large meals and spicy foods, eating at least 2–3 hours before lying down and not wearing tight clothes.

Treatments are given to reduce stomach acidity and to strengthen the opening from the stomach. Surgery may be necessary if symptoms persist or if complications such as **gastro-oesophageal reflux** occur. In gastro-oesophageal reflux, the contents of the stomach pass back into the oesophagus.

Diaphragmatic hernia

In some babies the diaphragm does not form properly, with the result that one of the abdominal organs pushes up into the chest cavity. This generally leads to a collapsed lung. Symptoms include:
- severe breathing difficulties;
- skin turning blueish;
- pauses in breathing.

If your child has any of these symptoms, seek urgent medical advice.

Paralysis of the diaphragm

This condition most commonly affects babies, particularly those born in the breech position or with the aid of instruments. If the muscles of the diaphragm weaken, the contents of the

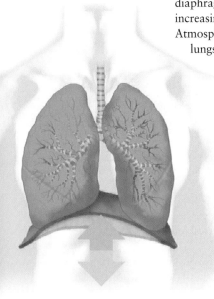

▲ **Flexible muscle**
The diaphragm is attached to the lower ribs at the sides and to the breastbone and backbone at the front and back. When it relaxes it forms a dome shape, forcing air out of the lungs. When it contracts , it flattens out and moves downwards, causing the lungs to fill with air.

abdomen push up into the chest cavity. Breathing capacity, especially when lying down, can be significantly reduced. A typical symptom is night-time breathlessness.

SEE ALSO *Chest pain; Respiratory system*

Diarrhoea

Diarrhoea is the frequent passage of loose, watery stools, often with explosive bowel movements. It is a common symptom of a wide range of conditions. Travellers' diarrhoea is one of the commonest illnesses experienced in tropical or subtropical countries (see **Travel and health**).

Diarrhoea can be very serious in babies and in elderly people because of the associated dangers of **dehydration**. It kills more than 3 million children each year, mainly in developing countries.

SYMPTOMS
- Frequent, loose, watery bowel movements.
- Abdominal pain (sometimes).
- Fever (sometimes).
- Nausea and vomiting (sometimes).
- Loss of appetite (sometimes).
- Dehydration – signs that a person is dehydrated include concentrated dark urine, dry skin and mouth, loss of skin elasticity, sunken eyes and, in severe cases, lightheadedness or confusion.

DURATION
- Acute diarrhoea comes on suddenly and lasts from a few hours to two or three days.
- Chronic diarrhoea can last for more than three weeks and may recur.

CAUSES
Diarrhoea is a symptom of many illnesses.
- Bacterial and viral infections that irritate the intestinal lining, with the result that more fluid passes from the blood into the intestines.
- Food that is contaminated, usually by *Staphylococcus* bacteria (see **Food poisoning**).
- A food allergy, such as hypersensitivity to gluten in wheat, or lactose or glucose intolerance (see **Coeliac disease; Food allergy and intolerance**).
- Anxiety and **stress**.
- A reaction to certain **drugs** such as antibiotics, some antacids, and blood pressure and arthritis medications.
- The abuse of **laxatives**.
- More rarely, **dysentery** or **typhoid fever**.
- Chronic diarrhoea may be caused by intestinal disorders such as **Crohn's disease** and **colitis**.

TREATMENT
You can usually treat diarrhoea at home using over-the-counter medicines.

How to deal with diarrhoea in babies and toddlers

Diarrhoea in babies is normally caused by a viral infection. Other causes include lactose intolerance and coeliac disease (gluten-sensitive enteropathy).

- Check there is nothing irritating in your child's diet – or yours if you are breastfeeding.

- Give plenty of fluids but do not give solid food.

- Give oral rehydration sachets, available from the chemist, dissolved in water that has been boiled.

- Gradually re-introduce solid foods for toddlers when the diarrhoea stops.

- Wash your hands thoroughly after handling or changing your child.

Call a doctor

- If there are signs of dehydration.

- If your child is vomiting, feels pain, is not gaining weight or has blood in his or her stools.

- If your child has a high fever or is floppy.

What a doctor may do

- Prescribe a special baby milk containing no sugars.

- Refer the child to a paediatrician.

What you can do
- Rest, take 3–4 litres (5–7 pints) of fluids a day and avoid food, especially dairy products.
- Buy oral rehydration sachets from your pharmacist. Alternatively, make up a solution of 4 level teaspoons of sugar and ½ a level teaspoon of salt dissolved in 1 litre (1.75 pints) of clean water.
- Take over-the-counter antidiarrhoeal medicines unless you have blood or pus in your motions.

When to consult a doctor
Go to your doctor if:
- diarrhoea lasts more than 24 hours in a baby or in frail or elderly people;
- there is blood or pus in your motions;
- symptoms are severe and persist for longer than three days;
- others are simultaneously affected;
- you have returned recently from abroad;
- there are signs of dehydration.

What a doctor may do
- Prescribe oral rehydration salts.
- Prescribe an antidiarrhoeal drug, such as loperamide.
- Arrange for testing of the faeces.

Complementary therapies
Relaxation techniques and **meditation** may be helpful if diarrhoea is stress-related.

PREVENTION
Follow good hygiene practices. Wash your hands thoroughly after using the lavatory and make sure children do the same.

COMPLICATIONS
Dehydration can be life-threatening, especially in babies or elderly people.

OUTLOOK
Most people recover from an acute attack within a few days with no side effects.

Diathermy

Diathermy is the use of a high-frequency electrical current to generate heat within the body to treat certain conditions. The current passes between the electrodes which are placed on the skin. To treat rheumatic conditions and sciatica, diathermy skin pads are used. These direct a diffuse heat inward to body tissues – stimulating blood flow and promoting healing. Powerful currents concentrated at a point with a diathermy needle or knife can be used to destroy tumours, warts, ulcers and polyps.

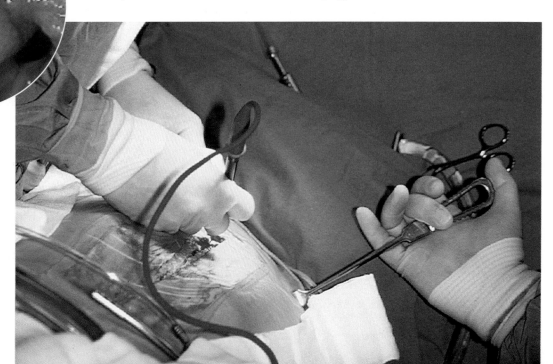

▲ **Diathermy**
The intense heat generated by a diathermy needle can be used to stop bleeding during conventional surgery or bloodlessly to destroy an ulcer (right). The electricity used in diathermy runs at 10 to 25,000 million oscillations per second.

Diet

We are what we eat, so the saying goes. Food affects the way we look and feel, our quality of life – and even how long we live. So how do we achieve a healthy and well-balanced diet?

Food supplies the raw materials for the growth of the body from a single cell to a full-grown adult, and for the production of sperm and egg cells to produce the next generation. These raw materials are also needed to maintain and repair body tissues, both throughout your life.

The human body is a complex, biochemical machine that has specific requirements for health. In addition to proteins, fats, carbohydrates and water, the body needs some 40 or more vitamins, minerals, essential fatty acids, essential amino acids and other components in order to remain healthy. A deficiency in any essential nutrient can make you ill – mildly or seriously – and in extreme cases it can lead to death.

THE FOOD PYRAMID

The main food groups are often shown as a pyramid. This makes it easy to see what types of food, eaten in what proportions, provide a balanced diet. Carbohydrates form the base of the pyramid and should be eaten in larger quantities than any of the foods higher up. The higher up you go, the less of that food type you should eat. So, for example, a balanced diet includes only small amounts from the sweets, nuts and oils group at the top of the pyramid, as they provide calories but very few nutrients.

All body cells need chemical energy to function. This is supplied mainly in the form of glucose – from carbohydrates, fats and sometimes protein. Proteins, fats and minerals are needed to build the structural parts of the body such as the bones, and vitamins and minerals are required to make active substances such as enzymes. Good nutrition, then, is based on a well-balanced diet with a varied intake of foods.

A balanced diet

Planning a balanced diet is simple if you follow a few guidelines about which foods to include from which groups and in which proportions.

First, aim to get about 50 per cent of your total daily intake of energy from carbohydrates. Try to include a portion of unrefined, starchy food, such as cereals, potatoes or bread, as part of each meal.

Eat plenty of fruit and vegetables as these are an excellent source of vitamins and minerals, as well as antioxidants and phytochemicals. Research has shown that eating a 'colour mix' of fruit and vegetables daily will help to prevent cancer and heart disease. Plan menus ahead so that meals include a lean-to-moderate portion of fat protein. Choose from fish, game, poultry, extra-lean meats and pulses (especially soya or soya-based foodstuffs such as tofu).

Oils, nuts and sweets
These foods should be eaten in very small amounts.

Proteins
Protein-rich foods are needed in moderate amounts, so total intake should be 4–6 servings daily. A serving could be a chicken breast or half a tin of beans.

Fruit and vegetables
It is recommended that you eat five or more servings a day from this group. A serving could be a large piece of fresh fruit, a handful of dried fruit, a small salad or two tablespoons of vegetables.

Carbohydrates
At the bottom of the food pyramid are carbohydrates. Breads, cereals, rice, pasta and potatoes are most people's main source of complex carbohydrates, and should form one-third of the total diet, or 6–11 servings daily. A serving could comprise either two pieces of bread, a bowl of cereal or a jacket potato.

Be sure to incorporate small quantities of olive and sesame oils, a little butter, or seeds and nuts in their raw state. Try pouring or sprinkling such small amounts over the rest of your meal. Don't forget liquids. Use drinks to obtain more nutrients – vitamin C from fruit and vegetable juices, calcium from low-fat or fortified soya milk.

Lastly, limit alcohol and other treats. They have little nutritional value and should make up no more than 10 per cent of your day's food intake.

THE MAIN FOOD GROUPS

Food is categorized into five main groups according to the type of nutrient it provides. These groups are carbohydrates, fruit, vegetables, proteins and fats. Each one has a different role to play in keeping the body in good health.

CARBOHYDRATES FOR ENERGY

Carbohydrates fuel the body. The main sources of carbohydrate in the Western diet are bread, cereals and potatoes. These are all starches. They occur in all foods made from flour, including bread, cakes, pastries, biscuits and pasta, as well as in rice and starchy vegetables such as potatoes, parsnips, sweet potatoes, pumpkin, squash, sweetcorn and broad beans. Starches also make up a large proportion of pulses such as peas, beans and lentils. For a healthy balanced diet, you should eat more carbohydrates than any of the other food groups. The healthiest come from wholegrain foods, fruit and vegetables.

Sugar, too, is a carbohydrate. It occurs naturally in some foods – in the form of fructose in fruit or lactose in milk – but processed sugar can cause harmful fluctuations in blood sugar levels: large amounts are used in processed foods, both sweet and savoury, and in commercially made drinks.

FRUIT AND VEGETABLES

Fruit and vegetables are loaded with the vitamins and minerals our bodies need to grow, develop and function. With the exception of vitamin D, which can be made in the skin by the action of sunlight, vitamins cannot be produced by the body and must therefore be provided by food and, in some cases, supplements. You need to obtain the full range of nutrients offered by fruit and vegetables, because vitamins and minerals depend on each other to function properly in the body.

The British government recommends eating 'five-a-day' – five portions of different fruit or vegetables a day – as part of a healthy balanced diet. A portion of fruit may be a single fruit, such as an apple or a banana, a cup of berries or grapes or a glass of fruit juice. A portion of vegetables is an average helping, a small salad or a glass of vegetable juice. Frozen, canned, dried or bottled fruit and vegetables all count, but avoid any with added any salt or sugar.

It's a good idea to eat fruit at breakfast, salad with lunch – if you are having a sandwich, add salad to the filling – and to use plenty of vegetables in stir-fries or stews. If you drink fruit juice and snack on fresh fruit you will quickly reach or exceed the five-a-day target.

There is clear evidence that a diet rich in fruit and vegetables helps to prevent cancer and heart disease. Also, the indigestible parts of plant material, such as fruit and vegetable skins, act as dietary fibre or roughage. This is essential to maintain healthy intestines, prevent constipation and reduce the risk of bowel disease.

PROTEINS – THE BUILDERS

Proteins are vital for growth, repair and replacement of body tissues: muscles, bones, hair and fingernails. They are needed to provide the body with amino acids. These are compounds containing the four elements that are necessary for life: carbon, hydrogen, oxygen and nitrogen. The body can make many amino acids itself, but there are eight – called essential amino acids – that it is unable to make, and so must be obtained from food.

When you eat protein, your digestive system breaks it down into amino acids that are then used to build new proteins. There are many types of protein molecule in the body, and each has a specific function. Haemoglobin, for example, is the oxygen-binding protein in the blood; keratin gives strength to nails; collagen gives skin its elasticity; while enzymes – a very important protein group – direct all the body cells' chemical reactions. Proteins are also the basis of many hormones, antibodies, neurotransmitters, and carriers of oxygen, fats and other substances within the body.

A healthy vegetarian diet

A vegetarian diet can provide adequate protein as long as it is planned properly.

With few exceptions – for example, tofu – plant proteins are deficient in one or two of the essential amino acids required by the body. By contrast, animal proteins such as meat, fish and dairy foods each contain all of these vital nutrients. However, by combining plant proteins – such as eating pulses with grains – strict vegetarians can still attain their full amino acid quota. Baked beans on toast, or pasta with a lentil-based sauce, for example, will provide the full complement of essential amino acids.

All living organisms, animals and plants, have these functions, so protein is found in all food. But the richest food sources of protein are:
- lean meat;
- fish and seafood;
- poultry and game;
- dairy foods including yoghurt;
- eggs;
- pulses, especially soya beans, soya milk and tofu;
- seeds and nuts.

The UK government guidelines recommend that we should aim to receive 10–15 per cent of our energy from protein. This is an indication of how much concentrated protein should appear on your plate. The average man needs about 55g (2oz) of protein a day.

A diet containing too much protein can put the liver and kidneys under stress. This is because the body cannot store protein, so any that is excess to requirement is converted by the liver into glucose and by-products such as urea, which are excreted. A high-protein diet also makes urine very acidic, which in turn causes the excretion of calcium from the bones, leading, in the long term, to **osteoporosis**.

FATS – BOTH GOOD AND BAD

Fats have several vital roles to play within the body. They are the main form in which energy is stored by the body and provide a layer of insulation under the skin and around certain organs. Fats are a vital structural part of cells, nerve coatings and body substances such as sex hormones. They also allow fat-soluble vitamins to enter the body.

The fats group includes all animal fats and plant oils. Natural fats are found as:
- visible fat on meat;
- less visible 'marbling' in meat;
- the skin of poultry;
- solid fats such as butter, margarine, lard and cheese;
- full-fat milk, cream, soft margarines and cream cheeses;
- oils in fish, particularly the fattier fish such as mackerel, salmon, herring and sardines;
- oils in seeds and nuts;
- refined vegetable, seed and nut oils.

In addition, since the flavour of some food depends on fat, much processed food has a high fat content.

◄ **Planning a balanced diet**
Grilled, skinned chicken is both low in fat and high in protein. Served with a varied mix of colourful vegetables, it makes a well balanced, nutrient-packed meal that is also appetizing.

Weight for weight, fat supplies twice as much energy as either carbohydrate or protein. So it is sensible to limit fat in your diet, particularly if you want to lose weight.

Government guidelines state that fat should provide no more than 30 per cent of our total energy from food: no more than one-third of this should come from saturated fats. Higher intakes of saturated fats, which occur naturally in meat and dairy products and also in coconut oil and palm oil, are associated with increased blood cholesterol levels and the associated risk of coronary heart disease (see **Heart and circulatory system**). The other two-thirds should come from unsaturated fats. There are two basic types: polyunsaturates and monounsaturates. Polyunsaturates are found in oily fish and vegetable oils; monounsaturates are provided by olive oil, rapeseed oil, avocados, nuts and seeds.

Polyunsaturates are essential fatty acids that the body cannot manufacture by itself; they must come from food. There are two main types: the Omega-6 fatty acids, which are found in corn and sunflower oils, almonds and walnuts, are needed as part of the make-up of all the body's cells; omega-3 fatty acids, which are present in oil-rich fish such as salmon, sardines and mackerel, help to reduce blood clotting and are necessary for brain development. Nutritionists recommend eating fish twice a week, and at least one of these servings should be oily fish.

Another group of fats is known as trans fats. These include hydrogenated oils such as margarine and fats that have been industrially hardened to prevent them becoming rancid. They are used a lot in the preparation of processed foods such as pies, biscuits, cakes and crisps. When fats are cooked at high temperatures or burnt they also become trans fats. Trans fat tends to accumulate in the arteries and other areas of the body and is linked to heart disease. Some research indicates that trans fats are carcinogenic (cancer-promoting).

ORGANIC FOOD

The healthiest food is food that is as close as possible to nature, such fresh, recently harvested fruit and vegetables and fresh meat and fish. Some studies suggest that these foods are even better for you if they have been grown or reared organically (see also **Organic food**).

Fruit and vegetables that are grown organically contain lower levels of pesticides than produce that has been industrially farmed. Organically reared meats are free of the antibiotics, hormones and antiparasite drugs, which are fed as a matter of course to all intensively reared animals – whether or not they are suffering from parasites or any other type of infection.

How to make the most of your food

By observing some basic principles when buying, storing, preparing and cooking foods, you can make the most of their nutritional value.

- Buy fruit and vegetables daily if possible, to access maximum vitamins and minerals; choose the best quality you can afford. Quick-frozen vegetables, such as peas, are useful on occasion, as are tinned beans, lentils and tomatoes (but avoid those with added salt and sugar).

- Prepare vegetables just before you cook them. Cook for a minimum amount of time to prevent loss of vitamins B and C – steaming is best for vitamin retention. Use any cooking water in soups, stews and gravies.

- Buy wholefoods (grains, seeds, nuts) from a reputable shop with a fast turnover, so that the foods have not had time to lose their nutritional value or become rancid.

- Dried and packaged food can be bought on a weekly or monthly basis, but rotate these items in your store cupboard so you use the oldest first.

- Use freshly baked produce, such as breads, within a day or two of purchase; moulds grow rapidly on these foodstuffs.

- Avoid foods advertised as 'packaged for extended shelf life'; they almost always contain preservatives.

- Try to avoid packaged foods containing additives, except those containing natural dyes and antioxidants.

- Store chilled food such as dairy food or meat quickly after purchase. Raw meats should be wrapped in greaseproof paper (or left in their packaging) and put on the lowest shelf, in case any blood leaks. Keep cooked meats and cheeses well away from any raw meat.

- Never re-freeze food. If you take too much uncooked food from the freezer, cook it and then freeze it. When preparing cooked meals in bulk for the freezer, cover and cool the food as quickly as possible before freezing.

- Always follow basic hygiene rules: wash your hands before preparing food and keep raw and cooked foods apart.

Research has also found that fresh organic produce contains on average 50 per cent more vitamins, minerals, enzymes and other micronutrients than intensively farmed produce.

Organic foods are usually more labour-intensive to produce and therefore tend to be more expensive than the equivalent non-organic foods. As the demand for organic foods increases, however, and more farmers and growers turn to organic methods, production costs will come down. This in turn will make organic foods cheaper to buy, and therefore more affordable for increasing numbers of consumers.

SEE ALSO *Mineral dietary supplements; Nutritional supplements; Vitamin dietary supplements*

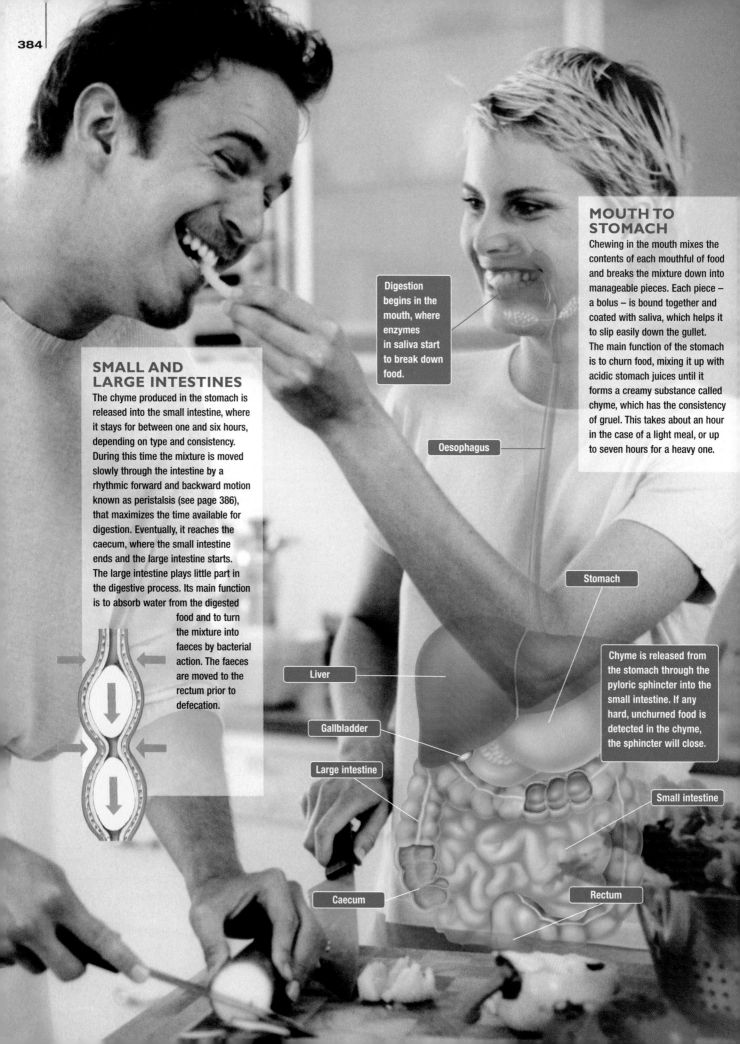

MOUTH TO STOMACH

Chewing in the mouth mixes the contents of each mouthful of food and breaks the mixture down into manageable pieces. Each piece – a bolus – is bound together and coated with saliva, which helps it to slip easily down the gullet. The main function of the stomach is to churn food, mixing it up with acidic stomach juices until it forms a creamy substance called chyme, which has the consistency of gruel. This takes about an hour in the case of a light meal, or up to seven hours for a heavy one.

Digestion begins in the mouth, where enzymes in saliva start to break down food.

Oesophagus

SMALL AND LARGE INTESTINES

The chyme produced in the stomach is released into the small intestine, where it stays for between one and six hours, depending on type and consistency. During this time the mixture is moved slowly through the intestine by a rhythmic forward and backward motion known as peristalsis (see page 386), that maximizes the time available for digestion. Eventually, it reaches the caecum, where the small intestine ends and the large intestine starts. The large intestine plays little part in the digestive process. Its main function is to absorb water from the digested food and to turn the mixture into faeces by bacterial action. The faeces are moved to the rectum prior to defecation.

Stomach

Chyme is released from the stomach through the pyloric sphincter into the small intestine. If any hard, unchurned food is detected in the chyme, the sphincter will close.

Liver

Gallbladder

Large intestine

Small intestine

Caecum

Rectum

Digestive system

The digestive system consists of a 6.5m (21ft) tube called the digestive tract, which runs from mouth to anus, together with the pancreas, liver and gallbladder. Problems can affect any part of the system.

In the digestive tract, food is broken down so that the sugars, fats, proteins, minerals, vitamins and water that it contains may be absorbed into the blood and used to fuel the body. People usually think of digestion as taking place in the stomach. But in fact it occurs mainly in the intestines, where most of the nutrients are absorbed. The enormous surface area of the lining of the small intestine, together with the thinness of the lining, and the closeness of the interior blood and lymph vessels to it, make absorption possible.

The motion that passes out at the anus consists of the unuseable elements of food – mainly cellulose – and the bacteria that aid the breakdown of food in the intestines. However, even though some elements of food do not nourish the body they do play an important part in digestion. The roughage, or fibre, in food helps to carry away wastes and may even help to protect against diverticular disease and cancer of the colon and rectum.

THE DIGESTIVE TRACT

Food may take many hours to pass along the convoluted, looping and twisting tube of the digestive tract from the mouth to the anus via the oesophagus, the stomach and the small and large intestines. The muscular walls of the tube contract rhythmically to propel the food along, while a series of valves normally prevent digested or semi-digested food from passing in the wrong direction, back up the tract to the mouth.

SPECIALIZED LINING

The stomach is lined with glands that secrete the gastric juices involved in the digestion of food (see page 387). The glands open into the main stomach cavity through gastric pits, which are visible in this micrographic image as dark holes. The lining of the small intestine contains numerous finger-like projections called villi. These are made up of cells that are specialized for absorbing nutrients.

Blood carried by arteries to the intestines flows through capillaries in the villi, where it picks up absorbed nutrients. The nutrient-rich blood is then delivered by veins to the liver for further digestion. Lymph vessels transport digested fats from the villi into the bloodstream.

How the body regulates digestion

Unconscious processes govern our appetite and the breaking down of nutrients in the food we eat.

Your appetite for food is a biological response. The hypothalamus, one of the parts of your brain that governs unconscious responses, monitors the levels of glucose circulating in your blood. When levels of blood glucose fall, the hypothalamus sends messages both to the higher centres of your brain in the cerebrum, which makes you think consciously of the need for food, and to your digestive system, preparing it for action (see **Brain and nervous system**).

Normally, you then find and eat some food, your blood glucose levels rise and the situation is stabilized. However, if you don't eat anything the signals from the hypothalamus become stronger. Your stomach starts to rumble and your appetite slowly starts to turn to hunger. As this grows sharper, you may feel hunger contractions, in which the muscles of your stomach wall contract forcefully for several minutes, causing you quite considerable discomfort.

HOW FOOD MOVES THROUGH THE SYSTEM

Rhythmic muscular movements, known as peristalsis, move the products of digestion through the digestive tract. The muscles in the walls of the digestive tract contract and relax in a rhythm which is controlled by the autonomic (unconscious) nervous system. The muscles in front of a parcel of food relax, while the ones behind it contract – and the result is a rippling, wave-like motion that moves food through the system. Food in the stomach is churned back and forth by three layers of muscle, so that it is thoroughly mixed. In the small intestine, food is moved more slowly and in both directions so that more time is allowed for digestion and absorption of nutrients. The muscles of the large intestine contract only a few times a day, usually after a meal. This is a forceful wave of contractions that pushes waste products down to the rectum so that they can be expelled when we defecate.

Factfile

Digestive enzymes and bacteria

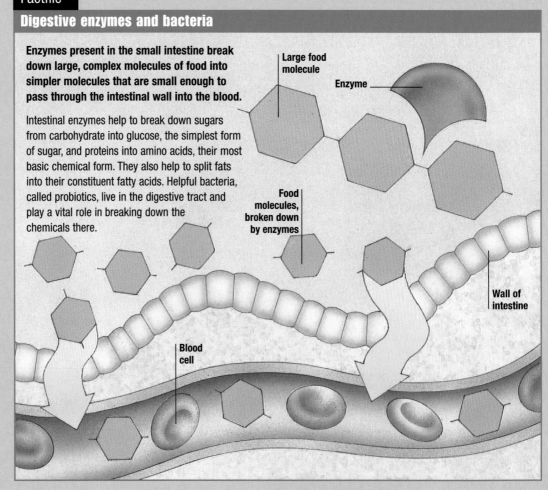

Enzymes present in the small intestine break down large, complex molecules of food into simpler molecules that are small enough to pass through the intestinal wall into the blood.

Intestinal enzymes help to break down sugars from carbohydrate into glucose, the simplest form of sugar, and proteins into amino acids, their most basic chemical form. They also help to split fats into their constituent fatty acids. Helpful bacteria, called probiotics, live in the digestive tract and play a vital role in breaking down the chemicals there.

Large food molecule

Enzyme

Food molecules, broken down by enzymes

Wall of intestine

Blood cell

How nutrients are extracted from food

Juices released in the mouth, stomach and small intestine break down the complex molecules of proteins, carbohydrates and fats in food. The molecules of vitamins and minerals are small enough for the body to absorb as they are.

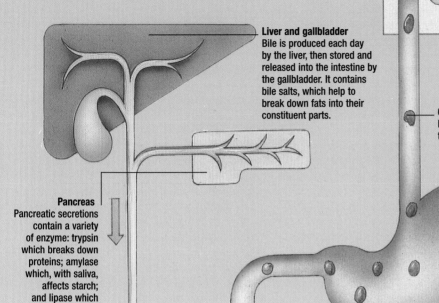

Saliva glands
Saliva is released by glands under the tongue, on the side of the face and under the lower jaw. Saliva contains the enzyme amylase, that starts the process by which starch is broken down into forms of sugar.

Liver and gallbladder
Bile is produced each day by the liver, then stored and released into the intestine by the gallbladder. It contains bile salts, which help to break down fats into their constituent parts.

Oesophagus
Each bolus of food passes down the oesophagus to the stomach.

Pancreas
Pancreatic secretions contain a variety of enzyme: trypsin which breaks down proteins; amylase which, with saliva, affects starch; and lipase which breaks down fat.

Stomach
Juices secreted by the stomach lining contain enzymes and hydrochloric acid. They begin to break down protein in food. At the same time, enzymes in the saliva that has been swallowed continue to act on starch for about 30 minutes until they are neutralized by the acidity of the stomach juices.

Small intestine
Bile, pancreatic enzymes and enzymes produced in the small intestine break down food as it passes through. The small intestine has an absorptive surface area of around 30m^2 (36 sq yd)

▼ **Absorbing nutrients**
Villi increase the intestine's absorptive area. They also release mucus, which eases the movement of food through the intestine.

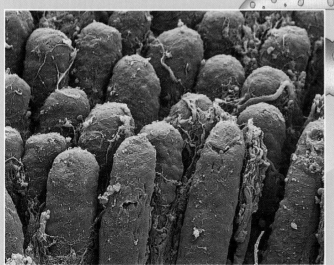

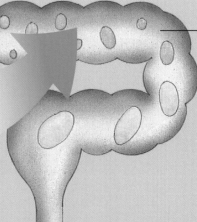

Large intestine
Bacteria in the large intestine manufacture vitamin K and some B vitamins and also break down cellulose – the material that forms the skeleton of plants – by using a process called fermentation. This creates gases, such as methane, hydrogen and carbon dioxide, which form wind.

What can go wrong

Damage to the liver, pancreas, or intestinal lining can cause painful disruptions of digestion and, ultimately, nutritional problems.

The most common cause of disruption to digestion and the absorption of nutrients is damage to the lining of the intestine or another part of the digestive tract.

Gastroenteritis is inflammation of the lining of the stomach and intestines. It leads to vomiting and diarrhoea, usually with abdominal cramps and colicky pains, a slightly raised temperature and perspiration. Traces of blood are sometimes found in vomit or stools. It is caused by bacterial or virus infection, usually from half-cooked or reheated food.

Gastritis is irritation of the stomach lining. It may be either acute (caused by something a person has eaten or drunk) or chronic (long-term and not linked to a specific incident). It also causes pain in the upper abdomen, nausea, vomiting and diarrhoea.

Ileitis, also known as **Crohn's disease**, is inflammation of the lower part of the small intestine. The cause is not known. Parts of the intestinal wall thicken and infection or ulcers may develop. It causes chronic diarrhoea, which is associated with poor appetite, fever, weight loss and abdominal pain. Sometimes ileitis may be mistaken for acute **appendicitis**.

Colitis is long-term inflammation of the colon (large intestine), which causes ulcers to form. It can cause frequent bloody diarrhoea, with fever, poor appetite, loss of weight and anaemia.

PROBLEMS WITH DIGESTIVE ENZYMES

Less common causes of digestive problems are metabolic disorders, in which there is a deficiency of one or more of the digestive enzymes. In addition, any problem that affects the pancreas, such as cancer or chronic inflammation, is likely to disrupt the supply of pancreatic enzymes to the

Keeping your digestive system healthy

Your digestive tract is tolerant of the wide variety of substances that pass through it, but reacts strongly against infected food and other irritants. You can keep your system healthy by taking care to eat only fresh foods and by eating plenty of the fibre that helps to carry wastes out of the system.

Try to avoid processed foods and to eat plenty of high-roughage foods such as fresh vegetables, meat, wholemeal bread and bran. Eat foods such as live yoghurt that contain bacteria that will boost the number of probiotics (see box, page 386) in your intestine. Eat regular, frequent meals and try not to bolt your food, even if you are very hungry. Try to stop eating before you feel completely full. Do not eat creamy foods, processed meat or fish that have been left more than eight hours at room temperature 18–21°C (65–70°F). Do not partly warm up cooked meat once it has gone cold. Either eat it cold or heat it through thoroughly. If you are constipated, do not strain too hard over motions.

▶ **Healthy approach**
Eating fresh green vegetables, fresh fruit, wholegrains, pulses and nuts will help you to maintain your digestive system in good shape. Keeping trim through regular exercise will also help, as allowing yourself to become overweight puts pressure on all your body's systems.

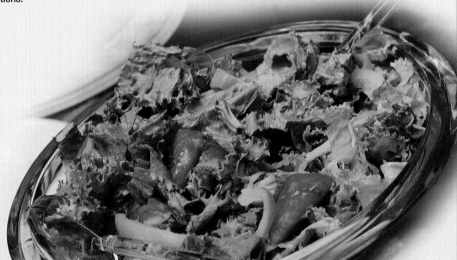

▶ **Stomach exam**
Doctors perform
an examination of
a woman's stomach
using an endoscope, a
flexible fibreoptic tube
with a video camera at
its end. The endsocope
is inserted through the
woman's mouth and
throat and passed down
the oesophagus. The
image is visible on the
screen (upper left).

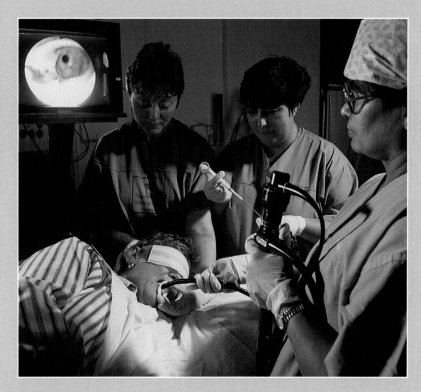

small intestine and disturb the process of
digestion there. Secretions from the pancreas
are released in response to a hormone that starts
to circulate when food is detected in the first part
of the small intestine (the duodenum).

Similarly, diseases that affect the gallbladder
or the liver will disrupt the supply of bile and
so affect the body's ability to digest fats. Bile,
which is produced in the liver and stored in the
gallbladder, contains complex chemicals called
bile salts, which help to break down fats into
their constituents. Bile production is stimulated
by a hormone whose release is triggered by the
presence of fatty foods in the duodenum.

PHYSICAL PROBLEMS

Physical problems such as the twisting or
displacement of the intestines also disrupt
the digestive process. In a hiatus **hernia**, the
stomach bulges through the diaphragm at the
weakest point where the oesophagus passes
through. The hernia is not visible and often
symptomless – symptoms where present are those
of indigestion (see below).

An **intussusception** is a twisted intestine, in
which part of the intestine pushes inside the
length of intestine next to it, like a glove finger
turning inside itself. It is most common in babies
under 12 months, and affects boys more than
girls, causing severe pain, vomiting and passing of
blood and mucus from the rectum. In adults it is
far less common and occurs where there is a
polyp or cancer within the bowel. Other physical
problems that obstruct the bowel, such as
impacted faeces and tumours, can also cause
serious digestive problems (see **Colorectal cancer**).

SYMPTOMS OF DIGESTIVE PROBLEMS

The general symptoms of mild digestive disorders
are familiar to us all – **abdominal pain**, loss of
**appetite, heartburn, indigestion, diarrhoea,
constipation, nausea, vomiting** and **flatulence**.
More serious ones include blood in the vomit or
stools, weight loss and yellow skin or eyes. Seek a
doctor's advice at once if there is a large amount
of blood in vomit or motions, if you or a person
for whom you are caring suffers prolonged or
severe vomiting with abdominal pain or diarrhoea
or if you notice a rapid deterioration in a baby or
elderly person who is vomiting or has diarrhoea.

Dealing with indigestion
Doctors define indigestion as discomfort in the
upper middle part of the abdomen, sometimes
speading up behind the breastbone. It is
associated with nausea and belching wind, which
may bring acid up to the mouth. If you suffer
from these or similar symptoms, try to work out
which foods make the pain worse, so that you
can avoid them. Alcohol can provoke digestive
problems and should never be taken to excess.
Stress can make indigestion worse, as can eating
irregularly and smoking. If you suffer from
indigestion, do not take aspirin or any drug
containing it, unless instructed to do so by your
doctor – aspirin irritates the stomach. Always tell
your doctor if the symptoms of your indigestion
grow worse or change in nature.

SEE ALSO *Bowel and disorders*

CONTACT **The Digestive Disorders
Foundation** 3 St Andrew's Place, London
NW1 4LB (020) 7486 0341
(www.digestivedisorders.org.uk)

Diphtheria

Diphtheria is a highly contagious bacterial infection that generally affects the throat but may also affect other mucous membranes and the skin. The bacteria release a toxin into the bloodstream; this toxin can obstruct the airways and damage the heart and nervous system. The infection is rare in most Western countries due to an effective vaccination programme.

SYMPTOMS

These can take the form of:
- sore throat;
- mild fever;
- tiredness;
- coughing and breathing difficulties;
- crusty scabs on the skin;
- enlarged lymph nodes in the neck;
- irregular heartbeat.

DURATION

The disease breaks out two to five days after infection. The affected person may be infectious for four weeks, sometimes longer.

CAUSES

The bacterium *Corynebacterium diphtheriae* is spread by coughs and sneezes. It can also be caught by touching people who have acquired immunity to the illness and may have no symptoms, but who harbour the organisms in their nose or skin (carriers).

TREATMENT

Early treatment is always required, so seek urgent medical advice at the earliest opportunity.

What a doctor may do
- Admit you to hospital.
- Prescribe **antibiotics** and diphtheria antitoxin.
- Treat complications as they arise.

Complementary therapies

Herbal remedies, including echinacea, may be used alongside orthodox medical treatment (see **Herbal dietary supplements**).

PREVENTION

The infection is best prevented by vaccination in childhood and boosters to maintain immunity.

COMPLICATIONS

The toxin produced by the diphtheria bacterium can cause asphyxiation and damage to the heart muscles or nervous system, resulting in heart failure or paralysis.

OUTLOOK

Diphtheria is potentially fatal, but most people recover fully with urgent medical treatment.

SEE ALSO *Bacterial infections*

Disability

Globally, almost one person in five has some kind of disability, ranging from mild impairments to severely disabling conditions.

Three-quarters of people affected by disability are mildly disabled: they are unable to do all the things they would like to do. One quarter are severely disabled, in that they cannot carry out the everyday activities associated with their age group, such as playing (in the case of children), going to work, or being able to look after themselves without assistance.

DEFINING DISABILITY

The term disability is used both as a general description and as a legal definition. There is an important difference between people with a temporary disability and those officially assessed and recognized as disabled. The latter are eligible to receive state benefits, which may include financial assistance with housing, nursing care, domestic help, physical aids such as wheelchairs, and concessions such as free parking.

Temporary incapacity due to acute illness does not usually qualify as disability, but repetitive functional impairment due to relapsing conditions such as **multiple sclerosis** or **rheumatoid arthritis** may do so. Certain disabilities may not be recognized as official disabilities. For example, the ten most common causes of disability in the developed world, as listed by the World Health Organization (see box, page 391), include alcohol abuse, depression and obsessive-compulsive disorders, but few people with these conditions are in receipt of disability benefits.

Disability may be primarily physical, marked by an inability to:
- sit, stand, or walk for long enough to allow the person to fulfil their daily tasks;
- lift or carry a weight;
- coordinate movements, such as manipulating objects by hand;
- remain alert for long periods without severe fatigue;
- breathe, eat and attend to bodily needs unaided;
- operate in a normal environment (for example, at normal temperature or both in and outside a building);
- see and hear well enough to function normally.

Or it may be primarily mental, marked by an inability to:
- understand, carry out or remember instructions;

Leading causes of disability in the developed world

Disability can have many causes and occur at any stage of life. It results in the inability to function normally because of physical or mental impairment.

■ **Depression** is the most common cause of disability worldwide, and affects between 13 and 15 per cent of the population. The condition is often overlooked because the symptoms are largely hidden.

■ **Alcohol abuse** affects about 10 per cent of people. This condition is rarely recognized as a disability.

■ **Osteoarthritis** affects 6 per cent of people. It is a progressive erosion of the bones in joints, preventing normal movement and causing chronic pain.

■ **Dementia** and other degenerative brain diseases, including Alzheimer's and Parkinson's diseases, affect about 5 per cent of people.

■ **Schizophrenia** affects 4 per cent of people. It is a brain disorder which, left untreated, causes apathy, paranoia, hallucinations and delusions.

■ **Manic depression** (bipolar disorder), a condition in which the affected person swings between depression and mania, affects 3.5 per cent of people.

■ **Cerebrovascular disease** (which affects the brain and its membranes) is a cause of disability in 3.2 per cent of people. It can take the form of a **stroke** or brain haemorrhage, and frequently causes brain damage.

■ **Diabetes**, mainly Type 2, affects 3.1 per cent of people. Left untreated, this condition causes visual impairment and kidney disease.

■ **Obsessions and compulsions** affect 3.1 per cent of people. Sufferers cannot function normally because they are restricted by obsessive thoughts or compulsions to carry out repetitive actions.

■ **Drug abuse** is the cause of disability in 2.9 per cent of people. The adverse effects of drug abuse may cause permanent mental and physical incapacity.

■ communicate through speech and the written word;
■ maintain the appropriate mood in a changing situation;
■ attend to relevant stimuli;
■ maintain a grasp of reality free of hallucinations and delusions.

Many disabilities are the result of a combination of physical and mental factors caused by a primary brain disorder such as **cerebral palsy** or **Parkinson's disease**.

CHILDHOOD DISABILITY

About half a million children in the UK are clearly disabled, and many more have mental or physical impairments that may or may not be recognized as a disability. The most common types of recognized disability are listed below.
■ Inherited disorders – **Huntington's disease** and Duchenne **muscular dystrophy**, for example.
■ Developmental abnormalities – including **autism**, cerebral palsy and **growth disorders**.
■ Disease-related disabilities – such as those caused by **polio** and bacterial **meningitis**.
■ Accidental disabilities – for example, severe head injury and damaged or amputated limbs.

The importance of early intervention
Children are in some ways more liable to disability because their brains and bodies are more fragile than those of adults. However, because they are young and still growing they also have a greater ability to recover. Early medical intervention or therapy can often help to restore the use of damaged limbs or a disordered brain by

're-training' the developing system. It is therefore important that a child's disability is recognized as soon as possible. Early signs differ according to the type of disability involved – inherited conditions may be detected by genetic tests and developmental abnormalities may be spotted during routine postnatal tests to monitor a child's progress.

Children reach developmental milestones at different rates, so a child who seems to be lagging

▼ **Self-expression**
Brain-activated computer technology can aid communication for people who are unable to use speech or the written word.

behind in things like crawling, walking or talking, may just be a late developer. Nonetheless, if parents notice that their child is different from others of the same age, they should take the child to a doctor for an assessment (see also **Child development**).

Obtaining assistance

Generally, all but the most severely disabled children are raised in the home environment. If a child is physically disabled, it may be necessary to provide aids such as a wheelchair or prosthetic appliances. Parents can usually get financial assistance with these, along with a disability caring allowance, from their local social services department. A number of high-tech devices have been developed for children who have severe movement and speech problems. They include electric wheelchairs, which allow the child to move around more independently and take part in most activities, including sports, and computers that can be operated by a movement as slight as the blink of an eyelid. Such products are not widely available and parents may have difficulty finding them – charities devoted to the type of disability concerned are often the most fruitful sources of advice.

Equipment can also be obtained through Motability. This is a charity partnership between the Government and charitable and private sectors that helps disabled people to become more mobile. Most schools can accept disabled children, but special schools are available for those who are unable to attend mainstream classes.

Children with severe mental disabilities may need such intensive supervision and special care that it is not feasible for them to live at home. This is particularly true of those with severe autism, for whom there are special institutions where they can live safely in the company of others like themselves.

DISABILITY AND AGEING

Advances in medicine have made it possible for people to live longer than they did in previous generations, and there is a greater proportion of elderly people in the community than ever before. The likelihood of developing a degenerative illness such as **osteoarthritis**, **Parkinson's disease**, **Alzheimer's disease** and **osteoporosis** increases sharply with age, and a disproportionate number of elderly people are therefore disabled.

Assistance in later life

Older people with minor disabilities can often live independently provided that they have immediate access to help if the need arises. Most local authorities, and some charities and private organizations, can provide a panic button, which is installed in the home or worn around the neck. A person can use it to summon help in an emergency. The local authority may provide a nurse or carer to call in on a daily basis to help with washing and dressing, or at less frequent intervals to help with household chores and shopping. Meal delivery services ensure that an elderly person's minimum nutritional requirements are met, and many charities provide volunteers to help elderly people with various aspects of living (see also **Elderly people, care of**).

TREATMENT AND PREVENTION

Treatment of a disability will depend on its cause, and in many cases there is no cure. However, several experimental medical techniques provide some hope for people with disabilities that are currently untreatable. They include:

■ electrical implants, which have been used with some success to take over the functions of lost nerve cells (for example, in Parkinson's disease);

■ specialized techniques to repair nerves damaged by spinal injuries;

■ antitoxic drugs, which may help to prevent brain damage caused by the release of neurotoxins after **stroke**;

Disability and employment

The Disability Discrimination Act (1995) makes it unlawful for an employer to discriminate against a disabled person solely on the grounds of their disability.

This legislation covers refusing to employ disabled people, withholding promotion, transfer or training and dismissing them because of their disability. To comply with the law, employers may be required to make adjustments to their premises, furniture or equipment, such as: installing easy-open or automatic doors with wheelchair access; ensuring that signs are easy to read for people with sight impairment; and putting in ramps for wheelchairs. Large corporations and government offices continue to offer the best opportunities for employment. However, statistics show that disabled people in the UK are three times more likely to be unemployed than able-bodied people, and those that are employed earn less. Only 12 per cent of the disabled workforce are in professional or managerial positions, compared with 21 per cent of non-disabled workers.

- **gene therapy**, which is being developed to treat disorders caused by single-gene mutations, such as Huntington's disease;
- **stem cell therapy**, which may be used to rebuild damaged or lost tissue resulting from degenerative diseases.

Prevention of age-related disabilities

Many of the most common causes of age-related disability can be prevented by good self-care and appropriate medical intervention at an early stage of development.

- Heart disease and **stroke**, for example, may be prevented by adherence to a regular exercise regime and a **diet** rich in antioxidants. A wide range of drugs is available to relieve symptoms of these diseases.
- Osteoporosis can be prevented to some degree by **hormone replacement therapy** in women and a high intake (starting as early as possible) of calcium-rich foods and regular exercise.
- Joint immobility can be minimized by undertaking exercise that gently stretches the limbs, such as swimming.
- **Depression** may be prevented by mental activity, social interaction and antidepressant drugs.
- Falls are a major cause of illness and subsequent disability in elderly people. The likelihood of falls can be reduced by using walking aids such as a walking stick or frame, and installing safety aids in the home.

SEE ALSO *Age and ageing; Brain and nervous system; Cerebral palsy; Child development; Community care; Mental health and problems*

▲ **On your marks**
Disability need not stop a person keeping fit or enjoying competitive sport. These disabled athletes are using wheelchairs specially adapted for racing.

Disability benefits in the UK

A number of benefits are available to help people with disabilities to deal with day to day life.

Make sure you apply for all the benefits to which you are entitled. Your local authority's social service department will send someone to your home to make an assessment of your needs. Some authorities provide a fuller range of services than others, and the assessment of need may vary from place to place. Should you feel that you are being refused benefits to which you are entitled you may appeal to the Secretary of State against the local authority's decision. The case may then be decided by a medical tribunal.

The State provides two main types of financial assistance for disabled people: disability living allowance (DLA) and attendance allowance (AA).

CONTACT **The Disabled Living Foundation** 380–384 Harrow Road, London W9 2HU; helpline 0845 1309 177 (www.dlf.org.uk) **Mencap** 123 Golden Lane, London EC1Y 0RT; helpline 0808 808 1111 (www.mencap.org.uk) **Motability** Goodman House, Station Approach, Harlow, Essex CM20 2ET (01279) 635999 (www.motability.co.uk) **Disability Rights Commission** Freepost MID 02164 Stratford-upon-Avon CV37 9BR; helpline 08457 622633; textphone 08457 622644 (www.drc-gb.org) **RADAR Royal Association for Disability and Rehabilitation** Head Office, 12 City Forum, 250 City Road, London EC1V 8AF; (020) 7250 3222 (www.radar.org.uk)

Discharge

Discharge means the production of fluid or mucus from a body surface. It is produced as part of the everyday functions of some body surfaces, such as the lining of the mouth, nose, airway, vagina and bowel. Such surfaces, called mucous membranes, differ from skin in that they are not protected by a dry outer layer of dead cells. They therefore secrete a protective mucus that lubricates them and carries away dirt, bacteria and dead skin cells.

Abnormal discharges can result from irritation or infection of the mucous membranes, or as a result of pus formation, for example, in an eye or ear canal infection.

Dislocation

Dislocation is the displacement of the bones of a joint from their normal position. A dislocation occurs when an injury wrenches the joint's ligaments and fibrous capsule, and moves the bones. These can be manipulated back into position, but recurrences may need surgery.
SEE ALSO *Joints and problems*

Diuretics

Diuretic drugs act on the kidneys to increase the production and excretion of urine, and so are used to remove excess fluid and salt from the body (hence the alternative term 'water tablets'). They are used to lower blood pressure in **hypertension**, to reduce **oedema** (fluid retention) and in other conditions where excess fluid accumulates.

ADVICE ON USAGE
■ All diuretics increase urine production.
■ Thiazide diuretics can increase the risk of gout and cause problems for diabetics.
■ Both loop and thiazide diuretics can cause potassium loss, which may need to be corrected with potassium supplements.
■ Potassium-sparing diuretics can cause digestive disturbances.
SEE ALSO *Drugs, medicinal*

Diverticular disease

The term 'diverticular disease' describes conditions caused by sacs (diverticula) that protrude through the wall of the intestines. Diverticula occasionally form in the small intestine, but more usually in the colon. The cause is thought to be a lack of dietary fibre.

There are two forms of diverticular disease: diverticulosis and diverticulitis. Diverticulosis simply means that diverticula are present. Often there are no symptoms, but there may be **irritable bowel syndrome** with abdominal cramps and, occasionally, rectal bleeding. Treatment is with a high-fibre diet and antispasmodic **drugs**. Diverticulitis means that diverticula have become infected. Symptoms include pain, vomiting, fever and bowel problems, and **peritonitis** if the intestine perforates. Treatment is with **antibiotics** and, sometimes, surgery.
SEE ALSO *Bowel and disorders*

Dizziness

Dizziness is a common symptom, often defined as being a sensation of lightheadedness without the illusion of movement characteristic of **vertigo**. It often precedes fainting.
CAUSES
The causes of dizziness include:
■ viral infection;
■ low blood sugar;
■ a drop in **blood pressure** on getting up (postural hypotension, which is common in elderly people and during pregnancy);
■ reduced blood flow to the brain – seen in elderly people with **osteoarthritis** of the neck;
■ anxiety and **hyperventilation**;
■ intoxication with drugs or alcohol, and the effects of chronic alcohol misuse;
■ occasionally, **carbon monoxide poisoning** (caused, for example, by a blocked flue in a domestic gas appliance).
DURATION
Dizziness usually starts suddenly, except in viral infection and anxiety, and lasts until the underlying cause settles down or is treated.
TREATMENT
The treatment varies depending on the cause. See your doctor if dizziness is continuous or recurs often. If other family members are affected, and domestic gas appliances are used, turn them off immediately and have them checked professionally for carbon monoxide emissions.
COMPLICATIONS
Usually none, unless the dizziness causes collapse resulting in injury.

Dog bite

Wounds caused by the teeth of a dog are very prone to infection. Anyone bitten by a dog should seek medical advice about the prevention of **tetanus** and, in some countries, **rabies**.
SEE ALSO *FIRST AID*

In the UK, 50 per cent of the population over 70 years old have diverticula, but in many cases the condition causes no trouble at all.

Doctor

The doctors and staff at your surgery or health centre are important first points of contact with the National Health Service system. Your treatment there will be completely confidential.

You have the right to register with any general practice surgery or health centre provided that you live within the catchment area of the practice. However, **general practitioners** also have the right to refuse to take a patient onto their list, without giving a specific reason. If this happens to you, the local health authority will allocate you another suitable doctor.

You register at a practice by filling in a medical card and taking it to your chosen surgery; an updated card will be returned to you from the health authority. It is possible to register at more than one surgery. If you are taken ill while staying away from home you can register temporarily at another surgery.

THE GP PRACTICE

As well as general practitioners (GPs) and locum (temporary) doctors, you may have access to practice nurses, community physiotherapists, counsellors and complementary therapists. You may have the option of being seen either under the NHS or as a private patient.

Many health centres offer minor surgery, such as the removal of warts, **health education** and targeted clinics for family planning, diabetics, 'well' women and men, and child development. In addition to the usual services, some rural surgeries dispense medicines for patients living a mile or more from a pharmacy.

Your GP will refer you for a second opinion or specialist treatment if necessary; you do not have a legal right to a specialist referral and you cannot attend a hospital clinic unless arranged by a GP.

MAKING APPOINTMENTS

You make an appointment to see your doctor at the surgery. Most practices are open during the day, although some offer evening surgeries. Most GPs are linked to medical call centres for out-of-hours treatment when trained staff will advise you about what to do.

If you think you are too unwell to attend the surgery, an assessment of need is made by telephone (usually by the GP). If the doctor is satisfied that you are too ill to move, a home visit will be made. You do not have an absolute right to a home visit. Lack of transport or unavailability of an escort is not a valid reason for a home visit, and your GP will usually try to find some solution to help you reach the surgery.

IF YOU ARE NOT SATISFIED

- You are entitled to change your GP – provided the new GP is willing to take you. There is no need to inform the first GP. Your medical notes will be transferred automatically when you change practice (see **Medical records**).
- The desire to obtain the best possible treatment or to confirm bad news may prompt you to seek a second opinion. You do not have an absolute legal right to a second opinion, but it is unlikely that any GP would refuse. The second opinion would normally be given by another GP within the same practice, since single GP practices are rare nowadays.

SEE ALSO *Health system, Medical staff and departments*

Visiting your doctor

Once you have arranged to see your doctor, a little advance preparation will help you to make best use of the appointment.

Do

✔ Describe your symptoms clearly.

✔ Write down a list of questions you have before your visit so that you do not forget anything.

✔ Have paper and pen handy to jot down information.

✔ Take someone else for support.

✔ Telephone early in the day for urgent appointments or home visits.

Don't

✘ Expect to be treated by your own doctor after surgery hours.

Donors

A donor is anyone who gives an organ or tissue for use by someone else, by transplantation or transfusion. Some people choose to donate their entire body after their death for use in medical research.

The donation of blood and organs helps save thousands of lives every year. Some donations, such as kidneys, blood and bone marrow, are made by living donors. The body can function perfectly well with only one kidney, as long as it is healthy, and blood and bone marrow are both constantly regenerating, so the donor's supply is rapidly replaced.

BLOOD DONATION
Blood donors are encouraged to give blood three times a year. Before you donate you will be asked a few confidential questions, such as whether you are an intravenous drug user, to assess your suitability. A drop of blood is taken from a fingertip and tested to check that you do not suffer from **anaemia**. Then a needle is inserted into a vein, and about a pint of blood is drawn off. It takes 10 minutes and, apart from the initial needle prick, the process is painless.

How to be an organ donor

It is important that others know about your intention to donate your organs.

- Fill in an organ donor card at your GP's surgery or online and carry it with you at all times.
- Register as an organ donor via the NHS website.
- Tell your relatives of your wishes.

The blood is screened for infection and classified by type before use to ensure compatibility between the blood groups of donor and recipient.

TISSUE MATCHING AND REJECTION
The body treats a transplanted organ as 'foreign' tissue and its immune system can attack it, leading to rejection. To minimize this possibility, tests are performed on donor and recipient to ensure as close a match as possible. Even so, organ recipients must take drugs to suppress their **immune system** and prevent rejection of the new organ. There is a global shortage of organs, and many people die while on the waiting list.

DONATION AFTER DEATH
A donor's corneas, kidneys, heart, lungs, liver and pancreas may be taken after death. Such donors have become brain dead, typically after a road accident. The donor's body is maintained on a **life support** machine. This ensures that the heart beats and respiration continues to keep organs as healthy as possible.

SEE ALSO *Blood and disorders; Bone marrow and disorders; Death and dying; Ethics, medical; Heart and circulatory system; Kidneys and disorders; Lungs and disorders; Transfusion; Transplants*

▼ **Precious drops**
The most frequently made donation is blood, a valuable gift that saves countless lives each year.

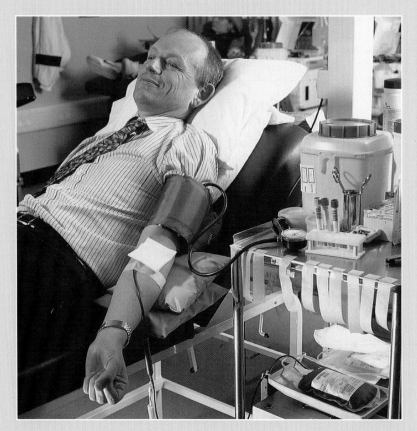

CONTACT Anthony Nolan Trust
0901 882 2234 (www.anthonynolan.com)
National Blood Service www.blood.co.uk, or call 0845 7 711 711 for your nearest centre. In the UK, call 0845 60 60 400 for a donor card and register as a donor.
(www.uktransplant.org.uk)

Double vision

Double vision is the perception of two distinct images. The condition is known medically as diplopia. Typically, double vision is caused by the two eyes looking in different directions as in a **squint** or strabismus.

If double vision comes on suddenly, seek medical help at once as it may be due to an underlying disease of the blood vessels. Double vision that is still present upon covering one eye (monocular diplopia) may be due to the onset of **cataract**: visit an optometrist.

SEE ALSO *Eye and problems*

Down's syndrome

Down's syndrome is a genetic disorder caused by the presence of an extra chromosome, giving a total of 47 instead of the usual 46. The extra chromosome is usually a duplicate of number 21, thus the most common form of Down's syndrome is also known as trisomy 21. This duplication mostly originates in the mother's egg, although in some cases it may be present in the fertilizing sperm.

Physical markers may include:
■ a flattish face with downward sloping eyes, heavy eyelids, a broad flat nose, thick lips and small ears flattened back to the skull;
■ a tongue which appears too large for the mouth cavity;
■ thick, short hands and feet;
■ undeveloped genitalia;
■ short stature, weak muscles and slow growth.

Children born with Down's syndrome can have health problems, such as heart or inner ear defects, and may be more susceptible to anaemia and infectious illnesses.

There is always some degree of learning disability, but this varies considerably – IQ can be between 30 and 80, and is sometimes higher. The vast majority of Down's syndrome children learn to talk and an increasing number learn to read. Today, some even attend mainstream schools and go on to live semi-independent adult lives.

Overall, about one in every 1000 babies is born with Down's syndrome. The chance of having an affected child varies greatly according to the age of the parents, especially the mother. For women under 30 the likelihood is less than one in 1000, while for a woman over 45 the chance is more than one in 60.

OUTLOOK

In the past many people with Down's syndrome died in infancy, often as a result of untreatable internal abnormalities or infections. Today, most reach adulthood, thanks to medical advances and the greater willingness of health professionals to offer life-saving treatment, where necessary. Most children with Down's syndrome can now look forward to a lifespan of 60 years or more.

Down's syndrome is not a disease, so there is no treatment. However, greater understanding of the condition and changes in attitude towards it now mean that affected individuals are more likely to get the support they need to develop their potential and enjoy a full life.

SEE ALSO *Disability; Genetics and genetic disorders; Learning difficulties*

Dreams and dream therapy

Dreams are the thoughts, ideas, images and events that fill the mind during sleep. They occur during the particular phase of the sleep cycle that is characterized by rapid eye movement or REM.

Therapists interpret the function of dreams in various ways. Psychologists are interested in the concept that dreams help to consolidate memories, or express experiences that are highly emotionally charged. Psychoanalysts are interested in the symbolic content – they believe that the events and images in the dream act as metaphorical commentary on aspects of the dreamer's life. This analysis of the symbolic content of dreams is called dream therapy.

SEE ALSO *Psychoanalysis; Psychological therapies; Psychology; Sleep and disorders*

Drowning

Drowning is death by inhalation of liquid, usually water, and is the third most common cause of accidental death in the UK. Young children are particularly at risk and should never be left unsupervised near pools, garden ponds or in the bath. Rescue requires immediate mouth-to-mouth resuscitation. Treatment for **hypothermia** may be needed.

SEE ALSO *Accident prevention; FIRST AID*

Drowsiness

Drowsiness is the halfway stage between wakefulness and sleep. The muscles become relaxed, and breathing and pulse rates slow down. Thought processes become slow and muddled, and the senses dim, reducing awareness of the outside world.

SEE ALSO *Sleep and disorders*

Drugs, medicinal

A drug is any chemical that alters the function or state of a living organism. In medicine, drugs are used to prevent or treat disease. Some drugs can be bought over the counter; others must be prescribed by a doctor.

Medicinal drugs have two names: the generic name and the proprietary name. The generic name refers to the drug's active ingredient, which is what a doctor writes on a prescription. The proprietary name is the drug's brand name. For example, Aspro, Anadin and Disprin are brands containing aspirin, the generic name for that drug, while Prozac is the brand name of the generic drug fluoxetine.

Some brand names may sound similar, but they contain different ingredients. For instance, Anadin Maximum Strength, Anadin Extra and Anadin Ultra all contain different active constituents. Many painkillers and cold-cure formulations contain several generic drugs in combination – ibuprofen, codeine and caffeine, for example. But not all drugs are suitable for everyone, so you should always read the list of constituents on the packaging, and the patient information leaflet that must by law be provided with all medicines.

HOW DO DRUGS WORK?

Many drugs kill invading disease-causing organisms. **Antibiotics, antibacterials, antivirals** and **antifungals** work in this way. Vaccines don't kill the organisms themselves, but stimulate the body to make antibodies that will. They also help the body to prepare itself against specific infections (see **Immunization**).

Other drugs work by replacing chemicals in which the body is deficient. Thyroid hormones, for example, are used to treat **hypothyroidism**, oestrogen helps to alleviate certain symptoms of the menopause in **hormone replacement therapy**, insulin is vital in **diabetes**, and iron is needed by people with iron-deficiency **anaemia**.

Then there are drugs that work by interfering with how cells normally function. For example, **calcium-channel blockers** work to reduce blood pressure in people with hypertension, and monoamine-oxidase inhibitors (MAOIs) interfere with certain enzymes and have an **antidepressant** effect.

ANIMAL, VEGETABLE OR MINERAL?

A number of drugs originally came from animals, including pigs and cows, or from human cadavers. These include **hormones** such as **steroids, insulin** and pituitary hormones, numerous human blood factors, including factors VII, VIII and IX for **haemophilia**, and vaccines. In their natural form these drugs sometimes carried dangerous infections. Creutzfeldt-Jakob disease (**CJD**), for example, could be transmitted via human growth hormone. Today these drugs are chemically manufactured replicas of the natural substances, so infection is no longer a problem. But since the synthetic version is almost identical to the natural one, it could still cause an allergic reaction.

Several drugs in use today come from plants. These include atropine from deadly nightshade, often used to treat eye infections; vinblastine, an anticancer drug which is derived from periwinkle; ergotamine, a migraine treatment which comes from the ergot fungus; and digitoxin, a heart medicine derived from foxgloves. Other widely used drugs came originally from plants but are now exact chemical copies of the natural active ingredient. Others are semi-synthetic, which means that chemists have modified the natural material to make the drug.

Antibiotics were originally obtained from fungi and moulds. Today, most are semi-synthetic or synthetic. They are best known for their antibacterial action in treating infections. Some can also be used in **chemotherapy**, to treat yeast infections or as immunosuppressant drugs.

Some drugs are mineral substances. Up to the 19th century, mercury, arsenic, antimony and other toxic salts were used to treat sexually transmitted diseases. Mineral drugs in use today include bismuth compounds for ulcers, calcium and magnesium carbonates and bicarbonates for dyspepsia, and lithium salts for manic depression.

MODERN DRUG DISCOVERY

In the past, discovering new drugs involved laborious and expensive experiments carried out almost entirely on live animals, or their organs. Today, most potential drugs are tested on biological materials made in a laboratory. These materials include enzymes and drug receptors that are almost identical to their counterparts in the human body. Researchers can screen thousands of compounds a day in order to identify those that might merit further development. Once a suitable compound has been identified, it must then, by law, be tested on both live animals and human beings before it can be marketed as a drug. This is a slow and expensive process.

Toxicity and drug safety

The **thalidomide** disaster in the late 1950s and early 1960s made doctors and scientists acutely aware of the need to test new drugs for safety. This is now a strict requirement and a top priority. Drugs are tested for all types of toxicity, such as cancer-causing potential. Any adverse results can lead to promising drugs being rejected.

How are drugs licensed?

Once a drug has been exhaustively tested in the laboratory it moves on to the next stage: **clinical trials** in people. The body that oversees this process in the UK is the Medicines Control Agency. The licensing authorities also decide whether drugs will be available only on prescription or over the counter. The use of a drug in its over-the-counter form is often more restricted than it is on prescription. For example, ranitidine – whose brand name is Zantac – is licensed as an over-the-counter drug only in a low-dose formulation for short-term use in cases of acid indigestion or **dyspepsia**. Its higher-dose form, available only on prescription, can be used for the long-term treatment of peptic ulcers and other gut problems.

The development of a new drug to the stage of marketing typically takes up to ten years and costs hundreds of millions of pounds.

CAN EVERYONE TAKE DRUGS SAFELY?

It is not always known why a drug is less safe for certain people, but some groups are more vulnerable than others. These include:

■ people with certain inherited medical conditions such as **porphyria**;
■ those with liver or kidney problems – a drug may have to be avoided or a lower dose taken so as to avoid excess strain on these organs;
■ babies and children – usually given much lower doses of medicines than adults;
■ pregnant and breastfeeding women – many medicines can harm a baby and it is best to avoid all drugs, including herbal or other complementary remedies, unless advised by a doctor;
■ people taking more than one medicine – one drug often influences the effects of another drug. For example, taking the herbal remedy St John's Wort with certain antidepressants can cause a dangerous rise in blood pressure;
■ older people – an older person's liver and

kidneys may function less well and remove drugs less efficiently than those of someone younger, so lower doses may be needed. They may be taking several medicines, and interactions are possible.

WHY DO DRUGS HAVE SIDE EFFECTS?

Side effects are unintended effects of a medicine that occur because drugs can be carried to parts of the body where they are not intended to work. They can be minimized by limiting where the drug goes, such as by applying it locally, as in eye ointment, rather than via an injection. Before prescribing a medicine, a doctor should assess its benefits against the risk of side effects.

Some side effects are predictable, such as the stomach irritation that can result from **aspirin**. Sometimes these are spotted during prelicensing testing; sometimes they are reported once the drug is marketed. Certain drugs, such as chemotherapy for cancers, have severe side effects, but their benefit makes it worth taking them. Others have unexpected and serious side effects, for example the allergic reaction that some people have to penicillin. If this occurs treatment should be stopped at once.

The Patient Information Leaflet that comes with each medication is obliged, by law, to list all reported side effects for that drug. This list, even for a common drug such as paracetamol, looks alarming. However, few people experience all, if any, side effects. If you do, tell your doctor.

Magic bullets

One of the main aims in the development of new drugs is to find compounds that can be targeted at the problem area and cause few side effects.

Drugs that affect their target site and very little else are known as 'magic bullets'. The term was coined by the German bacteriologist Paul Ehrlich, when he was researching a cure for syphilis. In 1910, he discovered an arsenic-containing substance – compound 606 – that cured his infected laboratory mice. This drug, later named Salvarsan, was Ehrlich's magic bullet, and its target was the syphilis-causing bacterium.

Other drug targets include enzymes and receptors. Receptors are found on all cells and organs in the body. Their role is to recognize chemical messages such as **hormones** and **neurotransmitters** – the chemicals that allow nerves to 'talk' to other nerves or tissues. Certain drugs bind to specific receptors and either mimic the natural messenger or block its action. These include antihistamines, beta-blockers, the contraceptive pill and morphine-like drugs.

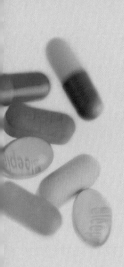

TAKING YOUR MEDICATION

Some drugs are taken as and when needed, while others must be taken regularly, often over a long period. You can stop taking medicines such as painkillers when you feel better, but for others, particularly antibiotics, you must finish the course to ensure that the disease-causing agent has been completely eradicated. If you are on long-term drug treatment for, say, epilepsy, depression or asthma, do not stop taking your medication without first talking to your doctor: your condition may worsen or you may suffer a serious reaction through stopping treatment suddenly.

It is important to follow any instructions that accompany your medicine, such as 'take with food', or 'avoid alcohol'. This will ensure that you get the most benefit from the drug, and in some cases avoid certain side effects. You should also know what to do if you miss a dose.

Drugs must get to the site where they are needed in order to work, which is why there are many different ways of administering them. They can be taken by mouth as tablets, capsules or liquids, by injection, by inhalation, as vaginal pessaries, as suppositories, as eye, ear, skin or nosedrops, as ointments or as skin patches.

PRESCRIBING POLICY IN THE UK

Doctors treating patients on the NHS have guidelines for prescribing. These limit choice and secure the cheapest version of a drug. A doctor will usually write the generic name of a drug on the prescription form; the pharmacist then supplies an economical brand.

Drug overdose

A drug overdose can be accidental or deliberate. Always call the emergency services if you suspect that someone has taken an overdose.

Accidental overdose commonly occurs when using illegal drugs. It also happens when children swallow drugs not kept safely out of reach, or when adults take a higher dose of a drug than is recommended. It sometimes occurs as a result of someone having an unusual reaction to a normal dose of a drug.

Deliberate drug overdose is a common means of attempting suicide – frequently with **paracetamol**.

If you think someone has taken an overdose, collect as much information about the drug as possible, such as the container or a sample of the drug, and send it to the hospital with the patient.

Some types of drug overdose can be treated with **antidotes**. These should be given as quickly as possible after the overdose has been taken.

! Warning

Remember: always store medicines according to instructions and keep them well out of children's reach, preferably in a locked cabinet.

An independent body, the National Institute for Clinical Excellence (NICE), has been set up to advise on the efficacy of treatments, particularly in terms of cost. It has investigated such issues as whether interferons can be prescribed for multiple sclerosis under the NHS, or for which cancers the expensive taxane drugs may be prescribed.

DRUGS IN THE FUTURE

Advances in drug therapy, particularly in the past 50 years, have led to new treatments that have played a major part in improving life expectancy and reducing long-term illness. However, despite billions of pounds being spent each year on drug development, many disorders still have no cure. These include high blood pressure, heart disease, arthritis, asthma and dementia.

There are also some modern diseases that were rare or previously unrecognized, such as chronic fatigue syndrome (known medically as myalgic encephalomyelitis or ME), extreme obesity and AIDS. Research offers hope for the future, though many of the breakthroughs reported in the media may not be available for years.

Cutting edge research

Pharmacological research is incorporating new technology into traditional drug design strategies. For example, 'monoclonal antibodies' are being harnessed as modern-day 'magic bullets' to target specific sites in the body. They are highly selective as to where they bind in the body and can be used to correct cell function, or convey a drug to a particular site. Such drugs are now used in some forms of cancer. Also, many antiviral agents are now available to give relief to AIDS sufferers.

The completion of the **Human Genome Project** has given researchers a new tool to assist in the design of medications targeted at an individual's genetic material, in much the same way as the modification of defective **genetic** material is being tried in gene therapy for cystic fibrosis.

There is still a wealth of medicinal plants to be discovered. These may well have properties that complement modern hi-tech drugs, and so may help to combat disease in the future.

CONTACT **Association of the British Pharmaceutical Industry** (www.abpi.org.uk) **Medicines and Healthcare products Regulatory Agency** (www.mhra.gov.uk)

Drugs and their uses

The glossary below lists the main generic drugs and the brand names by which they are most commonly known.

This alphabetical listing includes both branded and generic drugs. Some of them can be bought over the counter; others are only available on prescription. It also explains a number of common pharmacological terms such as 'antibiotic', 'chemotherapy', 'hormone replacement therapy' and 'painkiller'. Words in capital letters indicate cross-references to these general entries.

Where a brand name is given for a drug, it will give the generic name or names for any active ingredient in that drug. Under Actifed, for example, you will see that the active generic drugs contained in this medicine are triprolidine and pseudoephedrine. These each have their own entries in the glossary, informing you that triprolidine is used to treat allergic symptoms such as hay fever and urticaria; and pseudoephedrine is used to relieve general congestion in the airways.

A

ACARBOSE, used to treat non-insulin-dependent diabetes.

ACECLOFENAC, a PAINKILLER used to treat inflammation and pain, particularly that caused by arthritic conditions. It is an NSAID.

ACE INHIBITOR (angiotensin-converting enzyme inhibitor) drugs, used as ANTIHYPERTENSIVE agents and in the treatment of heart failure. They are widely prescribed, sometimes alone but often with other medicines such as DIURETIC drugs (for hypertension) or digoxin (for heart failure). They are taken by mouth either as tablets or capsules.

These drugs include captopril and enalapril. They work in a complex way to make the blood vessels dilate. This expansion of the vessels causes blood pressure to fall, which is beneficial to people who suffer from heart

failure or hypertension. Some people cannot safely take ace inhibitors: these include those with certain blood vessel conditions and pregnant women. Usually, ace inhibitors have few side effects but they may cause a severe fall in blood pressure, and some people get a persistent cough that can be troublesome.

ACICLOVIR, used to treat viral infections such as cold sores that have been caused by the herpes virus.

ACTAL, brand containing alexitol.

ACTIFED, brand containing triprolidine and pseudoephedrine.

ADALAT LA, brand name for nifedipine.

ADVIL, brand of ibuprofen.

ALENDRONIC ACID, used to prevent and treat osteoporosis.

ALEXITOL, an ANTACID.

ALFACALCIDOL, used to treat vitamin D deficiency.

ALFUZOSIN, used to treat urinary retention by men who have benign prostatic hypertrophy.

ALGINIC ACID, a sticky substance added to soothing mouthwashes and indigestion preparations.

ALLOPURINOL, used to prevent attacks of gout.

ALZHEIMER'S TREATMENT uses drugs aimed at restoring acetylcholine levels, such as donepezil, galamantine, memantine and rivastigmine.

ALUMINIUM HYDROXIDE, an ANTACID.

ALVERINE, used to relax intestinal muscles and so relieve the pain

of irritable bowel syndrome and diverticular disease. It is also used for period pain.

AMILORIDE, a DIURETIC.
AMINOPHYLLINE, used in ASTHMA TREATMENT.

AMIODARONE, used to treat arrhythmias of the heart.

AMITRIPTYLINE, an ANTIDEPRESSANT.

AMLODIPINE, used as an ANTIHYPERTENSIVE and to treat angina. It is a CALCIUM-CHANNEL BLOCKER.

AMOXICILLIN, an ANTIBIOTIC used to treat bacterial infections.

AMPHOTERICIN B, an ANTIBIOTIC used to treat fungal infections.

ANASTROZOLE, used in cancer CHEMOTHERAPY.

ANBESOL, brand containing lignocaine and cetylpyridium.

ANTACID drugs, chemicals that are used to treat indigestion. They work by neutralizing hydrochloric acid in the stomach. This acid, also called gastric acid, is produced by the stomach when food is being digested. However, sometimes too much hydrochloric acid is produced causing stomach pain and other indigestion symptoms. Indigestion is made worse by alcohol and drugs such as aspirin.

Antacids are taken by mouth, and are available over the counter. They can be used for occasional stomach upsets and also heartburn symptoms such as reflux oesophagitis – common in people with hiatus hernia and in pregnant women. Antacids can relieve some symptoms of peptic ulcers, but most ulcers are associated with a bacterium called Helicobacter pylori, and it is

usually treated with a combination of antibiotics and other drugs.

Antacids have side effects. Sodium bicarbonate and calcium carbonate can cause belching and flatulence; aluminium hydroxide can cause constipation; and magnesium carbonate, magnesium hydroxide and magnesium trisilicate can cause diarrhoea. Some antacids contain a lot of sodium and should not be taken by people who are on a sodium-restricted diet.

ANTIBIOTIC drugs, used to treat infections. Technically speaking, in medical circles, the term 'antibiotic' is restricted to drugs that are made by fungi and used for treating infections. Most antibiotics are used to treat infections caused by bacteria, but some treat infections caused by fungi. It is important to note that no antibiotic is effective against a viral infection so they will not treat a cold or flu.

Antibiotics make up a major proportion of the annual NHS drugs bill. The most-prescribed antibiotics are: amoxicillin, amphotericin, cefaclor, cefadroxil, cefalexin, cefradine, chloramphenicol, clarithromycin, doxycycline, erythromycin, flucloxacillin, fusidic acid, lymecycline, minocycline, mupirocin, neomycin, nystatin, oxytetracycline, phenoxymethylpenicillin and tetracycline.

The majority of antibiotics have few side effects, although some people are allergic to certain ones, such as cephalosporins and penicillins. It is important to tell anyone giving you medication – including your dentist – if you are allergic to any of these.

There is currently a growing problem in treating certain infections because overprescribing has led to the evolution of bacteria that are resistant to a number of common antibiotics.

ANTICOAGULANT drugs, sometimes called blood-thinners because they prevent blood clotting. They are used to stop clots forming in blood vessels and to treat clots that have already formed. Because of this, they are used to treat conditions such as thrombosis and embolism, especially following surgery to prevent deep vein thrombosis.

Many anticoagulants are versions of the blood's own natural anticoagulant, heparin. These must be injected and last for only a short time, so are mainly used in hospitals. Others, including warfarin, can be taken by mouth, and work for longer, so their use is not restricted to hospitals. It is important to get the right dose for each individual, so anyone taking warfarin will need frequent blood tests.

ANTIDEPRESSANT drugs, used to relieve the symptoms of depression. The most recently developed and best-known group includes fluoxetine (Prozac), sertraline (Lustral), paroxetine (Seroxat) and citalopram (Cipramil). These drugs are referred to as selective serotonin reuptake inhibitors (SSRIs). Although they can cause side effects – nausea and stomach upsets are quite common – most people cope well with them.

Other antidepressants include tricyclics such as imipramine, but these have pronounced side effects including sleepiness, sweating, blurred vision and dry mouth. Monoamine oxidase inhibitors (MAOIs) are not often prescribed now because they can have harmful interactions with constituents of food such as cheese, red wine and yeast extracts, causing a dangerous rise in blood pressure.

The herbal depression remedy St John's Wort should not be taken at the same time as antidepressants prescribed by your doctor because of the risk of serious interactions.

ANTIHISTAMINE drugs, used to treat allergic reactions. When people come into contact with a substance to which they are allergic, a chemical called histamine is released in the body. This causes allergic symptoms such as hay fever, urticaria, the itching of insect bites or stings, and wheezing. Antihistamines prevent histamine causing these effects. They can be taken by mouth, as a nasal spray, or applied to the skin as a cream. Certain antihistamines cause pronounced drowsiness and this can make it unsafe to drive when taking them. Some, such as promethazine, cause so much sedation that they are sold as over-the-counter SLEEP-AID medicines. More modern drugs, such as cetirizine, have a less sedative effect.

ANTIHYPERTENSIVE drugs, used to reduce high blood pressure, and so reduce a person's risk of heart attack, kidney failure and stroke. Several types of drug can be used and they are usually taken by mouth as tablets or capsules. They lower blood pressure either by reducing blood volume or by dilating blood vessels. Often a mild DIURETIC is all that is needed, but other drugs may also be prescribed.

Drugs that might be prescribed include CALCIUM-CHANNEL BLOCKERS such as nifedipine and verapamil; BETA-BLOCKERS such as acebutolol, atenolol, propranolol and timolol; and ACE INHIBITORS such as captopril and enalapril. Side effects depend on the particular antihypertensive drug you are taking. Some may cause dizziness at the start of treatment; beta-blockers can disrupt sleeping patterns and make your hands and feet feel cold; and ACE INHIBITORS can cause an irritating cough.

ANTIPLATELET drugs, used to reduce the stickiness of blood platelets, an important component of blood clots. They can help to prevent clots from forming in the arteries. Dipyridamole and low-dose aspirin are taken as a preventive measure by people who are at risk from blood clots, such as after a heart attack or stroke, or following bypass operations. If you have had a stroke or a heart attack, it may be necessary for you to take antiplatelet drugs for the rest of your life.

ANTIPSYCHOTIC drugs, used to treat schizophrenia and other severe psychiatric disorders. They control symptoms such as hallucinations and disturbed thoughts.

There are many antipsychotic drugs including chlorpromazine, haloperidol, flupentixol, thioridazine, prochlorperazine, sulpiride, olanzapine and risperidone. They work mainly by blocking the action of the neurotransmitter dopamine in the brain. However, this means that they have many unpleasant side effects and sometimes serious adverse effects. Because of this, they are only prescribed by specialists. Antipsychotic drugs, which are administered as long-lasting injection or taken by mouth under supervision, have allowed many people suffering from psychoses to rejoin the community rather than live in institutions.

ANXIETY TREATMENT drugs, used to relieve symptoms of anxiety. They are prescribed for people who do not respond to other therapies such as relaxation or psychotherapy. They are also used for short-term anxiety, such as experienced before surgery or job interviews. The best-known and most widely used are the BENZODIAZEPINE drugs, which include diazepam and lorazepam; and BETA-BLOCKERS, which are good for easing symptoms such as palpitations of the heart, sweating and tremors. Many of these drugs are addictive, so treatment should not be prolonged.

ARTHROTEC, brand of diclofenac.

ASCORBIC ACID, the chemical name for vitamin C. This is sometimes taken in high dosages as an antioxidant and free-radical scavenger. It can also be used to prevent and treat scurvy.

ASPIRIN, used as a PAINKILLER, and to reduce raised body temperature and inflammation such as in arthritis. It is a non-steroidal anti-inflammatory drug (NSAID). Low doses of aspirin may be taken as an ANTIPLATELET drug. Breastfeeding mothers and young children should not usually take aspirin.

ASPRO CLEAR, brand of aspirin.

ASTHMA TREATMENT drugs, used to relieve the symptoms of bronchial asthma or to prevent recurrent attacks. They are also used with other conditions that cause breathing difficulties, sometimes referred to as obstructive airways diseases. In an acute asthma attack, the air passages narrow and become blocked, and drugs called bronchodilators are taken to widen the airways and improve the passage of air. Most are inhaled so that they work quickly and where they are needed – in the lungs – and side effects in the body are minimized. Salbutamol and terbutaline are bronchodilators.

CORTICOSTEROID drugs used to prevent asthma attacks include beclometasone and budesonide. These can be inhaled or taken by mouth.

Anti-inflammatories such as sodium cromoglicate and nedocromil may also be used to treat asthma. Much research has been done to design devices that deliver the inhaled droplets or particles of drugs into the airways more efficiently, allowing the drug to reach the narrow bronchioles.

ATENOLOL, used as an ANTIHYPERTENSIVE, prescribed for cases of angina and heart arrhythmia.

ATORVASTATIN, a LIPID-REGULATING DRUG.

ATROVENT, a branded asthma drug containing ipratropium.

AZATHIOPRINE, used to reduce tissue rejection in people who have had organ transplants, and to treat autoimmune diseases such as myasthenia gravis and rheumatoid arthritis.

B

BACLOFEN, used to relax muscles that are in spasm, as is sometimes experienced by people with multiple sclerosis.

BAZUKA, brand of salicylic acid.

BECLOFORTE, brand of asthma medication, beclometasone.

BECLOMETASONE A, used in asthma treatment and to treat inflammatory conditions of the nose and the skin such as psoriasis and eczema. It is a CORTICOSTEROID.

BECOTIDE, brand of beclometasone asthma inhaler.

BENDROFLUMETHIAZIDE, a DIURETIC.

BENSERAZIDE, used together with the drug levodopa in treating PARKINSON'S DISEASE.

BENZHEXOL, see trihexyphenidyl.

BENZOCAINE, a local anaesthetic used on the skin and mouth to relieve pain.

BENZODIAZEPINES, drugs used for many purposes. Diazepam, temazepam, lormetazepam and lorazepam are used as sedatives in ANXIETY TREATMENT.
   Nitrazepam, oxazepam, temazepam and lormetazepam are prescribed as sleeping pills.
   Benzodiazepines are also used to treat epilepsy and as muscle relaxants.
   These drugs become addictive very quickly, so they should only be taken for short periods.

BENZOYL PEROXIDE, used to treat acne and other skin infections such as athlete's foot.

BENZYDAMINE, applied to the skin and mouth as pain relief.

BETA-BLOCKER drugs, used as ANTIHYPERTENSIVES, in MIGRAINE TREATMENT, in angina treatment, ANXIETY TREATMENT, and to treat glaucoma and heart arrhythmias. They are usually taken as tablets, except in glaucoma treatment when eyedrops are used. Those most frequently prescribed are atenolol, betaxolol, carteolol, celiprolol, levobunolol, metoprolol, nebivolol, propranolol, sotalol and timolol.

BETAHISTINE, used to treat Ménières disease of the ear.

BETAMETHASONE, a CORTICOSTEROID used to treat inflammation.

BETAXOLOL, used as an ANTIHYPERTENSIVE and to treat glaucoma. It is a BETA-BLOCKER.

BEZAFIBRATE, a LIPID-REGULATING DRUG.

BISACODYL, a laxative.

BISOPROLOL, an ANTIHYPERTENSIVE, also used to treat angina.

BRICANYL, brand of terbutaline.

BRIMONIDINE, used to treat glaucoma.

BROMPHENIRAMINE, used to relieve allergic symptoms such as hay fever and urticaria. It can also be used as a cough medicine. It is an ANTIHISTAMINE.

BUCLIZINE, used to prevent vomiting in MIGRAINE TREATMENT.

BUDESONIDE, used in ASTHMA TREATMENT and other inflammatory conditions such as rhinitis. It is a CORTICOSTEROID.

BUMETANIDE, a DIURETIC.

BUPRENORPHINE, a strong PAINKILLER used to treat moderate to severe pain, such as after surgical procedures.

BUPROPION, used to help people stop smoking.

C

CAFFEINE, a stimulant. It is added to some PAINKILLERS to increase their effect.

CALAMINE, incorporated into some lotions used to soothe itchy skin conditions such as eczema.

CALCIPOTRIOL, used to treat plaque psoriasis.

CALCIUM CARBONATE, an ANTACID. It is also prescribed for high levels of phosphate in the blood.

CALCIUM-CHANNEL BLOCKER drugs, mainly used as ANTIHYPERTENSIVE agents. They work by relaxing blood vessels allowing blood pressure to fall. They are also used in angina treatment, to correct heartbeat irregularities (arrhythmias), to limit brain damage after bleeding in strokes, for treating Raynaud's disease, and after heart attacks. Commonly prescribed calcium-channel blockers include amlodipine, lacidipine, lercanidipine, nifedipine and verapamil.

CALPOL, brand of paracetamol.

CANDESARTAN CILEXETIL, an ANTIHYPERTENSIVE.

CANESTEN, brand containing clotrimazole.

CANESTEN HC, brand containing clotrimazole and hydrocortisone.

CAPSAICIN, rubbed into the skin to relieve pain in underlying muscles and joints.

CAPTOPRIL, an ACE INHIBITOR used as an ANTIHYPERTENSIVE to treat heart failure and in diabetic neuropathy – a complication of diabetes mellitus.

CARBAMAZEPINE, used in EPILEPSY TREATMENT, to relieve the pain of trigeminal neuralgia, in manic depressive illness (bipolar disorder), and in diabetes insipidus and diabetic neuropathy (a complication of diabetes mellitus).

CARBIMAZOLE, used to treat the symptoms of thyrotoxicosis, a condition in which there are excess thyroid hormones in the blood.

CARBOMER, used in artificial tears for dry eyes caused as a result of disease.

CARDURA, brand of doxazosin.

CARTEOLOL, used to treat glaucoma. It is a BETA-BLOCKER.

CEFACLOR, an ANTIBIOTIC used to treat bacterial infections.

CEFADROXIL, an ANTIBIOTIC used to treat bacterial infections.

CEFALEXIN, an ANTIBIOTIC used to treat bacterial infections.

CEFRADINE, an ANTIBIOTIC used to treat bacterial infections.

CELECOXIB, a PAINKILLER used to reduce pain and inflammation in arthritis. It is an NSAID.

CELIPROLOL, used as an ANTIHYPERTENSIVE. It is a BETA-BLOCKER.

CERIVASTATIN, a LIPID-REGULATING DRUG.

CETIRIZINE, used for hay fever and urticaria. It is an ANTIHISTAMINE.

CETYLPYRIDIUM, a skin and mouth antiseptic.

CHEMOTHERAPY, commonly used to mean drug treatment of cancer; the drugs used are also called anticancer drugs. Most anticancer drugs are chemicals that are cytotoxic, meaning that they are poisonous to cancerous cells. They work by preventing new cancerous tissue from growing.

Inevitably, this means that production of normal body cells is also affected, which is why there are side effects, some of which can be serious. Common side effects of anticancer drugs include nausea, vomiting, temporary hair loss and bone-marrow suppression. Cytotoxic drugs are administered in low doses over a set period. They are often given with other drugs designed to lessen the adverse effects – such as drugs to stop nausea and vomiting – and sometimes in combination with radiotherapy. Treatment is often carried out in hospital. Certain cancers, including some childhood leukaemias, can now be treated successfully and permanently.

Some newer drugs work against cancers that in the past could not be treated. However, these can be very expensive. Taxanes such as paclitaxel and docetaxel are examples; they are used against ovarian and breast cancer. Other drugs used to treat, or even prevent, cancer in people at risk include tamoxifen for breast cancer and OESTROGENS for prostate cancer.

CHLORAMPHENICOL, an ANTIBIOTIC used to treat bacterial infections.

CHLORDIAZEPOXIDE, used in ANXIETY TREATMENT. It is also used to treat acute withdrawal symptoms experienced by alcoholics who are giving up drinking. It is a BENZODIAZEPINE.

CHLORHEXIDINE, used as an antiseptic – for example, as a mouthwash – and as a disinfectant.

CHLORPHENAMINE, used for hay fever and urticaria. It is an ANTIHISTAMINE.

CHLORPROMAZINE, an ANTIPSYCHOTIC drug used to treat schizophrenia. It can also be used to treat anxiety and prevent vomiting.

CHOLINE SALICYLATE, used to relieve pain such as teething pain.

Rubbed into the skin, it eases pain in underlying muscles and joints.

CICLOSPORIN, used after organ transplants to stop tissue rejection. It is also used for some other conditions including rheumatoid arthritis and severe dermatitis.

CILEST, brand of contraceptive pill that contains the hormones ethinylestradiol and norgestimate.

CIMETIDINE, an ULCER-HEALING DRUG.

CINNARIZINE, used to prevent vomiting and in the treatment of Raynaud's syndrome.

CIPRAMIL, brand of citalopram.

CIPROFIBRATE, a LIPID-REGULATING DRUG.

CIPROFLOXACIN, an ANTIBIOTIC used to treat bacterial infections.

CITALOPRAM, an ANTIDEPRESSANT.

CITRIC ACID, incorporated into drug preparations including cough-and-cold remedies and laxatives.

CLARITHROMYCIN, an ANTIBIOTIC used to treat bacterial infections.

CLARITYN, branded loratadine.

CLINDAMYCIN, an ANTIBIOTIC used to treat bacterial infections.

CLOBAZAM, a BENZODIAZEPINE used in ANXIETY TREATMENT. It is sometimes used, along with other drugs, in EPILEPSY TREATMENT.

CLOBETASOL, a powerful CORTICOSTEROID drug used to treat severe skin inflammation such as in eczema and psoriasis.

CLONAZEPAM, used in EPILEPSY TREATMENT. It is a BENZODIAZEPINE.

CLONIDINE, mainly used as an ANTIHYPERTENSIVE and in MIGRAINE TREATMENT.

CLOPIDOGREL, used as an ANTIPLATELET drug.

CLORAL BETAINE, a SLEEP-AID drug.

CLOTRIMAZOLE, used to treat fungal infections of the skin.

COAL TAR, used to treat psoriasis and eczema and other skin and scalp conditions such as dandruff.

CO-AMILOFRUSE, the name given to the combined DIURETICS amiloride and frusemide.

CO-AMILOZIDE, the name given to a combination of the DIURETICS amiloride and hydchlorothiazide.

CO-AMOXICLAV, the name given to a combination of the ANTIBIOTIC amoxicillin, and clavulanic acid. It is used for bacterial infections.

CO-BENELDOPA, the name given to a combination of benserazide and levodopa. It is used in PARKINSON'S DISEASE treatment.

CO-CARELDOPA, a combination of carbidopa and levodopa. It is used in treating PARKINSON'S DISEASE.

CO-CODAMOL, a combination of two PAINKILLERS, codeine and paracetamol.

CO-CYPRINDIOL, the name given to a combination of cyproterone and ethinylestradiol, which is used to treat severe acne.

CO-DANTHRUSATE, the name given to the combined laxatives dantron and docusate sodium.

CODEINE, a PAINKILLER. Also used to treat a dry cough and diarrhoea.

CODIS 500, brand containing aspirin and codeine.

CO-DYDRAMOL, the name for a combination of two PAINKILLERS, dihydrocodeine and paracetamol.

CO-FLUAMPICIL, a combination of the ANTIBIOTICS flucloxacillin and ampicillin.

COLCHICINE, used to treat gout.

CO-MAGALDROX, a combination of the ANTACIDS magnesium and aluminium hydroxide.

COMBIVENT, brand containing ipratropium and salbutamol.

CONJUGATED OESTROGEN, an OESTROGEN used in HORMONE REPLACEMENT THERAPY.

CO-PHENOTROPE, the name given to a combination of diphenoxylate and atropine used to treat diarrhoea.

CO-PROXAMOL is the name given to a combination of the two PAINKILLERS dextropropoxyphene and paracetamol.

CORTICOSTEROID drugs, often just called steroids, used on a wide scale to treat many inflammatory and allergic reactions of the skin, airways and elsewhere. They resemble the steroid hormones naturally secreted by the adrenal glands, so some are used to make up for the shortage of hormones in Addison's disease. Commonly prescribed corticosteroids include hydrocortisone, beclometasone, betamethasone, clobetasol, dexamethasone, fludrocortisone, flumetasone, fluticasone, methylprednisolone, prednisolone and triamcinolone.

The way in which corticosteroids are taken depends on what they are treating. However, because they can cause serious side effects, they are ideally administered close to where they need to act as this reduces potential problems. Many are used in ointments or creams such as for eczema and psoriasis. Others are inhaled as in ASTHMA TREATMENT and for other lung conditions. Nasal sprays are prescribed for rhinitis, and injections are given into the joints for conditions such as tennis elbow. A weak formulation will usually be tried first, progressing to stronger ones only if necessary. The likely side effects of taking a high-dose or potent corticosteroid over a period of time include frequent infections, water retention, weight gain and a moon-shaped face. When it is time to stop taking high-dose corticosteroid, the dose must be reduced gradually over time. Your doctor will give you a medical alert card explaining this. It should be carried with you at all times.

CO-TENIDONE, a combination of the BETA-BLOCKER atenolol and the DIURETIC chlortalidone. It is used as an ANTIHYPERTENSIVE.

CO-TRIAMTERZIDE, a combination of two DIURETICS, triamterene and hydchlorothiazide.

COVERSYL, brand of perindopril.

COZAAR, brand of losartan.

D

DAKTACORT, brand containing hydrocortisone and miconazole.

DEPO-PROVERA, brand of medroxyprogesterone.

DESLORATADINE, used to treat allergies such as hay fever and urticaria. It is an ANTIHISTAMINE.

DESMOPRESSIN, used to treat diabetes insipidus. It is also used to stop bedwetting.

DEXAMETHASONE, used to treat inflammation. It is a CORTICOSTEROID.

DEXTROMETHORPHAN, used to relieve dry coughs.

DIABETES TREATMENT, of two types. The treatment of Type 1 diabetes – known also as insulin-dependent diabetes mellitus and juvenile-onset diabetes – involves regular injections of insulin. This is because in this type of diabetes the pancreas does not secrete enough of the hormone insulin for the body's needs.
   The treatment of Type 2 diabetes – non insulin-dependent diabetes mellitus or maturity-onset diabetes – involves taking oral

hypoglycaemic drugs by mouth. These help the body to store sugar. This treatment is used when the pancreas is still able to produce some insulin. The main oral hypoglycaemics are glibenclamide, gliclazide, glimepiride, glipizide, tolbutamide and metformin. Researchers are looking for new drugs that work in different ways and suit different people.

DIAMORPHINE, also known as heroin. It is a powerful PAINKILLER used to treat severe pain. It is also given to very ill patients with severe and painful coughing.

DIANETTE, brand of co-cyprindiol.

DIAZEPAM, used as in ANXIETY TREATMENT, in EPILEPSY TREATMENT, and as a SLEEP-AID. It is a BENZODIAZEPINE.

DICLOFENAC, a PAINKILLER, also used to treat inflammation. It is an NSAID.

DICYCLOVERINE, used to relieve painful spasms of the gastro-intestinal tract.

DIDRONEL, brand containing disodium etidronate.

DIETHYLAMINE SALICYLATE, rubbed into the skin to relieve pain in underlying muscles and joints.

DIGOXIN, used to treat heart failure and heart arrhythmias.

DIHYDROCODEINE, a PAINKILLER.

DILTIAZEM, used as an ANTIHYPERTENSIVE and to treat angina.

DIMETICONE (simethicone), used to relieve flatulence.

DIOCALM, brand containing the antidiarrhoeal loperamide.

DIPHENHYDRAMINE, used for allergic conditions. It is also contained in some cough-and-cold remedies, and is used as a SLEEP-AID. It is an ANTIHISTAMINE.

DIPYRIDAMOLE, an ANTIPLATELET DRUG.

DISODIUM ETIDRONATE, used to prevent and treat osteoporosis.

DISPRIN, brand of aspirin.

DISPRIN EXTRA, brand containing aspirin and paracetamol.

DIURETIC drugs, used to reduce excess fluid in the body. They are used in ANTIHYPERTENSIVE TREATMENT, also in acute pulmonary (lung) oedema, congestive heart failure and some liver and kidney disorders.
   Diuretics act on the kidneys and increase the removal of water and sodium and other mineral salts from the body. They increase urine production and so are often called water tablets.
   Various diuretics are used, including amiloride, furosemide and spironolactone. Some deplete potassium from the body, so people taking these must take potassium salts as a supplement. On the whole, diuretics are safe and free from side effects – apart from the frequent need to urinate.

DOCUSATE SODIUM, a laxative. It is also used to soften ear wax.

DOMPERIDONE, used to relieve nausea and vomiting.

DORZOLAMIDE, used to treat glaucoma.

DOSULEPIN (or dothiepin), an ANTIDEPRESSANT.

DOXAZOSIN, an ANTIHYPER-TENSIVE. It is also used to treat urinary retention in men with benign prostatic hyperplasia.

DOXYCYCLINE, an ANTIBIOTIC used to treat bacterial infections.

DULCO-LAX, brand of bisacodyl.

E

EFEXOR, brand of venlafaxine.

EFORMOTEROL, used in ASTHMA

TREATMENT. It is now known as FORMOTEROL.

ENALAPRIL, used as an ANTIHYPERTENSIVE and to treat heart failure. It is an ACE INHIBITOR.

EPILEPSY TREATMENT, used to prevent the occurrence of epileptic seizures. Specialized drugs are used depending on the type of epilepsy and how severe it is. Drugs used include sodium valproate, phenytoin, phenobarbital and carbamazepine. Many of these drugs have side effects, and some are not recommended for use in women of childbearing age.

ERGOCALCIFEROL (vitamin D_2), used to make up deficiency of vitamin D.

ERYTHROMYCIN, an ANTIBIOTIC used to treat bacterial infections.

ESOMEPRAZOLE, an ULCER-HEALING DRUG.

ESTRADIOL, an OESTROGEN used in HORMONE REPLACEMENT THERAPY.

ESTRIOL, an OESTROGEN used to treat menstrual, menopausal and other gynaecological problems.

ETHINYLESTRADIOL, an OESTROGEN used as a constituent of the ORAL CONTRACEPTIVE pill.

ETHOSUXIMIDE, used in EPILEPSY TREATMENT.

ETYNODIOL, a PROGESTOGEN in the ORAL CONTRACEPTIVE pill.

F

FELBINAC, a PAINKILLER used for the relief of strains and bruises. It is an NSAID.

FELODIPINE, used as an ANTIHYPERTENSIVE and to treat angina. It is a CALCIUM-CHANNEL BLOCKER.

FENOFIBRATE, a LIPID-REGULATING DRUG.

FENOTEROL, used in ASTHMA TREATMENT.

FERROUS GLUCONATE, an iron-rich compound used in iron-deficiency anaemia.

FERROUS SULPHATE, used to treat iron-deficiency anaemia.

FEXOFENADINE, used for hay fever and other allergic conditions. It is an ANTIHISTAMINE.

FINASTERIDE, used to treat benign prostatic hyperplasia.

FLIXONASE and **FLIXOTIDE**, brands of fluticasone.

FLOMAX MR, brand of tamsulosin.

FLUCLOXACILLIN, an ANTIBIOTIC used to treat bacterial infections.

FLUCONAZOLE, used to treat fungal infections.

FLUMETASONE, used to treat inflammatory skin disorders. It is a CORTICOSTEROID.

FLUOXETINE, an ANTIDEPRESSANT.

FLUTICASONE, used to treat inflammatory skin disorders such as eczema. It is also used as an asthma treatment and to prevent hay fever. It is a CORTICOSTEROID.

FLUVASTATIN, a LIPID-REGULATING DRUG.

FOLIC ACID, a vitamin of the B complex. It is taken as a supplement by pregnant women, or women who plan to become pregnant, to help prevent neural tube defects in their babies.

FORMOTEROL, used in ASTHMA TREATMENT. It is also known as EFORMOTEROL.

FUCIBET, brand of betamethasone.

FUCIDIN, brand of fusidic acid.

FUCIDIN H, brand containing hydrocortisone and fusidic acid.

FUCITHALMIC, brand of fusidic acid.

FULL MARKS, preparations of phenothrin against headlice.

FUROSEMIDE, a DIURETIC.

FUSIDIC ACID, an ANTIBIOTIC used to treat bacterial infections.

FYBOGEL, brand of the laxative ispaghula husk.

FYBOGEL MEBEVERINE, brand containing mebeverine and ispaghula husk.

FYBOGEL ORANGE, brand of ispaghula husk, flavoured.

G

GABAPENTIN, used in EPILEPSY TREATMENT.

GAMOLENIC ACID, used to relieve symptoms of breast pain and eczema.

GAVISCON, branded ANTACID preparation that contains alginic acid, sodium bicarbonate and aluminium hydroxide.

GERMOLOIDS, branded preparations containing lignocaine and zinc oxide. They are used for the relief of haemorrhoids.

GLIBENCLAMIDE, used in DIABETES TREATMENT.

GLICLAZIDE is used in DIABETES TREATMENT.

GLIPIZIDE, used in DIABETES TREATMENT.

GLYCEROL, used as a laxative and for treating glaucoma.

GLYCERYL TRINITRATE, used to treat angina.

GOSERELIN, used in INFERTILITY TREATMENT, to treat endometriosis. It is also used in CHEMOTHERAPY for breast and prostate cancers.

H

HALF-INDERAL, brand of generic BETA-BLOCKER, propranolol.

HALOPERIDOL, an ANTIPSYCHOTIC drug that is also used in ANXIETY TREATMENT. It is sometimes used to prevent intractable hiccups and nausea and vomiting.

HEDEX, brand of paracetamol.

HEDEX EXTRA, brand containing paracetamol and caffeine.

HEPARIN, an ANTICOAGULANT.

HEPARINOIDS, drugs with ANTICOAGULANT properties, also used topically to give relief from haemorrhoids, chilblains, varicose veins and bruising.

HIRUDOID, branded heparinoid.

HORMONE REPLACEMENT THERAPY (HRT), used to treat menopausal symptoms. Drugs that act in a similar way to the female sex hormones are given to supplement the diminished production of OESTROGEN hormones by the body, which occurs during the menopause. Conjugated oestrogens, and estradiol (or oestrodiol), are often used. Most women will also be prescribed a PROGESTOGEN, such as levonorgestrel or norethisterone, because there is a small increased risk of uterine cancer if oestrogen is taken alone. Alternatively, a new drug called tibolone can be used. If you have had a hysterectomy, oestrogen alone will probably be prescribed.
    The main purpose of HRT is to alleviate menopausal symptoms such as flushing, night sweats and thinning and drying of the vagina. HRT also reduces postmenopausal osteoporosis and benefits some women by reducing the risk of atherosclerosis, heart attacks and strokes. However, in other women there is an increased risk of deep vein thrombosis and of pulmonary embolism. There is a slightly increased risk of breast cancer, but a reduced risk of some other cancers.
    HRT is usually taken as tablets but may also be applied as vaginal cream, skin gels or skin patches. Sometimes HRT causes side effects such as breast tenderness, nausea, headaches, mood swings and water retention. A doctor will recommend the best type for you, based on your medical history.

HUMAN MIXTARD, brand of insulin.

HYDROCORTISONE, used to treat many types of inflammation, including allergic conditions, skin conditions, inflammatory bowel disease and rheumatic disease. It is a CORTICOSTEROID.

HYDROXOCOBALAMIN, a form of vitamin B_{12} used to treat megaloblastic anaemia.

HYDROXYCHLOROQUINE, used to treat inflammatory disorders such as rheumatoid arthritis and lupus erythematosus.

HYDROXYZINE, used to treat allergic symptoms, and as an ANXIETY TREATMENT. It is an ANTIHISTAMINE.

HYOSCINE, used as a sedative and to prevent travel sickness and symptoms of Ménières disease of the ear. It is also used in some ophthalmic operations because it paralyses the muscles of the eye.

HYPROMELLOSE, a constituent of artificial tears, and is used to treat dry eyes.

I

IBULEVE, brand of pain-relieving cream containing ibuprofen.

IBUPROFEN, a PAINKILLER. It is also used to reduce a high temperature and to treat inflammation. It is an NSAID.

IKOREL, brand of nicorandil.

IMDUR, brand of isosorbide mononitrate, a vasodilator.

IMIGRAN, brand of sumatriptan.

IMIPRAMINE, an ANTIDEPRESSANT.

IMODIUM, brand of loperamide.

IMODIUM PLUS, brand containing loperamide and dimeticone.

INDAPAMIDE, a DIURETIC.

INDERAL, brand of propranolol.

INDOMETACIN (indomethacin), a PAINKILLER used to treat painful inflammatory conditions, such as rheumatic pain, and period pain. It is an NSAID.

INDORAMIN, an ANTIHYPERTENSIVE, also used to treat benign prostatic hypertrophy.

INFACOL, brand of dimeticone.

INFERTILITY TREATMENT drugs, used to help couples who have problems conceiving. The type of treatment depends on the cause of infertility.
   Sometimes drugs that help a woman to ovulate are used. These include gonadotrophins, goserelin and tamoxifen. A drug regime may also be used as part of assisted conception such as in vitro fertilization (IVF).
   In cases of male infertility caused by impotence, drugs such as sildenafil – better known as the brand Viagra – may be prescribed.

INNOVACE, brand of enalapril.

INSULIN, used in DIABETES TREATMENT.

IPRATROPIUM, used to treat chronic bronchitis and in ASTHMA TREATMENT for chronic asthma. It is also used to relieve a runny nose in people with rhinitis.

IRBESARTAN, used as an ANTIHYPERTENSIVE. It is an ACE INHIBITOR.

ISOSORBIDE DINITRATE, used to prevent angina attacks.

ISOSORBIDE MONONITRATE, used to prevent and treat angina.

ISPAGHULA HUSK, a laxative used for treating irritable bowel syndrome. It is also used as a LIPID-REGULATING DRUG.

ISTIN, brand of amlodipine.

K

KETOCONAZOLE, used to treat serious fungal infections.

KETOPROFEN, a PAINKILLER and anti-inflammatory drug. It is used to treat rheumatic and muscular pain. It is an NSAID.

KWELLS, brand of hyoscine.

L

LACIDIPINE, used as an ANTIHYPERTENSIVE. It is a CALCIUM-CHANNEL BLOCKER.

LACTULOSE, a laxative.

LAMICTAL, brand of lamotrigine.

LAMISIL, brand of terbinafine.

LAMOTRIGINE, used in EPILEPSY TREATMENT.

LANSOPRAZOLE, an ULCER-HEALING DRUG.

LASONIL, branded heparinoid.

LATANOPROST, used to treat glaucoma.

LERCANIDIPINE, an ANTIHYPERTENSIVE. It is a CALCIUM-CHANNEL BLOCKER.

LEVOBUNOLOL, used to treat glaucoma. It is a BETA-BLOCKER.

LEVODOPA, used to treat PARKINSON'S DISEASE.

LEVONORGESTREL, a PROGESTOGEN used in ORAL CONTRACEPTIVE pills, the 'morning-after pill', HORMONE REPLACEMENT THERAPY and intra-uterine devices (IUDs).

LEVOTHYROXINE SODIUM, see thyroxine.

LIGNOCAINE (lidocaine), a local anaesthetic used to relieve pain such as during dental procedures. It is also used to treat heart arrhythmias.

LIPID-REGULATING DRUGS, used to treat people with high levels of certain cholesterol lipids and triglycerides (natural body fats) in the blood. The condition is known medically as hyperlipidaemia. The main drugs used are the statins, which include atorvastatin, cerivastatin, fluvastatin, pravastatin and simvastatin; and the fibrates: bezafibrate, ciprofibrate and fenofibrate. These are all taken by mouth.
   Lipid-regulating drugs, along with dietary changes, are used to lower levels of harmful low-density lipoprotein (LDL) cholesterol while raising beneficial high-density lipoprotein (HDL) cholesterol. This can slow down the development of coronary atherosclerosis, a diseased state of the arteries of the heart in which plaques of deposited lipid material cause a narrowing of blood vessels.
   Because atherosclerosis contributes to angina pectoris attacks and the formation of the clots that cause heart attacks and strokes, lipid-regulating drugs can be used to help reduce this risk. Lipid-regulating drugs used to be prescribed only for people who had a family history of hyperlipidaemia, or who had very high cholesterol levels. However, large-scale clinical trials have shown that many people, including those with angina or heart failure, as well as those who have really high blood lipids, may benefit. It is likely that these drugs will be used more widely in future to prevent certain cardiovascular diseases.

LIPITOR, brand of atorvastatin.

LIPOSTAT, brand of pravastatin.

LISINOPRIL, used as an ANTIHYPERTENSIVE and to treat

heart failure. It is an ACE INHIBITOR.

LITHIUM CARBONATE, used to treat manic depressive illness (bipolar disorder).

LOPERAMIDE, used to treat diarrhoea.

LOPRAZOLAM, used in ANXIETY TREATMENT, in EPILEPSY TREATMENT, and as a SLEEP-AID. It is a BENZODIAZEPINE.

LORATADINE, used to treat allergic conditions such as hay fever and urticaria. It is an ANTIHISTAMINE.

LORAZEPAM, used in ANXIETY TREATMENT, in EPILEPSY TREATMENT, and as a SLEEP-AID and sedative before operations. It is a BENZODIAZEPINE.

LORMETAZEPAM, a SLEEP-AID used to treat insomnia. It is a BENZODIAZEPINE.

LOSARTAN, used as an ANTIHYPERTENSIVE.

LOSEC, brand of omeprazole.

LUSTRAL, brand of sertraline.

LYCLEAR, brand of permethrin.

LYMECYCLINE, an ANTIBIOTIC used to treat bacterial infections

M

MACROGOL 3350, used in laxative preparations.

MAGNESIUM HYDROXIDE, an ANTACID. It is also used as a laxative.

MAGNESIUM SULPHATE, a laxative.

MAGNESIUM TRISILICATE, an ANTACID.

MALATHION, used to kill head lice and their eggs, and the mites that cause scabies.

MEBENDAZOLE, used to treat worms.

MEBEVERINE, used to treat gastro-intestinal disorders such as irritable bowel syndrome.

MECLOZINE, used to prevent nausea and vomiting such as in travel sickness. It is an ANTIHISTAMINE.

MEDROXYPROGESTERONE ACETATE, a PROGESTOGEN that is a constituent of the ORAL CONTRACEPTIVE pill, HORMONE REPLACEMENT THERAPY and of contraceptive implants. It is also used to boost hormone levels in women who need it, and is used in CHEMOTHERAPY for some cancers.

MEFENAMIC ACID, used as a PAINKILLER and to treat the inflammation of arthritis. It is also used for period pain and heavy menstrual bleeding. It is an NSAID.

MELOXICAM, used as a PAINKILLER and to treat the inflammation caused by arthritis. It is an NSAID.

MEPTAZINOL, a powerful PAINKILLER.

MESALAZINE, used to treat ulcerative colitis.

METFORMIN, used in DIABETES TREATMENT.

METHADONE, best known as a heroin substitute for addicts undergoing detoxification therapy. It is also used as a strong PAINKILLER and to stop coughing in terminally ill people.

METHOCARBAMOL, used to treat muscle spasms.

METHOTREXATE, used in cancer CHEMOTHERAPY, and to treat rheumatoid arthritis and severe psoriasis.

METHYLDOPA, used as an ANTIHYPERTENSIVE.

METHYLPHENIDATE, used to treat attention deficit hyperactivity disorder (ADHD) in children.

METHYLPREDNISOLONE, used to treat inflammation such as in allergic reactions. It is a CORTICOSTEROID.

METOCLOPRAMIDE, used to prevent vomiting.

METOPROLOL, used as an ANTIHYPERTENSIVE, to treat angina and heart arrhythmias, in MIGRAINE TREATMENT and, in the short term, to treat thyrotoxicosis. It is a BETA-BLOCKER.

METRONIDAZOLE, used to treat infections including amoebic dysentery and giardiasis, bacterial infections and worms.

MICONAZOLE, used to treat fungal infections.

MICROGYNON, brand of ORAL CONTRACEPTIVE containing ethinylestradiol and levonorgestrel.

MIGRAINE TREATMENT drugs, used in two ways. Some, such as BETA-BLOCKERS like propranolol, are taken to prevent attacks. Others are taken at the beginning of or during an attack to alleviate symptoms. This type must be rapidly absorbed into the body, so newer drugs such as sumatriptan – marketed under the brand-name Imigran – have been developed that can be self-injected or taken as a nasal spray.
Ordinary PAINKILLERS such as aspirin, codeine and paracetamol, available in quick-absorption formulations, along with drugs to prevent vomiting, such as metoclopramide and domperidone, may be helpful.

MIGRALEVE, brand of migraine medication containing codeine, paracetamol and buclizine.

MINOCYCLINE, an ANTIBIOTIC used to treat bacterial infections such as bacterial meningitis.

MINOXIDIL, best known as a topical treatment for male pattern baldness.
It is also used orally as an ANTIHYPERTENSIVE.

MIRTAZAPINE, an ANTIDEPRESSANT.

MOMETASONE, used to treat severe inflammatory skin conditions and allergic rhinitis. It is a CORTICOSTEROID.

MONTELUKAST, used in ASTHMA TREATMENT.

MORNING-AFTER PILL, see ORAL CONTRACEPTIVES.

MORPHINE, a strong PAINKILLER. It is also used to treat dry coughs and diarrhoea.

MOXONIDINE, an ANTIHYPERTENSIVE.

MUPIROCIN, an ANTIBIOTIC used to treat bacterial infections.

MYCIL, branded anti-fungal, tolnaftate.

N

NABUMETONE, a PAINKILLER used particularly for arthritis. It is an NSAID.

NAFTIDROFURYL, used to treat peripheral vascular disease.

NAPROXEN, a PAINKILLER and treatment for inflammation. It is an NSAID.

NARATRIPTAN, used in MIGRAINE TREATMENT.

NEBIVOLOL, used as an ANTIHYPERTENSIVE. It is a BETA-BLOCKER.

NEDOCROMIL, used in ASTHMA TREATMENT to prevent recurrent attacks. It is also used to treat hay fever and other allergic conditions.

NEOMYCIN, an ANTIBIOTIC used to treat bacterial infections.

NICORANDIL, used to prevent and treat angina.

NICORETTE PREPARATIONS, brand of nicotine used to help smokers to give up.

NICOTINE, used in replacement therapy to help smokers to quit.

NICOTINELL PREPARATIONS, brand of nicotine to help smokers to give up.

NIFEDIPINE, used as an ANTIHYPERTENSIVE and to treat angina and Raynaud's disease. It is a CALCIUM-CHANNEL BLOCKER.

NIGHT NURSE PREPARATIONS, brand of cold remedy containing paracetamol, promethazine and dextromethorphan.

NIQUITIN, brand of nicotine to help smokers to give up.

NITRAZEPAM, used as a SLEEP-AID. It is a BENZODIAZEPINE.

NITROFURANTOIN, used to treat bacterial infections.

NIZATIDINE, an ULCER-HEALING DRUG.

NORETHISTERONE, a PROGESTOGEN used in the ORAL CONTRACEPTIVE pill, in HORMONE REPLACEMENT THERAPY and contraceptive implants. It is also used for other gynaecological problems, and in CHEMOTHERAPY for some cancers.

NSAID (non-steroidal anti-inflammatory drugs), used as anti-inflammatories, analgesics and antipyretics to lower temperature.

NUROFEN, brand of ibuprofen.

NUROFEN COLD AND FLU, brand containing ibuprofen and pseudoephedrine.

NUROFEN PLUS, brand containing ibuprofen and codeine.

NYSTATIN, an ANTIBIOTIC used to treat fungal infections.

O

OESTROGEN, a hormone that is frequently combined with PROGESTOGEN hormones in ORAL CONTRACEPTIVES, HORMONE REPLACEMENT THERAPY and to treat various gynaecological and menstrual problems. Oestrogen is also used to treat certain cancers, such as prostate cancer. Those used include natural oestrogens, estradiol and estriol, and synthetic versions, including ethinylestradiol and diethylstilbestrol (stilboestrol).

OLANZAPINE, used to treat schizophrenia. It is an ANTIPSYCHOTIC drug.

OMEPRAZOLE, an ULCER-HEALING DRUG.

ORAL CONTRACEPTIVE drugs, taken by women to prevent conception, commonly referred to as the Pill. Most contain both an OESTROGEN and a PROGESTOGEN, and this type of Pill is known as the combined oral contraceptive.

Another type of Pill is the progestogen-only pill; this is safe to use if you are breastfeeding. Contraceptive oestrogens and progestogens can also be given by injection or implant. The so-called 'MORNING-AFTER' pill is an oral contraceptive taken after unprotected sex. All oral contraceptives have side effects, and you need expert advice to find the one best suited to you.

ORIGINAL ANDREWS SALTS, brand containing sodium bicarbonate, magnesium sulphate and citric acid.

ORLISTAT, used to treat obesity.

ORPHENADRINE, used to treat PARKINSON'S DISEASE.

OXAZEPAM, used in ANXIETY TREATMENT and as a SLEEP-AID. It is a BENZODIAZEPINE.

OXITROPIUM, used to treat chronic bronchitis and as an ASTHMA TREATMENT.

OXY PREPARATIONS, brand containing benzoyl peroxide.

OXYBUTYNIN, used for urinary problems such as bedwetting.

OXYTETRACYCLINE, an ANTIBIOTIC used to treat bacterial infections.

P

PAINKILLER drugs, known medically as analgesics. NSAID (non-steroidal anti-inflammatory drugs) such as aspirin and ibuprofen work by reducing the inflammation that is often a cause of pain. These drugs are widely taken to treat arthritic and rheumatic pain, and inflammation and pain in other musculoskeletal disorders. Other NSAIDs include diclofenac, etodolac, felbinac, ketoprofen, indometacin, meloxicam, nabumetone, naproxen, piroxicam and rofecoxib. Most can cause gastro-intestinal upsets ranging from dyspepsia to serious haemorrhage.

Paracetamol is a painkiller. It can also be used to reduce body temperature and can be given to children including babies after immunization.

Narcotic analgesic painkillers can be used to alleviate more intense pain such as that experienced after operations, dental pain and for the severe pain of some cancers. Morphine and diamorphine (heroin) are powerful narcotic analgesics used only for severe pain. Codeine, which has weaker action, is available over the counter only when it is combined with paracetamol. Other narcotic analgesics include buprenorphine, methadone, pentazocine and pethidine. They mimic the actions in the brain of the body's natural analgesics, the encephalins and endorphins. However, most can be addictive and are prescribed with caution.

PANCREATIN, taken to make up a deficiency of pancreatic enzymes in people who have conditions such as cystic fibrosis, or who have had pancreatic surgery.

PANOXYL PREPARATIONS, brand containing benzoyl peroxide.

PANTOPRAZOLE, an ULCER-HEALING DRUG.

PARACETAMOL, a popular PAINKILLER also used to reduce high body temperature.

PARACODOL, brand containing paracetamol and codeine.

PARIET, branded rabeprazole.

PARKINSON'S DISEASE treatment, used to alleviate some of the symptoms of Parkinson's disease. In Parkinson's disease the level of the neurotransmitter dopamine, relative to the level of the neurotransmitter acetylcholine is reduced. Drugs, used to try to restore the correct balance, include levodopa, co-beneldopa, co-careldopa, benzhexol and procyclidine. Specialist medical advice is needed in order to choose the best drug for a given stage of the condition.

PAROXETINE, an ANTIDEPRESSANT.

PEPPERMINT OIL, used to relieve the discomfort of conditions such as irritable bowel syndrome.

PERINDOPRIL, used as an ANTIHYPERTENSIVE and to treat heart failure. It is an ACE INHIBITOR.

PERMETHRIN, used to eradicate lice and their eggs, and the mites that cause scabies.

PETHIDINE, a powerful PAINKILLER often administered to women in labour.

PHENOBARBITAL (or phenobarbitone), a barbiturate used in EPILEPSY TREATMENT.

PHENOTHRIN, used to treat head lice and pubic lice infestations.

PHENOXYMETHYLPENICILLIN (or penicillin V), an ANTIBIOTIC used to treat bacterial infections.

PHENYLPROPANOLAMINE, used to relieve congestion in the airways and nose.

PHENYTOIN, used in EPILEPSY TREATMENT and also for trigeminal neuralgia.

PHOLCODINE, used to treat a dry cough.

PILOCARPINE, used to treat glaucoma.

PINDOLOL, used as an ANTIHYPERTENSIVE. It is a BETA-BLOCKER.

PIRITON PREPARATIONS, brand containing chlorphenamine.

PIROXICAM, a PAINKILLER. It is used to treat pain and inflammation in musculo-skeletal conditions such as arthritis. It is an NSAID.

PIZOTIFEN, used in MIGRAINE TREATMENT.

PLAVIX, brand of clopidogrel.

PLENDIL, brand of felodipine.

POLYVINYL ALCOHOL, used as a constituent of artificial tears to treat dry eyes.

POTASSIUM BICARBONATE, a potassium supplement taken to make up potassium loss from the body, such as after chronic diarrhoea.

PRAVASTATIN, a LIPID-REGULATING DRUG.

PREDNISOLONE, used to treat many inflammatory conditions. It is also used in cancer CHEMOTHERAPY, and for some autoimmune conditions. It is a CORTICOSTEROID.

PREMARIN, brand of conjugated oestrogens.

PRIMIDONE, used in EPILEPSY TREATMENT.

PROCHLORPERAZINE, an ANTIPSYCHOTIC drug for schizophrenia and mania. It is also used to prevent vomiting and as an ANXIETY TREATMENT.

PROCYCLIDINE, used to treat PARKINSON'S DISEASE.

PROGESTOGEN, the natural female progesterone hormone that prepares the lining of the uterus for pregnancy, maintains it throughout pregnancy, and prevents the further release of eggs. Natural progesterones used medically include levonorgestrel, medroxyprogesterone and norethisterone. The hormones are used in ORAL CONTRACEPTIVES, HORMONE REPLACEMENT THERAPY, and to treat various menstrual and gynaecological problems. Sometimes progestogen is used in the treatment of breast, endometrial and prostate cancers.

PROMETHAZINE, used to treat allergic conditions, travel sickness and as a SLEEP-AID. It is an ANTIHISTAMINE.

PROPRANOLOL, used as an ANTIHYPERTENSIVE, to treat angina, thyrotoxicosis and heart arrhythmias. It is also used as a MIGRAINE TREATMENT and ANXIETY TREATMENT. It is a BETA-BLOCKER.

PROZAC, brand of fluoxetine.

PSEUDOEPHEDRINE, used to relieve congestion in the nose and airways.

PULMICORT, brand of budesonide.

Q

QUINAPRIL, used as an ANTIHYPERTENSIVE and to treat heart failure. It is an ACE INHIBITOR.

QUININE, used to treat malaria and also to relieve night time leg cramps.

QUINODERM PREPARATIONS, brand of benzoyl peroxide.

R

RABEPRAZOLE, an ULCER-HEALING DRUG.

RALOXIFENE, used to prevent and treat osteoporosis.

RAMIPRIL, used as an ANTIHYPERTENSIVE and to treat heart failure. It is an ACE INHIBITOR.

RANITIDINE, an ULCER-HEALING DRUG.

REGAINE, brand of minoxidil.

RESOLVE, brand containing paracetamol, ascorbic acid, sodium bicarbonate, sodium carbonate, potassium bicarbonate and citric acid.

RISEDRONATE, used to prevent and treat osteoporosis.

RISPERIDONE, an ANTIPSYCHOTIC drug.

RIZATRIPTAN, used in MIGRAINE TREATMENT.

ROFECOXIB, a PAINKILLER and anti-inflammatory drug used in arthritis. It is an NSAID.

ROSIGLITAZONE, used in DIABETES TREATMENT.

S

SALBUTAMOL, used in ASTHMA TREATMENT.

SALICYLIC ACID, used on the skin to treat minor infections and conditions such as athlete's foot, and to relieve muscle and joint pain. It is also used to remove warts and callouses.

SALMETEROL, used in ASTHMA TREATMENT.

SEA-LEGS, brand of meclozine.

SENNA, a laxative.

SENOKOT, brand of senna.

SEREVENT, brand of salmeterol.

SEROXAT, brand of paroxetine.

SERTRALINE, an ANTIDEPRESSANT, also used to treat obsessive-compulsive disorders.

SILDENAFIL, used as an impotence treatment.

SILVER SULPHADIAZINE, used to treat bacterial infections, particularly to prevent bedsores and burns becoming infected.

SIMETHICONE (dimeticon), used to relieve flatulence.

SIMVASTATIN, a LIPID-REGULATING DRUG.

SINUTAB, brand containing paracetamol and phenylpropanolamine.

SLEEP-AID DRUGS, known medically as hypnotics. These help to induce sleep and work by acting on the brain. They are used mainly to treat insomnia and to sedate patients who are mentally ill, but they may also be used for the short-term treatment of insomnia due to jet lag, shift work, emotional problems or serious illness.

The best known and most often taken are the BENZODIAZEPINE drugs, such as diazepam and temazepam. Other drugs that are used include zopiclone, zolpidem and chloral betaine. Most are available only on prescription, but over-the-counter sleep-aids include promethazine. Some can cause you to feel drowsy the following day.

SODIUM BICARBONATE, an ANTACID.

SODIUM CARBONATE, an ANTACID.

SODIUM CITRATE, used as a laxative and as an enema.

SODIUM CROMOGLICATE, used in ASTHMA TREATMENT and other allergic conditions such as allergic conjunctivitis.

SODIUM FEREDETATE, rich in iron and is used to treat iron-deficiency anaemia. It is also known as SODIUM IRONEDETATE.

SODIUM FUSIDATE, a compound of FUSIDIC ACID, used in the same way.

SODIUM IRONEDETATE, see sodium feredetate.

SODIUM PICOSULFATE, a laxative.

SODIUM VALPROATE, used in EPILEPSY TREATMENT.

SOLPADEINE, brand containing paracetamol, codeine and caffeine.

SOTALOL, used to treat heart arrhythmias. It is a BETA-BLOCKER.

SPIRONOLACTONE, a DIURETIC.

STATINS, see Lipid-regulating drugs.

SULEO-M, brand of malathion.

SULFASALAZINE, used to treat Crohn's disease, ulcerative colitis and rheumatoid arthritis.

SULPIRIDE, used mainly as an ANTIPSYCHOTIC drug for schizophrenia.

SUMATRIPTAN, used in MIGRAINE TREATMENT.

T

TAGAMET 100, brand of the ulcer-healing drug cimetidine.

TAMOXIFEN, used as an INFERTILITY TREATMENT and in cancer CHEMOTHERAPY to prevent or treat breast cancer.

TAMSULOSIN, used to treat urinary retention by men who have benign prostatic hyperplasia.

TEMAZEPAM, used as a SLEEP-AID. It is a BENZODIAZEPINE.

TENORMIN, brand of atenolol.

TERBINAFINE, used to treat fungal infections such as ringworm.

TERBUTALINE, used in ASTHMA TREATMENT.

TETRACYCLINE, an ANTIBIOTIC used to treat bacterial infections.

THEOPHYLLINE, used in ASTHMA TREATMENT.

THIORIDAZINE, an ANTIPSYCHOTIC drug. It is sometimes used as an ANXIETY TREATMENT for elderly people.

THYROXINE, a hormone administered to make up for deficient hormone production by the thyroid gland.

TIBOLONE, used in HORMONE REPLACEMENT THERAPY.

TIMOLOL, used as an ANTIHYPERTENSIVE and to treat angina and glaucoma. It is also used as a MIGRAINE TREATMENT. It is a BETA-BLOCKER.

TOLBUTAMIDE, used in DIABETES TREATMENT.

TOLNAFTATE, used to treat fungal infections such as athlete's foot.

TOLTERODINE, used to treat urinary problems.

TRAMADOL, a strong PAINKILLER.

TRANDOLAPRIL, used as an ANTIHYPERTENSIVE. It is an ACE INHIBITOR.

TRANEXAMIC ACID, used to stem bleeding such as might occur during tooth extraction, or for excessive menstrual bleeding.

TRAZODONE, an ANTIDEPRESSANT.

TRIAMCINOLONE, used to treat inflammatory conditions, especially when caused by allergy. It is a CORTICOSTEROID.

TRIFLUOPERAZINE, an ANTIPSYCHOTIC drug. It is also sometimes used to treat anxiety and severe nausea and vomiting.

TRIHEXYPHENIDYL, used to treat PARKINSON'S DISEASE.

TRIMETHOPRIM, used to treat bacterial infections.

TRIMIPRAMINE, an ANTIDEPRESSANT.

TRIPROLIDINE, used to treat allergic symptoms such as hay fever and urticaria. It is an ANTIHISTAMINE.

TRITACE, brand of ramipril.

TYROZETS, brand of lozenge containing benzocaine.

U

ULCER-HEALING DRUGS, used to promote healing of ulcers in the lining of the stomach and small intestine. The proton-pump inhibitors such as omeprazole (Losec) may be prescribed for peptic ulcers. These drugs may be used in conjunction with antibacterial drugs which eliminate the bacterium *Helicobacter pylori* in the stomach. *H. pylori* is known to be one of the main causes of peptic ulcers.

Many different types of drug may be used, including so-called H2-antagonist drugs such as ranitidine (known by the brand name Zantac) and cimetidine (branded as Tagamet).

V

VACCINES, used to give immunity against infections and so prevent the vaccinated person from catching that disease. They work by causing a person's own body to create a defence in the form of antibodies. Vaccines can be made from dead microbes, live but weakened microbes, or extracts of the toxins released by the invading microbes. They are usually injected, but some, such as the polio vaccine, are taken by mouth. There are vaccines to treat a range of infections, but they are less effective against viruses that can change rapidly into new forms, as do influenza and HIV. A vaccine for HIV is still in the research stages.

VALSARTAN, used as an ANTIHYPERTENSIVE.

VENLAFAXINE, an ANTIDEPRESSANT.

VENTOLIN, brand of salbutamol.

VERAPAMIL, used as an ANTIHYPERTENSIVE, and to treat angina and heart arrhythmias. It is a CALCIUM-CHANNEL BLOCKER.

VIAGRA, brand of sildenafil.

VIOXX, brand of rofecoxib.

VISCOTEARS, brand of carbomer.

W

WARFARIN, an ANTICOAGULANT

X

XALATAN, brand of latanoprost.

Z

ZANTAC, brand of ranitidine.

ZANTAC 75, brand of ranitidine.

ZESTRIL, brand of lisinopril.

ZINC OXIDE, used to treat skin conditions such as eczema.

ZIRTEK, brand of cetirizine.

ZOCOR, brand of simvastatin.

ZOLADEX, brand of goserelin.

ZOLMITRIPTAN, drug used in MIGRAINE TREATMENT.

ZOLPIDEM, a SLEEP-AID drug.

ZOPICLONE, a SLEEP-AID drug.

ZOTON, brand of lansoprazole.

ZOVIRAX, brand of aciclovir.

ZYPREXA, brand of olanzapine.

Drugs, misuse of

Drug misuse is the taking of drugs that can harm health, make it hard to function socially or are simply illegal. It can lead to physical or psychological dependency on the drug, and may be a sign of other behavioural problems.

The misuse of drugs in the UK occurs in all sectors of society, particularly the taking of illegal drugs amongst younger people. Drug traffickers are known to target this age group providing easy access to cannabis, stimulants such as ecstacy, as well as a range of the more addictive drugs.

ADDICTIVE DRUGS
Not all drugs are addictive. Those that are will lead to a psychological – and sometimes physical – state which is characterized by a compulsion to take the drug. This is known as drug dependence. Addiction is a severe form of drug dependence. It is an actual physical need for the drug and results from changes in the body that have been caused by regularly taking that drug. Addiction is preceded by tolerance. Tolerance can develop to any drug if it is taken regularly. What it means in physical terms is that more of the drug is needed in order to achieve the same effects.

Some drugs, when used repeatedly, can cause withdrawal symptoms if suddenly stopped. In the case of opiates, withdrawal involves nausea, diarrhoea, pain and 'goose-flesh', though symptoms vary with the type of drug.

Psychological dependence is regarded as the compulsion to take a drug purely for the mind-altering effects, even in the absence of physical withdrawal symptoms.

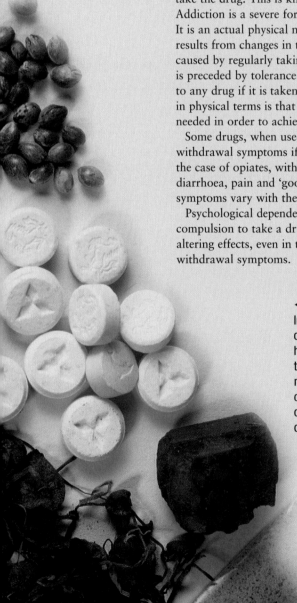

◀ **Popular drugs**
In the UK, over 50 per cent of the population under 24 have used illegal drugs more than once. Cannabis is the most popular drug with those over 16, while 11 to 12 year-olds prefer to sniff glue and other solvents.

Drugs producing major psychological and physical dependence include the opiates, nicotine, alcohol, benzodiazepines and barbiturates.

THE LEGAL POSITION
In the UK, drugs are regulated by the *Misuse of Drugs Act, 1971*, which makes illegal certain activities in relation to 'Controlled Drugs'. The penalties for offences involving the different drugs are graded broadly according to the perceived harmfulness of the drug when it is misused. For this purpose the drugs are defined as three classes, A, B and C.

Class A drugs are the most harmful. They include many opiates (opium, heroin, morphine, methadone, pethidine), cocaine, LSD, Ecstasy, phencyclidine. They also include Class B drugs which have been prepared for use by injection.

Class B drugs include oral amphetamines, barbiturates, codeine and pholcodine.

Class C covers a broad range of drugs related to the amphetamines, most benzodiazepines, and a number of drugs used in sport and body building, including androgenic steroids and anabolic steroids, and growth hormones (somatotropin, somatrem and somatropin).

In January 2004, the Government lowered the classification of cannabis from Class B to Class C. The main legal consequence is that the maximum legal penalty for possession of cannabis has been reduced down to 2 years plus a fine. While it remains illegal, most adults found in possession of cannabis will receive only a warning and the drug will be confiscated. Those under 18 are still likely to be arrested and receive a formal warning. The maximum penalty for supplying or dealing remains at 14 years imprisonment.

COMMONLY MISUSED DRUGS
Most drugs that can be described as being misued are taken to alter the user's state of mind. Some cause a depression or a calming of brain function, while others act as stimulants, elevating mood and reducing appetite and the need for sleep. Others have powerful hallucinogenic properties.
Relaxants and stimulants
The **opiates**, such as **heroin**, are some of the most powerful and popular relaxants. Initially they

◀ **Dance culture**
Use of illegal drugs, such as Ecstasy, is often associated with dance and youth culture. Increasingly clubs and venues, together with local authorities, are offering information and advice to clubbers regarding drugs misuse.

produce a state of euphoria, a general numbing of feeling and alleviation of pain. At higher doses, they bring drowsiness and sleep. A brown or white powder, heroin is often diluted with other substances and injected, sniffed or smoked.

Cannabis is also a relaxant, probably the most widely used. Although it causes some stimulation, giddiness and euphoria at first, this is quickly followed by a feeling of calm and an increased perception of the senses. Sedative-hypnotics such as benzodiazepines and the **barbiturates**, are also used to depress alertness, producing symptoms similar to those caused by large amounts of alcohol.

Nitrates, nicknamed 'poppers', are commonly used for an almost immediate, though short-lived, feeling of light-headedness, followed by a sense of relaxation and well-being. Some users also claim they have an aphrodisiac effect. But continued sniffing of such drugs can damage the circulatory system and the blood's capacity to carry oxygen, as well as causing skin problems around the mouth and nose. They are particularly harmful for people with anaemia, glaucoma, or breathing or heart problems, and may be fatal if swallowed. Mixing nitrates with Viagra is very dangerous.

There is also a range of powerful stimulants that act on the central and peripheral nervous systems to heighten alertness, creating a feeling of euphoria and of having boundless energy. These include **cocaine, ecstasy** and amphetamines ('speed') and their derivatives. Nicotine from smoking is also a stimulant, reducing the appetite and raising blood pressure.

Hallucinogenic drugs
Some drugs are used to produce changes in perception. A good example is LSD – a psychoactive drug with extremely powerful hallucinogenic properties. Mescaline, from the Mexican peyote cactus, and magic mushrooms have similar effects but are less potent. Some

other drugs, such as cannabis, opiates and ecstasy, can promote vivid dreams and experiences, but are not regarded primarily as hallucinogens.

IF YOU THINK SOMEONE IS ABUSING DRUGS
There are often no definite signs that a person is misusing drugs. If you suspect that someone in your care has a drug problem, try not to be too alarmed; if you can, attempt to air your worries with them. Listen to what they have to say. Discuss the legal and health implications of drug taking – including alcohol and tobacco – and try to suggest ways of avoiding harm or preventing an escalation of the abuse.

If the person has a serious problem, it may help to discuss it with a health professional, perhaps your GP, in the first instance, or to phone one of the dedicated organizations that can offer advice and support (see below).

SEE ALSO *Addictions; Alcohol and abuse; Narcotics; Nicotine and nicotine replacement therapy; Smoking; Solvent abuse; Tranquillizers*

CONTACT **Talk to Frank** 0800 77 66 00 (English language); 0800 917 6650 (Asian). All calls from a landline are free. (www.talktofrank.com) The organization gives free confidential advice and will tell you about local services and rehabilitation clinics.
Cascade (0121) 788 3436 (theteam@cascade-drug.org.uk). An information service on drugs, for young people from the age of 11. It advises drug users, parents and friends of users or those with a professional interest.
ADFAM (020) 7928 8898. A charity for families and friends of drug users.
Families anonymous 0845 1200 660. A self-help support group for the parents of drug users. (www.famanon.org.uk)
Narcotics Helpline (020) 7730 0009 (www.ukna.org)

DTP vaccine

DTP vaccine is a triple vaccine, used routinely to immunize children, that protects against the infectious diseases **diphtheria**, **tetanus** and pertussis (**whooping cough**). The first dose is given at two months followed by a second at three months and a third at four months. The vaccine is administered by an injection into a muscle or deep into the skin. It consists of a diphtheria vaccine and a tetanus vaccine, which neutralize the toxins produced by the bacteria causing these diseases, and a pertussis vaccine that works by reacting with the actual bacteria.

SEE ALSO *Immunization*

Duchenne muscular dystrophy

Duchenne muscular dystrophy is the most common and severe form of **muscular dystrophy**. Often referred to as DMD, this hereditary muscle disease almost exclusively affects boys. Its incidence is estimated to be between one in 3000 and one in 4000 boys born in the UK. The disease usually manifests between the ages of four and seven, and is characterized by a waddling movement and curvature of the lumbar spine. The calf muscles, shoulders and upper limbs often become firm and bulky. Most DMD patients die before the age of 30.

Dumping syndrome

Also called rapid gastric emptying, dumping syndrome is the excessively rapid movement of undigested food from the stomach to the lower end of the small intestine. It is usually the result of the disruption of the stomach's normal mechanisms by surgery (see **Gastrectomy**). It can sometimes be caused by stress.

If the stomach empties straight after a meal – early dumping – the symptoms include vomiting, bloating, diarrhoea and shortness of breath. Late dumping occurs one to three hours after eating; it causes weakness, sweating and dizziness as a result of a rise and then a fall in blood sugar levels. Some people experience both early and late dumping.

Treatment is primarily dietary: frequent small meals that are low in carbohydrates and sugars, and plenty of liquids consumed between meals rather than with them have been found to be helpful.

SEE ALSO *Digestive system*

Duodenal ulcer

An erosion in the wall of the duodenum, the first part of the small intestine, is referred to as a duodenal ulcer. In the UK, 10–15 per cent of people have a duodenal ulcer at some time in their life. It is more common in men than in women. Duodenal ulcers are two to three times more common than **gastric ulcers**.

The cause is an attack on the duodenal wall by acidic digestive juices, often when the bacterium *Helicobacter pylori* is present in the stomach. Cigarette smoking and the use of aspirin and other non-steroidal anti-inflammatory drugs (NSAIDs) contribute. Symptoms include abdominal pain – often at night – nausea and vomiting, tarry stools and weight loss.

Complications include an obstruction, perforation of the duodenum, **peritonitis** and bleeding. Treatment is with **antibiotics** and drugs such as cimetidine.

SEE ALSO *Ulcer*

Dupuytren's contracture

Dupuytren's contracture is a gradual puckering of the skin and bending of the fingers, which is caused by the painless thickening of the fibrous tissues of the hand. The ring and little fingers are usually affected, and may be drawn down onto the palm. It often occurs in both hands, and usually develops from the age of 40 onwards. It is more common in men than women.

SYMPTOMS
- A small lump develops on the palm, spreading to form a band of hard tissue under the skin, which may pucker.
- Over a period of months or years, the affected fingers gradually close over the palm in a fixed position.

CAUSES
The exact cause is unknown but abnormal activity of cell growth factors may be involved. The condition sometimes runs in families and it is more common in those suffering from **epilepsy** and alcoholic liver disease (see **Liver and disorders**).

TREATMENT
Surgery, in which the bands of thickened tissue under the skin are cut and separated, is the only effective treatment. The condition may return in time. Some sufferers benefit from exercise and warm water baths.

Complementary therapies
A combination of **acupuncture** and **homeopathy** may help. Some researchers in the USA have claimed that high doses of vitamin E can improve symptoms.

Dysentery

Dysentery is a bowel infection that causes severe **diarrhoea**. There are two forms: bacillary dysentery and amoebic dysentery (see **Amoebiasis**). In the UK, between 2000 and 10,000 cases are notified annually, mostly the mild form of bacillary dysentry caused by poor hygiene. Amoebic dysentery is very rare in the UK but common in tropical countries. Symptoms can include diarrhoea, stools streaked with blood, pus or mucus, vomiting, griping pains in the abdomen and an urgent desire to defecate. Rest and fluids may settle mild bacillary dysentery in a few days; severe cases can last for weeks. Amoebic dysentery needs at least ten days' treatment. Left untreated, it may persist for years.

CAUSES
- A group of bacteria called *Shigella* are the cause of the bacillary form.
- A parasite called *Entamoeba histolytica* is the cause of the amoebic form.
- Both types are spread by contaminated food and poor hygiene.
- Amoebic dysentery is also spread by water.

WHAT YOU CAN DO
- Take plenty of fluids.
- If the symptoms are not too severe, try an antidiarrhoeal medicine.

WHEN TO CONSULT A DOCTOR
- If symptoms are severe or persistent, or start to get worse.
- If blood, pus or mucus occur in the stools.
- If symptoms occur in a country where amoebic dysentery is present.

WHAT A DOCTOR MAY DO
- Send the patient's stools for testing.
- Prescribe **antibiotics** for bacillary dysentry and anti-microbial drugs for amoebic dysentery.
- Arrange for specialist treatment.

COMPLEMENTARY THERAPIES
Homeopathy and **acupuncture** may help when used alongside conventional treatments.

COMPLICATIONS
- The main risk is **dehydration**.
- Amoebiasis is more serious, because the parasite is hard to kill and may cause **abscesses** in the liver and lungs.

PREVENTION
- Strict hygiene measures if contact with dysentery sufferers is likely.
- Boil water in countries where amoebic dysentery occurs and do not eat raw food, salad or fruit that cannot be peeled.

OUTLOOK
The outlook for bacillary dysentery is good, but it is more difficult to cure amoebic dysentery completely.

Dyslexia

A person with dyslexia has problems acquiring reading and writing skills despite having average or high intelligence and normal opportunities to learn. The disorder can vary from a slight difficulty (which may not be recognized) to complete incomprehension of the written word. There may also be problems with basic mathematics, processing information and short-term memory. Dyslexia is more common in boys than girls. It is thought to be caused by a developmental abnormality, with a strong genetic component.

Three kinds of dyslexia have been identified. It is unclear whether they are separate disorders or different manifestations of the same one:
- Visual: the person can read individual letters but cannot put them together to make words.
- Phonological: the person is unable to match written words to their sounds – an essential skill as normal reading involves internally 'speaking' words that are read and then understanding them by 'listening in' to this inner speech.
- Semantic: the person is unable to match written symbols to their meaning; a rough meaning may be grasped, but a precise match is elusive – hence 'dog' may be read as 'cat'.

What's going on in the brain?
Different areas of the brain may be involved in different types of dyslexia. Visual dyslexia is linked with a functional abnormality in the magnocellular system – a nervous pathway that carries sensory information to the part of the brain concerned with directing attention.

Phonological dyslexia may also be due in part to such an abnormality, but another possibility is that people with this type of dyslexia process the visual component of writing satisfactorily but cannot transfer it from the part of the brain that 'comprehends' it to the part that turns it

It is not known how many people are dyslexic because reading difficulties have often been assumed to be the result of a general learning disability.

▼ **Forming words**
Writing skills are affected in varying degrees by dyslexia. One of the most common manifestations is misspelling – the right letters may appear, but in the wrong order.

into articulated speech. Semantic dyslexia may similarly involve a blockage between the area of the brain that attaches meaning to a word and that which expresses the meaning.

TREATMENT

There is no medical treatment for dyslexia, but some studies have found that symptoms improved in children who took supplements, including fish oils, evening primrose oil, thyme oil and vitamin E.

People with dyslexia can be taught strategies to help them to overcome their problems. Some education authorities offer tuition for dyslexic children and may give them extra time in examinations.

CONTACT **British Dyslexia Association** 98 London Road, Reading RG1 5AU (0118) 966 8271 (www.bda-dyslexia.org.uk)

Dysmenorrhoea

Dysmenorrhoea is painful menstruation. It affects up to 60 per cent of women at some time. In primary dysmenorrhoea, the pelvic organs are healthy but abdominal cramps, low backache, and sometimes gastro-intestinal symptoms, develop during the first two days of a period. Antiprostaglandin medications, such as mefenamic acid (Ponstan) or the contraceptive pill usually relieve the pain. Secondary dysmenorrhoea is caused by a pelvic abnormality, such as infection, **endometriosis**, **fibroids** or the presence of an intra-uterine device (see **Contraception**). The pain is often a dull ache that starts before a period and lasts right through it. The cause should be treated.

SEE ALSO *Menstruation and problems; Pelvis and disorders*

Dyspepsia

Dyspepsia is the medical name for indigestion: a discomfort or pain in the middle of the chest, often felt after eating but sometimes present at other times. Other symptoms include nausea, **heartburn**, bloating, flatulence and belching.

Generally the cause is eating too quickly or eating highly spiced or fatty foods, although stress may also be a factor. Sometimes dyspepsia is a symptom of another condition, especially when it persists or recurs. Often this is a gastric

ulcer or oesophagitis, but other possibilities include gallstones or a hiatus hernia.

SEE ALSO *Diaphragm and disorders, Gallbladder and disorders; Hernia; Oesophagus and disorders; Stomach and disorders*

Dysphasia

Dysphasia is a communication disorder caused by disease in the dominant hemisphere of the brain – most often the left half of the brain. It can affect understanding, speaking, reading or writing, and may occur after a stroke, head injury or neurological disease. Speech and other therapies can help people to learn cues and short-cuts to improve communication.

SEE ALSO *Brain and nervous system; Speech disorders and therapy; Stroke*

Dyspraxia

Dyspraxia is due to an immaturity in the brain, resulting in difficulty in planning and carrying out complex movements. This disorder of the cerebral cortex affects at least 10 per cent of the population, and almost three-quarters of those affected are male. Symptoms include clumsiness and poor posture, coordination and short-term memory. Children are often slow to develop, and their speech may be hard to understand. They may be of average or above-average intelligence, but their behaviour is immature.

Occupational and other therapies can help sufferers to overcome or minimize symptoms.

SEE ALSO *Child development; Occupational therapy*

Dystonia

Dystonia refers to involuntary muscle spasms that result in abnormal movements, postures or sounds, such as frequent blinking, facial or neck twitching or a creaky voice. This disorder is often associated with disease of the basal ganglia – an area of the brain that is involved in regulating voluntary movement.

When the condition affects only one part of the body, such as the eyes, neck, or an arm, it is known as focal dystonia. When it affects a larger area, it is called segmental dystonia. The rare, generalized form tends to be genetic.

Focal and segmental dystonia can be treated with injections of botulinum toxin A or B into the affected muscles. Treatment usually has to be repeated every 8 to 16 weeks.

SEE ALSO *Brain and nervous system*

The creativity connection

Dyslexia is often associated with left-handedness, which in turn is linked with visual creativity.

The human brain is divided into two hemispheres – the left is dominant for language, while the right mainly processes visual and emotional information. For right-handed people, this division holds true, but left-handers tend to process all kinds of information more equally across both hemispheres. The ability to bring both brain hemispheres to bear in this way is thought to be the key to their creativity, especially in the visual arts. Brain scans have shown that the same may be true of dyslexics, which is useful if the left hemisphere does not function properly and a word cannot be read – a signal can then be sent to the right hemisphere to process the word instead.

Ear and problems

The ear is a dual-purpose organ. It is responsible for the sensation of sound as well as helping us to maintain our sense of balance. The external part of the ear is the gateway to an intricate piece of biological engineering made up of bones, membranes and channels. The ear normally does a superb job of keeping us in tune with the world around us. But its direct connection to the outside also makes it vulnerable to infection, while even minute disruptions in its workings may give rise to hearing loss or balance problems.

HOW THE EAR WORKS

To understand the workings of the ear, it is easiest to think of the way sound is conducted through its three major components – the outer ear, the middle ear, and the inner ear.

The outer ear consists of the auricle (or pinna), which is the part you can see, and the 2.5cm (1in) long auditory canal, which ends at the eardrum. While the curves of the auricle and the shape of the earlobe vary in subtle ways from person to person, they all have the function of collecting and channelling sound vibrations into the auditory canal. The auricle (except for the earlobe) is composed of a tough material called **cartilage**. Researchers are now learning how to create cartilage in the laboratory and it may not be too long before they can fashion a replacement to repair ears that have been damaged through injury. The whole of the outer ear is lined with fine hairs (in some people, you can see these hairs sprouting) and glands that produce earwax – both of which have a protective function.

The outer ear is separated from the middle ear by a membrane called the eardrum, which vibrates when sound impinges on it. It is well supplied with blood vessels and nerves, which is

Foreign bodies in the ear

Doctors are often called upon to deal with foreign bodies in the ear.

Children sometimes put small objects, such as peas, beads or stones, into the auditory canal. If these get stuck, they have to be removed by a doctor. Attempts to remove them with hairgrips or cotton buds may drive them further into the ear. A doctor uses a syringe or forceps (syringing with water is not recommended for organic objects, such as peas, because the moisture makes them swell).

Sometimes small insects may crawl into the ear. This is unpleasant and may be very frightening for a young child – but be assured, there is no way in which the insect can penetrate the brain. Tilting the head and washing out with water or olive oil may remove the insect. Or a doctor may remove a persistent insect from the ear after first 'knocking it out' with a local anaesthetic.

why a punctured eardrum – caused by sudden exposure to very loud noise or a sharp blow to the ear – causes excruciating pain and bleeding from the ear. Sound is conducted through air in the outer ear, but through bone in the middle ear – chiefly through the auditory ossicles, three tiny linked earbones called the hammer (malleus), the anvil (incus) and the stirrup (stapes), which is the smallest bone in the human body. While the eardrum cuts off the middle ear from the outside, the middle ear space is filled with air from the Eustachian tube, which runs forwards and downwards from the middle ear to the back of the nose. Normally, the Eustachian tube is closed, but it opens up if you yawn or swallow. The Eustachian tube allows equalization of air pressure on either side of the eardrum, enabling it to function properly.

The base of the stapes lies up against a structure called the oval window, which separates the middle ear from the inner ear. From here on in, sound is transmitted through

Anatomy of the ear

The ear is a complex organ divided into three sections – the outer, middle and inner ear.

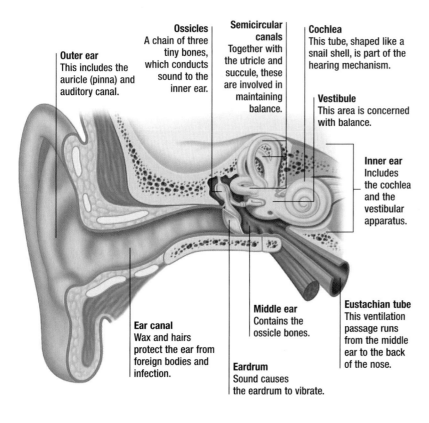

Outer ear
This includes the auricle (pinna) and auditory canal.

Ossicles
A chain of three tiny bones, which conducts sound to the inner ear.

Semicircular canals
Together with the utricle and succule, these are involved in maintaining balance.

Cochlea
This tube, shaped like a snail shell, is part of the hearing mechanism.

Vestibule
This area is concerned with balance.

Inner ear
Includes the cochlea and the vestibular apparatus.

Ear canal
Wax and hairs protect the ear from foreign bodies and infection.

Middle ear
Contains the ossicle bones.

Eardrum
Sound causes the eardrum to vibrate.

Eustachian tube
This ventilation passage runs from the middle ear to the back of the nose.

▶ **Earache**
Children have narrow Eustachian tubes and are prone to blockages that result in middle ear infections. Outer ear infections may follow swimming in infected water.

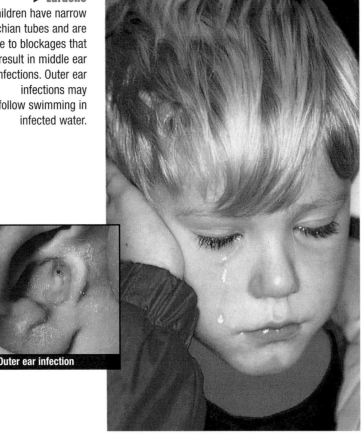

Outer ear infection

fluids contained within the complex structures of the inner ear, which is also known as the labyrinth because of its intricacy. At the front is the cochlea, named after the Greek word for shell because of its shape. Inside the cochlea is a fluid-filled tube containing microscopic hairs. It is these hairs that form the interface between the ear and the brain. Stimulated by sound vibrations coming from the oval window, they send electrical impulses to the acoustic nerve, which are received and interpreted by the brain.

The auditory region of the brain can respond to the frequency, intensity (decibel level) and direction of a sound – thereby making sense of all the vibrations arriving at the eardrum; the brain can also readily distinguish between meaningful sound, carried by regular vibrations, and meaningless noise, where the vibrations are irregular.

Noise may have damaging health effects. Loud noise can impair hearing, but noise is also recognized as a stress factor, which can lead to learning difficulties in children.

According to research done in Sweden, noise can lead to an increase in blood pressure in adults, which raises the risk of heart disease and **strokes**.

Keeping a balance

The rear part of the inner ear is concerned with maintaining balance, re-orienting you relative to your surroundings whenever you change position. The three structures involved with balance are the saccule, the utricle and three semi-circular canals, which lie at right angles to one another and are connected to a cavity called the vestibule. The whole ensemble is known as the vestibular apparatus. The utricle and saccule help static (standing) equilibrium. The canals contain hairs that are bathed in fluid. Each responds to a different element of balance – such as gravity, acceleration, position or head movement. Nerve fibres interfaced with the hairs convey this information to the brain. The brain merges this information with that from the eyes and muscles. All this together keeps you balanced.

WHAT CAN GO WRONG

The ear is susceptible to a range of disorders which, in some cases, can cause deafness.

Ear infections

Both the outer and middle ear are vulnerable to infection by fungi, bacteria or viruses. An outer ear infection is often linked to swimming in infected water, or poking down the auditory canal. Middle ear infection (otitis media) occurs when bacteria infect the mucous membranes that line the spaces within the temporal bone, which surrounds this area. Acute otitis media is generally triggered by a cold or flu, which leaves the Eustachian tube swollen or blocked. The infection may become chronic and may then lead to rupture of the eardrum (see also **Glue ear**). Before the widespread use of **antibiotics** and **grommets**, complications from otitis media, such as mastoiditis (infection of the bone behind the ear) or even brain abscesses, were not uncommon.

Referred pain in the ear

Earache is not always the result of a problem in the ear. Problems occurring in other parts of the face may at first appear to be ear-related.

The cause of earache can be an obvious infection of the outer or middle ear, or a ruptured eardrum. But the nerves that serve the ear also connect into the face, jaw and neck. The brain may interpret an impulse coming from these regions as coming from the ear instead. Such referred pain is quite frequent. For instance, temporomandibular joint (TMJ) syndrome is a common cause of ear pain: it is caused by misalignment of the jaw and is made worse by stress and teeth grinding. Other dental problems, such as tooth decay, could also cause referred earache. (See also Teeth and problems.)

The inner ear can be affected by **labyrinthitis**. This inflammation of the inner ear, believed to be caused by a viral infection, results in vertigo (see below), vomiting, loss of balance and deafness. Labyrinthitis may follow cold or flu-type infections and can last for six to eight weeks.

Hearing loss

A complete inability to hear is rare, and usually present from birth. Degrees of hearing loss occur from ear disease, injury or degeneration of the hearing process with age. Hearing loss is divided into two categories – conductive and sensorineural. In conductive deafness, there is a fault in the transmission of sound vibration from the outer to the inner ear. The most common cause is earwax blocking the auditory canal. Conductive deafness can also occur from **otosclerosis**, in which the stapes loses its mobility, from otitis media, or from barotrauma – damage to the eardrum or middle ear occurring because of unusually rapid pressure changes in an aircraft or when diving.

Sensorineural deafness is linked to damage to the cochlea or inner ear, which degenerate in function as people age. It can also be caused by **Ménière's disease**, by acoustic neuroma (a benign tumour affecting the acoustic nerve) or by certain drugs, such as streptomycin.

Vertigo

Vertigo is a disabling sensation of spinning, falling or the feeling that the ground is moving beneath your feet. It occurs when someone is stationary, or is quite out of proportion to the movement they are actually making. It is different from feelings of lightheadedness, dizziness or faintness, which have various causes. Vertigo is not a fear of heights (known as acrophobia). In the true sense it is linked to a problem in the vestibular system, such as labyrinthitis, a viral infection of the inner ear, or Ménière's disease. Vertigo is often accompanied by nausea and vomiting, and sometimes by **tinnitus**, a ringing or buzzing sound in the ears.

SEE ALSO *Deafness*

Effects of noise on hearing

Risk of damage to hearing depends not just on the intensity of sound but the length of time that you are exposed to it. Noise levels over 80dB are potentially damaging.

EXAMPLES	DECIBELS	PERCEPTION	EXPOSURE BEFORE DAMAGE OCCURS
Jet engine 25m (27 yards) away	140	Painful	All exposure dangerous
Jet takeoff at 100m (110 yards), air raid siren	130	Barely tolerable	1–5 minutes
Live rock band	110	Very noisy	26 minutes
Pneumatic drill	100	Very noisy	2 hours
Average street traffic	90	Noisy	16 hours per week
Alarm clock	80	Noisy	No known limit
Vacuum cleaner	70	Moderately noisy	No known limit
Conversation, singing birds	60	Comfortable	No limit
Light traffic, quiet office	50	Quiet	No limit
Quiet radio music, dripping tap, library	40	Quiet	No limit
Whisper at 5m (5$\frac{1}{2}$ yards)	30	Very quiet	No limit
Leaves rustling	10	Very quiet	No limit
Lower limit of hearing	0	Silence	No limit

Eating disorders

Eating disorders are the outward signs of emotional or psychological distress. For people who have such problems, eating or not eating is used to block out painful feelings and so becomes a way of coping.

▼ **Delusions of size** Some people with anorexia nervosa have persistent images of themselves as overweight – even though they may in fact be very thin.

Patterns of eating vary, so it is difficult to define normal eating. Habits may change if people are depressed, anxious or under stress. At these times a person may eat much more or much less, or crave a particular food. Most people find their eating returns to normal when the upset passes, but for some food becomes the centre of their lives. They may not eat even when they are very hungry, or they may eat constantly. Recognizing an eating disorder and getting help early on leads to a much better chance of recovery.

Anyone can develop an eating disorder, but young women between the ages of 15 and 25 are the most vulnerable group. Ten per cent of all people with eating disorders in the UK are men, about 20 per cent of whom are homosexual.

Eating disorders are on the increase, with a rise in conditions such as **bulimia nervosa** and binge eating. Cases of **anorexia nervosa** have remained fairly constant over time.

In any year, around 60,000 people in the UK are receiving treatment for anorexia or bulimia, but some estimates put the total number of people affected by an eating disorder at more than one million, with many sufferers undiagnosed and not receiving treatment.

There are many different eating disorders and overlaps between them. Variations include 'chew and spit' behaviour, where food is not swallowed, or eating non-foods such as paper tissues, to fill up without taking in calories.

BINGE EATING

Like bulimia nervosa, binge eating has only recently been recognized as a distinct condition. It involves uncontrollable bouts of overeating without vomiting or purging. A person afflicted by binge eating consumes large amounts of food more rapidly than usual and in private, resulting in feelings of shame, depression and guilt. Binge eating is thought to be more common than either anorexia or bulimia, and can lead eventually to obesity.

CAUSES

Genetic make-up and personality are important factors in the development of eating disorders. A sufferer may have been affected by a family member's attitude to food, or may use food to cope with the pressure of high academic expectations or social pressures.

Traumatic events such as bereavement, divorce or sexual abuse can also trigger eating disorders. Some blame may also lie with our image-obsessed culture, which puts enormous emphasis on body shape and appearance. People with eating disorders often have low self-esteem or suffer from anxiety or depression.

TREATMENT

'Giving up' an eating disorder that has become a way of coping with emotional problems is hard. The starting point is to seek help – or persuade a sufferer to seek help – from a specialist who understands the problem. An organization such as the Eating Disorders Association will offer advice.

There are several approaches that will help a person suffering from an eating disorder. They may be offered talking therapies such as **counselling**, **psychotherapy**, family therapy or **cognitive behavioural therapy**. Antidepressant drugs may be prescribed and diet or nutritional advice may be offered. Non-verbal therapies such as dance, music, art and drama can be helpful.

SEE ALSO *Anorexia nervosa; Bulimia nervosa*

CONTACT Eating Disorders Association First Floor, Wensum House, 103 Prince of Wales Road, Norwich NR1 1DW (0845) 6341414 for adults or (0845) 6347650 for young people (www.edauk.com). Support, help and information for people with eating disorders, their families and friends. **Overeaters Anonymous** PO Box 19, Stretford, Manchester M32 9EB 07000 784985 (www.oagb.org.uk)

Ebola virus

Ebola, also known as haemorrhagic fever, is a severe and largely fatal infectious disease. It is caused by a virus of African origin, which was first recognized in 1976 when there were major outbreaks in the Sudan and the Democratic Republic of Congo (formerly Zaire). In 1995, there was another major outbreak in Congo.

The temperate climate and environmental conditions in the UK do not support the virus, although cases are occasionally imported.

Initial symptoms include muscle and joint pain, fever and headache, and there may be nausea, vomiting and diarrhoea. The disease progresses rapidly until there is massive bleeding either from the major organs or from tiny blood vessels within the digestive tract and in the gums.

Seven out of every ten people affected by the ebola virus die, usually within a week of contracting the disease. There is no readily available treatment but scientists are working on developing therapies against the virus.

SEE ALSO *Tropical diseases*

E. coli

E. coli (*Escherichia coli*) is the name for a number of bacterial organisms found in the intestines of healthy human beings and animals. Most are harmless but one strain, E. coli 0157, which is found in the intestines of healthy cattle, can cause serious and sometimes fatal **food poisoning**. The bacteria are passed into the environment in the animals' manure. If the faeces spread on to their hides or get into the water system, the bacteria can infect those who handle the cattle and even contaminate meat and other farm products entering the food chain.

People most commonly develop E. coli food poisoning from eating contaminated foods, particularly inadequately cooked minced beef. This is often in the form of beefburgers which, typically, have not been grilled, fried or barbecued until they are cooked through. Contaminated milk can also be a source of infection. Outbreaks have been linked to yoghurt, cooked meats, meat pies, cheese, dry-cured salami, raw vegetables, unpasteurized apple juice and water. Direct contact with farm animals, particularly with cattle, can also be a cause.

Once caught, the infection can be passed from person to person.

SYMPTOMS
- Severe abdominal cramps (haemorrhagic colitis).
- Mild to bloody diarrhoea.

DURATION
- The incubation period, before the onset of diarrhoea, can range from one to 14 days.
- The E. coli bacteria are usually excreted from the body within a week, but the process can take much longer, especially in children and elderly people, who are more at risk from the infection.
- Those with mild symptoms usually recover within two weeks.

TREATMENT
See a doctor as soon as there are food-poisoning symptoms, especially if you notice blood in the stools or watery diarrhoea in children. The doctor may prescribe **antibiotics**. Serious cases may be referred to hospital.

COMPLICATIONS
Up to 10 per cent of people with E. coli develop haemolytic uraemic syndrome, which kills red blood cells and leads to kidney failure (see **Kidneys and disorders**). It usually affects young children and is a major cause of acute kidney failure in children in the UK. Some adults with E. coli develop haemolytic uraemic syndrome together with neurological complications.

PREVENTION
Government bodies have issued guidelines for the food and farming industries on minimizing the contamination of meat. Guidance on farm visits have also been issued to farmers and teachers. Preventive measures include the following:
- Cook all beef and meat products thoroughly. Minced beef, especially beefburgers, should be cooked until the juices run clear and there are no pink areas.
- Ensure good kitchen hygiene, and store raw and cooked foods separately. Wash your hands after handling raw meat.
- Do not drink unpasteurized milk.
- Do not touch manure and avoid handling animals on visits to farms or animal centres.
- Ensure children wash their hands thoroughly after stroking farm animals.

OUTLOOK
If the infection is severe, it can cause permanent kidney damage and may even be fatal. Those most vulnerable include babies, young children and elderly people.

SEE ALSO *Urinary system*

The number of cases of E. coli infection in the UK trebled in less than a decade, increasing from 360 cases in 1991 to more than 1000 in 1997.

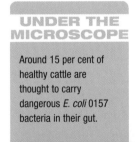

UNDER THE MICROSCOPE

Around 15 per cent of healthy cattle are thought to carry dangerous E. coli 0157 bacteria in their gut.

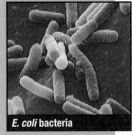

E. coli bacteria

Eclampsia

Eclampsia is a condition affecting pregnant women. It is characterized by sudden convulsive fits that starve both the pregnant woman and her unborn baby of oxygen. These fits are followed by a period of coma and sometimes further convulsions. Eclampsia occurs in one in 2000 pregnancies; it is fatal for one in 50 affected women and one in 14 affected babies.

Eclampsia is more common among very young mothers, first-time mothers and women who are carrying more than one baby. The causes are not fully understood, but the condition can run in families.

SYMPTOMS

Eclampsia is usually preceded by pre-eclampsia, in which there is raised blood pressure, protein in the urine, and often swelling, headaches and visual disturbance. Eclampsia may develop so quickly that pre-eclampsia goes unnoticed.

TREATMENT

A woman with pre-eclampsia is advised to rest, is closely monitored and may be admitted to hospital. Treatments include anti-convulsant drugs, magnesium sulphate, low doses of aspirin and mild sedatives. In severe cases, with an advanced pregnancy, the baby may be induced.

PREVENTION

High doses of vitamins C and E reduce the risk of eclampsia in high-risk women; low doses of aspirin may also help – but neither should be taken without medical supervision.

SEE ALSO *Pregnancy and problems*

CONTACT **Action on Pre-eclampsia (APEC)** 84–88 Pinner Road, Harrow, Middlesex HA1 4HZ (020) 8427 4217 (www.apec.org.uk)

Ecstasy

Ecstasy, a derivative of amphetamine, has stimulant and sometimes mild hallucinogenic effects. It is a Class A drug in the UK, along with cocaine, heroin and other opiates. It has no medical uses and is associated with club culture.

Ecstasy enhances alertness and heightens the emotions. Users can also experience anxiety, panic, confusion and unpleasant distortion of the senses. They may feel tired and depressed for three or four days after taking the drug.

The effects of taking a moderate dose start after 20 to 60 minutes (longer if taken on a full stomach) and can last for up to several hours. Physical effects include dilation of the pupils, raised blood pressure and heart rate, sweating, dry mouth, often brief nausea, and a tightening of the jaw. Loss of appetite is common.

RISKS

In the short term, users risk overheating and dehydration if they dance without taking breaks or drinking enough fluids. But, conversely, drinking large quantities of water over a short period has led to deaths from heavy loss of sodium from the body, kidney failure and water on the brain (cerebral oedema).

Ecstasy has been linked to liver and kidney problems. Some experts are concerned that it may lead to brain damage, causing **depression**, memory loss and other psychiatric conditions in later life. Psychological dependence on the feelings of euphoria can develop.

SEE ALSO *Drugs, misuse of*

Ectopic pregnancy

If a fertilized egg implants outside the womb, the pregnancy is described as ectopic. In most cases, the egg implants in a Fallopian tube, but it may become attached to an ovary or the cervix, or in the abdominal cavity instead.

About one pregnancy in 80 is ectopic. Such a pregnancy has virtually no chance of lasting more than two months, and if not recognized and treated, it can be fatal.

CAUSES

Ectopic pregnancies have increased in the past 15 years, possibly owing to the rise in pelvic inflammatory diseases, such as those caused by **chlamydia** bacteria, which can damage the Fallopian tubes, as can previous surgery. Other risk factors include the use of an intra-uterine contraceptive device, some types of fertility treatment and a previous ectopic pregnancy.

SYMPTOMS

Symptoms usually occur around the sixth week of pregnancy. An ectopic pregnancy may be signalled by vaginal bleeding and pain in the lower abdomen. Symptoms may subside briefly but worsen as the embryo grows. If it grows large enough, it may rupture the Fallopian tube, causing heavy bleeding, severe pain and shock.

TREATMENT

Diagnosis is confirmed by a positive pregnancy test, where necessary, followed by an **ultrasound** scan or laparoscopy, when a tiny telescope is inserted into the abdomen through an incision under the navel.

The embryo is removed, although the method depends on its size and location. This may involve **keyhole surgery** to remove the embryo on its own, or with a small section of Fallopian tube. It may also be possible to inject drugs during a laparoscopy to stop the embryo growing; the embryo dies and is reabsorbed into the body.

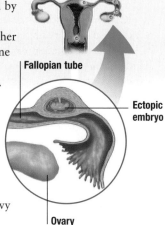

▼ **Doomed pregnancy** A fertilized egg normally travels from the ovary to the uterus, where it can develop. An ectopic pregnancy occurs when the fertilized egg implants in the wall of the ovary, Fallopian tube or cervix.

Fallopian tube

Ectopic embryo

Ovary

A few women who have had an ectopic pregnancy are left infertile, but 65 per cent become pregnant again within 18 months. A woman who has had an ectopic pregnancy is carefully monitored in future pregnancies.

SEE ALSO **Pelvis and disorders**

Ectropion

Ectropion is an outward turning of the eyelid or lids, away from the eyeball. It generally affects the lower lid. Ectropion is commonest in elderly people, whose muscles around the eye have lost their elasticity. It may also result from scarring of the surrounding facial skin or a loss of nerve function in the area, for example, in **palsy**.

Ectropion causes tears to flow onto the cheek, and the eyeball becomes dry, leading to grittiness and discomfort, occasional blurred vision, increased risk of **conjunctivitis** and, in severe cases, inflammation of the cornea. Rubbing the eye aggravates the condition.

Ocular lubricants or artificial teardrops may give temporary relief but a more permanent solution generally involves surgery.

SEE ALSO **Eye and problems**

ECG

An ECG, or electrocardiogram, is a test used to record the minute electrical impulses generated by heart muscle. It gives detailed information about the physical condition of the heart, and helps in diagnosing disorders such as **coronary artery disease, coronary thrombosis** and **pericarditis**. An ECG may be carried out in the following instances.

■ To aid diagnosis in anyone with a suspected heart disorder.

■ After a heart attack, when the test can show the extent of heart damage, and to monitor the patient's progress after recovery.

■ During exercise, as a test of fitness.

WHAT'S INVOLVED

Electrodes leading to a recording machine are attached to the chest, wrists and ankles using a conducting jelly. The machine displays the electrical activity of the heart as a trace on a screen or paper graph. An ECG causes no discomfort and there are no health risks associated with it.

WHO ADMINISTERS AN ECG?

Electrocardiography is available on the NHS, generally by GP referral to a hospital. In some cases, it may be possible for an ECG to be carried out in a GP's surgery or in a patient's

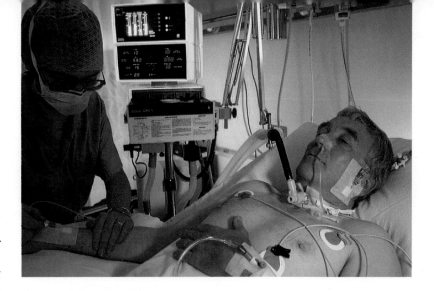

home using portable equipment. Some patients wear a miniature ECG device that gives a 24-hour readout, which is useful in diagnosing some heart conditions.

SEE ALSO **Heart and circulatory system**

ECT

ECT, or electroconvulsive therapy, is used to treat severe mental illness. Electric shocks are used to induce short seizures or fits, which have a beneficial effect on conditions such as serious **depression**. Although there is clear evidence of its effectiveness, ECT has side effects, including short-term memory loss, and is therefore used sparingly, with medication usually the first choice of treatment. Its use is confined to severe **depression**, mania and occasionally **schizophrenia**.

ECT may be offered as part of a package of care to people with severe mental illness. The patient will be under the care of a consultant psychiatrist, who will explain why ECT is being considered as treatment in this case, and answer any questions, before asking the patient to sign a consent form, as is usual for other medical and surgical procedures.

WHAT'S INVOLVED

ECT follows a clear pattern.

■ The patient is given a general **anaesthetic**, with muscle relaxant.

■ Electric pads are placed on the temples.

■ A short controlled electric pulse is delivered to the electrodes.

■ A mild fit occurs.

■ Oxygen is usually given as the anaesthetic wears off.

■ Consciousness is gradually regained.

■ Immediate effects include headache, some confusion and memory loss.

■ Between four and eight treatments is usual.

SEE ALSO **Mental health and problems**

▲ **Instant results**
An ECG picks up any abnormal patterns of electrical activity in the heart and shows them on a screen or paper graph.

Eczema

Eczema is an inflammatory condition of the skin. It causes scaly, red patches, itching and small fluid-filled blisters which burst, making the skin moist and crusty. The disease, also known as **dermatitis**, affects about one in 12 people in the UK and incidence is increasing.

There are several types of eczema. The most common types are atopic and contact. Atopic eczema runs in families and often appears in the first year of life. Like other atopic diseases, it is caused by an overreaction of the immune system to an allergen – a substance that triggers an allergic response. This type of eczema is linked to other atopic diseases such as **asthma** and allergic rhinitis – more commonly known as **hay fever**.

Contact eczema is caused by contact with any of a wide variety of substances, ranging from washing powders to nickel watch-straps.

The discomfort caused by the condition can lead to extreme distress, which is made worse if the itching leads to sleep deprivation.

Different types of eczema

Eczema can appear anywhere on the body, but different types have different manifestations and tend to affect specific areas.

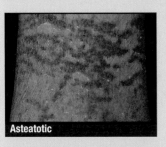
Asteatotic

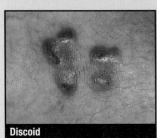
Discoid

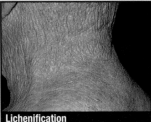
Lichenification

- **Atopic** – mainly affects the face, neck and inner creases of the elbows and knees. It is linked with an increased risk of asthma and hay fever.

- **Contact** – most commonly seen on the hands; it is caused by contact with nickel, for example.

- **Seborrhoeic** – affects the face or scalp; the greasy crusts of cradle cap are one example.

- **Asteatotic** – often on the legs of older people; it causes dry, crazy-paving skin patterns.

- **Stasis** – affects the lower legs; it is associated with poor circulation in the area.

- **Pompholyx** – mostly on the fingers, palms or soles of the feet; it causes small, itchy blisters.

- **Discoid** – usually on the legs and trunk; it appears as round – disc-shaped – areas of irritation.

- **Neurodermatitis** – a thickening of the skin known as **lichenification**.

- **Photo-allergic** – caused by the action of sunlight on skin sensitized by absorbed drugs or chemicals.

SYMPTOMS

Eczema commonly affects skin on the hands, inside the elbows and behind the knees, but it may be found anywhere on the body. Atopic eczema is commonly found in skin folds, whereas contact eczema is more usually seen on the hands. Seborrhoeic eczema affects areas such as the scalp and ears, and in men may also affect the back and chest. In severe cases it can spread to affect skin covering most of the body. Symptoms vary from mild to severe and can include:

- dry, scaly, thickened skin; crusting; redness;
- itching (skin may be rubbed raw by scratching); blisters may form;
- weeping sores that may become infected;
- a flaky scalp.

CAUSES

Although external factors can trigger a flare-up of atopic eczema, it is usually hereditary. One in every eight children and 1–2 per cent of adults suffer from it. If both parents have eczema, there is about a 40 per cent chance that their offspring will also have it.

Many factors can trigger eczema. A common cause of hand eczema in healthcare workers is an allergy to the latex rubber gloves that they sometimes wear.

Some people also find that eczema symptoms are brought on or made worse by eating certain foods, such as eggs or milk. There is, however, no firm evidence to show that diet plays a major part in causing flare-up of eczema.

Stress or anxiety can cause sudden flare-ups, however, although the cause of worry may not always be obvious, especially in children.

The skin bacterium *Staphylococcus aureusis* is associated with flare-ups of the condition, but eczema itself is not infectious.

TREATMENT

Dry and itchy skin should be treated with emollients, special moisturizers in the form of oils, lotions or creams that soothe, smooth and cleanse the skin. Eczema sufferers should wash with aqueous cream rather than soap, which can be very drying.

A doctor may prescribe a corticosteroid cream to reduce inflammation and to improve symptoms, but this will not cure the condition. Such creams should be applied as prescribed and should not be used on the face or genitals.

Antibacterial bath additives help to reduce *staphylococcus* infection. Oral **antihistamines** may reduce itching and swelling in allergic eczema. In severe cases, immunosuppressive drugs may be prescribed in hospital.

Complementary therapies

Evening primrose oil contains gammalinolenic acid, an essential fatty acid that may help to reduce itchiness and dryness in some people with essential fatty acid deficiency. It needs to be taken in large doses of around 240mg twice a day for at least three months before its effectiveness can be properly evaluated.

SEE ALSO **Skin and disorders**
CONTACT **National Eczema Society**
Hill House, Highgate Hill, London N19 5NA; helpline 0870 241 3604 (www.eczema.org)

EEG

An EEG (electroencephalogram) is a test that records the electrical activity of the brain. It can help in the diagnosis of many diseases affecting the nervous system, but is particularly useful in confirming the existence of **epilepsy** in someone with a history of **fits**, and in monitoring the progress of this condition.

The test is a painless procedure in which leads are applied to the scalp. These relay electrical transmissions from the brain, which are then converted into a brainwave tracing on paper. Normal brain activity is demonstrated by wave forms of predominantly two types – alpha and beta waves.

Abnormal waves are either much slower and of higher amplitude (that is, bigger) than normal, or consist of very fast spikes.

Interpretation of an EEG can pinpoint the area in the brain where discharges of abnormal electrical activity originate. This area is called the epileptic focus. The results of an EEG are highly relevant when deciding on treatment, whether with medication or with surgery.

Usually an EEG is carried out when a patient is resting but not sedated. However, brain activity may also be recorded during sleep, or when epileptic fits are deliberately provoked to aid diagnosis, or during anaesthesia to monitor brain function. In special circumstances, the absence of electrical activity on an EEG may aid in the confirmation of brain death.

SEE ALSO **Brain and nervous system; Brainstem death**

Elbow and problems

The elbow is the junction of the upper arm and the forearm. It is made up of two joints. The main elbow joint is a simple hinge joint between the bone of the upper arm and the two bones of the forearm. The second joint, called the superior radio-ulnar joint, is a pivot; its function is to rotate. An arrangement of ligaments, tendons and muscles stabilize and move the joint.

WHAT THE ELBOW DOES
The movements that take place at the elbow's hinge joint are called flexion and extension – bending and straightening the elbow. Both movements are limited – in the case of flexion by the upper arm and forearm muscles; and in

A complex arrangement of bone and muscle
There are two joints at the elbow. A hinge joint that lies between the bones of the upper arm and the forearm and the superior radio-ulna joint which allows the bones of the forearm to rotate. Both are encased in a single fibrous capsule filled with lubricating synovial fluid.

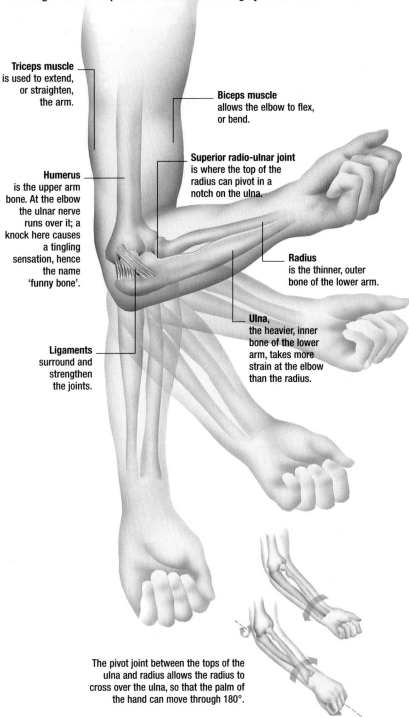

Triceps muscle is used to extend, or straighten, the arm.

Biceps muscle allows the elbow to flex, or bend.

Superior radio-ulnar joint is where the top of the radius can pivot in a notch on the ulna.

Humerus is the upper arm bone. At the elbow the ulnar nerve runs over it; a knock here causes a tingling sensation, hence the name 'funny bone'.

Radius is the thinner, outer bone of the lower arm.

Ulna, the heavier, inner bone of the lower arm, takes more strain at the elbow than the radius.

Ligaments surround and strengthen the joints.

The pivot joint between the tops of the ulna and radius allows the radius to cross over the ulna, so that the palm of the hand can move through 180°.

the case of extension by the configuration of the joint's bones, which allow movement to only 180° – you cannot bend your elbow backwards.

The only movement that takes place at the elbow's second joint – the superior radio-ulnar joint – is rotation. It is this joint, combined with the wrist joints, that allows you to turn your hand palm-down or palm-up.

WHAT CAN GO WRONG INSIDE THE JOINT

A number of conditions can arise within the elbow. They involve damage to the bones, tendons or nerves.

Osteochondritis dessicans

After the knee, the elbow is the commonest site of osteochondritis dessicans. In this condition, the cartilage that lines the bones where they meet at the elbow joint breaks down and eventually breaks away from the bone to form a 'loose body' (see below). The cause is unknown, but injury and a poor blood supply are thought to play a part.

Loose body formation

A loose body is any small, loose piece of bone, cartilage or fibrous membrane. The main causes are osteochondritis dessicans, **osteoarthritis** or a minor **fracture** in which a fragment of bone separates.

A loose body can also be caused by synovial chondromatosis, a rare condition in which the cells of a joint's fibrous inner lining turn into cartilage and detach themselves from the membrane, forming numerous minute loose bodies. The main symptom is a sudden 'locking' of the elbow during movement, accompanied by a sharp pain; this may be relieved by movement or it may clear up itself. If the locking happens frequently, treatment is by surgical removal of the loose body.

Rheumatoid arthritis

Rheumatoid arthritis frequently affects the elbows. The main symptoms are pain and swelling of the thickened synovial membrane surrounding the joint.

Pyogenic arthritis

Pyogenic arthritis is a rare condition that can occur if the humerus becomes infected. The sufferer has a raised temperature, and the elbow joint becomes inflamed, swollen with fluid and hot. A doctor will treat the condition by sucking out the fluid with a needle and syringe and prescribing a course of antibiotics.

WHAT CAN GO WRONG OUTSIDE THE JOINT

Several conditions can affect the outside of the elbow, which is especially vulnerable to damage caused by repetitive movements.

Tennis elbow

Tennis elbow is so-called because it can result from playing backhand strokes during tennis, but in reality its most common cause is ironing or polishing, because of the strenuous, repetitive movements of the forearm with the wrist held up that these activities entail.

Tennis elbow involves a tearing of the wrist extensor tendons at the elbow, where they are attached to the outside of the upper arm bone (humerus). Since this area is particularly rich in nerve endings, someone with tennis elbow feels acute pain, but there is also a dull ache felt as a broad band down the forearm. The condition makes it impossible to carry anything heavier than a sheet of paper, turn a doorknob or shake hands, for example.

Most cases of tennis elbow clear up of their own accord, but the process can take up to two years. Initial treatment involves the administration of anti-inflammatory drugs, with a hydrocortisone injection into the tendon. In severe cases, a surgeon may separate the tendon from the bone and re-site it.

Golfer's elbow

Golfer's elbow is similar to tennis elbow, but affects the wrist flexors (rather than the wrist extensors), where they attach to the humerus at the elbow. The condition is caused by overuse of the flexors when playing golf, but can also result from activities such as using a screwdriver. Golfer's elbow is treated in the same way as tennis elbow.

Student's elbow

Student's elbow is also known as olecranon bursitis. The bursa, a fluid-filled sac behind the funny bone (see **Bursitis**), can become inflamed as a result of minor injury – such as by leaning on a desk for extended periods of time. The bursa may also be affected by **gout** or **blood poisoning**. The condition is treated by sucking out any fluid, a hydrocortisone injection and, in persistent cases, surgical removal of the bursa.

Neuritis of the ulnar nerve

The ulnar nerve passes behind the bone of the upper arm (humerus) before passing down to the forearm and hand. It lies very close to the surface as it crosses the elbow and is easily injured by fracture or dislocation in this area. Osteoarthritis can also cause damage by putting prolonged pressure on the nerve, as can friction from a muscle tendon.

Once damaged, fibrous tissue is laid down over time and gradually the nerve ceases to function correctly. The result is neuritis, a condition characterized by numbness, pins and needles and muscle wasting.

Treatment is by surgery to free the nerve from the groove and move it so that it passes over the front of the elbow.

SEE ALSO *Arm and problems; Muscular system; Skeletal system*

> The most common cause of tennis elbow is not playing tennis but ironing.

Elderly people, care of

As people grow older, they may become a little more dependent on daily support. Relatives who provide healthcare can make things easier with one or two adaptations to the home and to daily routines.

Caring for an elderly relative or friend may involve no more than popping in to see him or her each day. Loneliness can be a problem for many older people, particularly those who have lost a husband or wife. Emotional and mental well-being are important aspects of physical health, and a central part of your role as a carer may be to help your elderly relative or friend to maintain an optimistic, self-sufficient frame of mind.

A QUESTION OF ATTITUDE

Many of the diseases that occur in old age are the same as those that affect younger people, but the attitude of elderly people towards them may be different. Some elderly people may be unnecessarily fatalistic, believing that deteriorating health is a natural consequence of their age. They may accept loss of mobility or deteriorating hearing, say, as inevitable and be unwilling to seek

help – even though these problems can be improved. If you are able to persuade your relative to use a hearing aid and a walking stick, then his or her ability to converse and move around may be greatly increased.

Unspoken fears may lie beneath the unwillingness of some elderly people to help themselves or to seek medical attention. Fear of being put in a residential or nursing home may make an old person reluctant to admit that there is something wrong, while fear of falling and being unable to get up may make an old person reluctant to go out or to use a walking stick. It is essential to find out if any of these fears exist and, if they do, to reassure the person as much as possible.

MENTAL HEALTH AND DEPRESSION

Many people find it harder to remember things as they age. It seems that the older we are, the longer it takes us to access information in our memories when we need it. A more serious trigger for memory problems is **dementia** (the most common cause of which is **Alzheimer's disease**). Dementia usually affects people over the age of 65. There is no cure, but staying mentally and physically active can help. Studies have shown that taking the herb ginkgo biloba appears to delay deterioration of mental function.

Fewer than one in 30 elderly people are so depressed that doctors would diagnose them with a depressive illness. However, events that might be expected to trigger depressed feelings tend to become more common as we grow older – for example, having to stop work or experiencing a drop in income, physical problems such as arthritis, or the death of a loved one. If you think that a person for whom you are caring is suffering from depression, consult a doctor. You can also help the person by encouraging him or her to keep active and to talk about how he or she is feeling to other people.

HEALTHY LIVING

As a carer you may well be in charge of cooking and planning the daily activities of the person for whom you are caring. Try to encourage a healthy diet and regular exercise. Following a good **diet**

▼ Regular medication
Elderly people often need to take a variety of drugs. These must be taken at the right times and in the right dosage to be effective.

will help to reduce the risk of illnesses such as heart disease, **osteoporosis, diabetes** and **cancer**. Many people find that their appetite decreases as they age; if the person you look after feels like eating only a small amount, avoid foods that give little nourishment, such as cakes and biscuits and ensure that they eat meals at regular intervals.

Regular physical activity, whatever a person's age, has many benefits, including strengthening the bones, heart and lungs. As well as the physical benefits, most older people discover a marked improvement in their mood and morale after starting regular exercise. An older person should get a little breathless every day, and can achieve this by doing energetic household jobs such as polishing the window vigorously or raking the lawn.

The key is gradually to increase the person's level of activity, be it through gardening, walking, swimming or a class at a local sports centre.

Safe house

As people age, their reactions slow down, their eyesight may deteriorate and they become less mobile. Keeping in shape through physical activity will help, but there are also many ways to adapt a home to make it safer to live in.

Many local authorities run classes for older people and some have classes designed for people with medical conditions, such as heart disease and arthritis.

HOUSING OPTIONS

There is a variety of living arrangements that may suit people who find it difficult to manage in their own homes. Sheltered housing enables people to live independently in a self-contained flat, while an alarm system and on-site warden or scheme manager ensures that help is at hand in an emergency. Different types of sheltered housing provide varying levels of service: some have communal areas and group activities, others provide laundry and some meals.

Care can be provided in a residential or nursing home. In a residential home, a person will receive help with personal tasks, such as washing and dressing, if needed. Staff can look after people during short illnesses but are not qualified to provide continuous nursing. For those needing more consistent medical attention, a nursing home is probably the best option since a qualified

If possible, redesign the bathroom so that the washbasin is positioned close to the lavatory and at a convenient height.

Good lighting will make slips and trips less likely.

Automatic garage doors and bright outdoor lighting help to prevent accidents if an elderly person is returning home in the dark.

In the bathroom, a raised lavatory seat, grab-rails for either side of the bath and a non-slip bath mat can help to prevent falls.

Install press-down lever door handles and sliding doors.

Adapt your kitchen to make it more convenient for an elderly person who finds lifting and bending difficult. Worktops, cookers and sinks should be at the same level to make it easier for a person with a weaker grip to slide pots and pans along the worktop rather than having to lift them.

Handrails on both sides of the stairs make them easier to climb. For some people a stairlift may be more appropriate than handrails.

Place a non-slip mat in the hall and on any wooden or polished floors. Stick rugs down with backing tape.

Caring for the carer

Looking after a partner or a relative can be satisfying: it is an opportunity to deepen an existing relationship and learn new skills as you find solutions to fresh challenges. But to be a successful carer, you need to look after yourself.

■ Eat regular meals and follow a well-balanced diet. As a carer, your energy requirements are higher than those of a sedentary office worker.

■ Drink plenty of fluids and exercise regularly.

■ Make time to relax, socialize and enjoy yourself – keep up your interests and pursue new ones.

■ Do not ignore symptoms of fatigue and ill health: rest or see your doctor.

■ Be careful not to drink too much alcohol.

■ If you feel low or under emotional strain, talk to your doctor or a professional counsellor.

■ Always encourage older people to be as independent as possible. For example, if a person is incontinent or growing deaf, make sure that he or she seeks medical help.

■ Take advantage of grants and organizations that offer help with labour-saving devices and safety aids, and provide other assistance.

▲ **Contact with others** Learning new skills is an excellent way to make new friends and maintain mental agility.

nurse will be on duty 24 hours a day. An elderly person can also go into a residential home for a short respite period – if he or she needs to convalesce after an illness, for example, or in order to give a carer a break. Most homes keep beds free for this purpose.

If you are considering whether the person you look after should move into a residential home, contact your local authority's Social Services Department (England), the Families and Communities Department (Wales), the Social Work Department (Scotland) or your local health and social services trust (Northern Ireland) for an assessment. You may also like to contact Age Concern for advice. If you are unsure about whether residential care is suitable, arrange for the person to have a short stay in a home as a temporary resident to see how he or she finds it.

HEALTH CHECKS AND BENEFITS

Around one million people over the age of 60 fail to claim extra help from the government with their day-to-day expenses, housing costs or council tax, even though they are entitled to it. The benefits available include regular financial aid for those on low incomes, help with rent (housing benefit) or council tax and payments to help with the expense of a spouse's funeral.

Anyone aged 60 or over can receive prescriptions for medicine free of charge and a free sight test at any opticians. An elderly person may also be entitled to help with the costs of dental checkups and treatment, glasses or with fares to and from hospital for medical treatment. Contact your local Benefits Agency or Citizens Advice Bureau for advice on making a claim.

A person who is 65 years or over is entitled to free flu vaccinations from their GP; a person who is 75 or over should be offered a free annual health check, which can take place either at the doctor's surgery or at home.
SEE ALSO *Age and ageing; Community care; Home care and nursing*

CONTACT **Age Concern England** Astral House, 1268 London Road, London SW16 4ER (www.ace.org.uk); helpline 0800 009966
Alzheimer's Society Gordon House, 10 Greencoat Place, London SW1P 1PH (020) 7306 0606; helpline 0845 300 0336 (www.alzheimers.org.uk)
Counsel and Care Twyman House, 16 Bonny Street, London NW1 9PG; helpline 0845 300 7585 (www.counselandcare.org.uk)
Help the Aged 207-221 Pentonville Road, London N1 9UZ (020) 7278 1114; helpline 0808 800 6565 (www.helptheaged.org.uk)
Learndirect 0800 100 900
Royal Society for the Prevention of Accidents (RoSPA) Edgbaston Park, 353 Bristol Road, Birmingham B5 7ST (0121) 248 2000

Electrical injuries

An electric shock can cause effects varying from a minor tingling to instant death. Often an electric shock leaves **burns** – which can be deep and serious – where the current enters and leaves the body. The shock may also disrupt heart rhythm or breathing; children are particularly vulnerable to these symptoms. Such disruption may involve quivering of the heart muscles (fibrillation) or interference with a proper heartbeat, or the heart may stop altogether. If the injured person is still in contact with the electric current, rescuers are in danger, too.

The most common cause of electric shock is a faulty electrical appliance in the home. A lightning strike can cause similar injuries.

Anyone who has been unconscious or has suffered a burn due to electricity should go to hospital. Electrical burns can be more serious than they appear, and heart rhythm may need to be monitored for a while.

DEALING WITH AN EMERGENCY

If you are rescuing someone who has been electrocuted from a domestic supply, observe the following guidelines.

■ Don't touch the person until contact with the electricity supply has been broken.

■ Switch off the power at the socket or at the mains and pull out the plug.

■ If it is not possible to disconnect the power, stand on some insulating surface (a rubber mat, thick towel or folded newspaper) and use a non-conducting implement – such as a wooden broom handle, walking stick or chair leg – to push the person away from the source of electricity, for example, by knocking the person's hand clear of the electrical appliance. Avoid anything wet or metallic.

■ Check the affected person's breathing and pulse and start resuscitation if necessary and if trained to do so.

■ Put the person into the **recovery position**.

■ Look for and treat burns and **shock**.

■ Call an ambulance.

PREVENTION

There are several precautions you can take to reduce the danger of electrical injuries.

■ Have damaged cables and flexes mended before using an appliance.

■ Never take electrical equipment into a bathroom.

■ Don't touch electrical items with wet hands.

■ Don't overload sockets or adaptors.

■ Always have wiring jobs carried out by a competent professional.

SEE ALSO *Accident prevention; FIRST AID; Heart and circulatory system*

Electrolysis

Electrolysis is the removal of superfluous body hair by electrical means. Practitioners say that the technique removes hair permanently. It can be used on most parts of the body, although in unskilled hands it can damage delicate skin and may cause disfigurement.

WHAT'S INVOLVED

A short-wave electrical current is introduced into each follicle of unwanted hair through a needle electrode. The current is applied for a fraction of a second; the aim is to stop blood flow to the base of the hair follicle to prevent regrowth. Afterwards the hair itself is loose and can be lifted out. If properly applied, the needle should not cause any pain, but the current may be experienced as a tingling sensation.

Hair may grow back after treatment, but becomes gradually weaker. Several treatments may be necessary before hair growth stops completely. After electrolysis, there may be inflammation and swelling of the skin but this should disappear quickly.

Electromagnetic radiation

Electromagnetic radiation is the form of radiation given off by electrical devices. It is increasingly regarded as a form of pollution and has been linked with possible health hazards, but the evidence for such links continues to be a matter of scientific controversy.

Environmental sources of electromagnetic radiation include power lines and pylons, as well as domestic items such as microwave ovens, televisions, computers, satellite dishes, mobile phones and electric blankets. Children are thought to be particularly vulnerable to the effects of electromagnetic radiation, and there

Minimizing exposure to radiation

If you are worried about your level of exposure to radiation, use a hand-held radiation monitor to measure the electric and magnetic fields in your home. To minimize risk, you can:

■ avoid electric blankets;

■ turn off appliances such as TVs and computers when not in use;

■ restrict use of mobile phones to a few minutes at a time, or use a phone shield or a hands-free device;

■ place children's beds away from walls that have a high concentration of electrical devices on the other side.

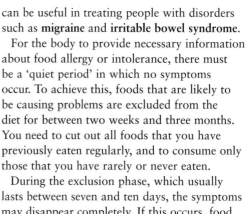

▶ **Keeping it short**
To limit the risk of radiation, mobile phones should be used for only a few minutes at a time. It is always advisable to use a hands-free device.

are reports of increased incidence of **leukaemia** among children living near power pylons and high-voltage lines. Other disorders suspected of possible association with electromagnetic radiation include **Alzheimer's disease**, birth defects, **cancers**, headaches, lethargy, memory loss, muscle pains and sleep disturbances, as well as such events as miscarriage, **sudden infant death syndrome** (cot death) and suicide.
SEE ALSO *Environmental health*

Elephantiasis

Elephantiasis is a rare disease of the **lymphatic system**, which causes massive swellings of a limb, the scrotum or the torso. The skin thickens and darkens, so that it resembles the skin of an elephant. It occurs most commonly in tropical regions, particularly in parts of Africa.

The most common cause of elephantiasis is small parasitic roundworms, which can be transmitted to human beings by mosquitoes; they then lodge in the lymphatic system and obstruct the lymph flow. Treatment usually involves surgery to remove the excess skin.

Elimination diet

An elimination diet aims to identify foods that are causing illness by first excluding all possible problem foods from the diet, then re-introducing them one by one. It must be rigorously followed if it is to fulfil this purpose Elimination diets

can be useful in treating people with disorders such as **migraine** and **irritable bowel syndrome**.

For the body to provide necessary information about food allergy or intolerance, there must be a 'quiet period' in which no symptoms occur. To achieve this, foods that are likely to be causing problems are excluded from the diet for between two weeks and three months. You need to cut out all foods that you have previously eaten regularly, and to consume only those that you have rarely or never eaten.

During the exclusion phase, which usually lasts between seven and ten days, the symptoms may disappear completely. If this occurs, food intolerance is confirmed. If it does not, it is improbable that food intolerance is to blame.

In the second phase, assuming that symptoms have disappeared, foods can be re-introduced to the diet, usually at a rate of one food per week. Any re-introduced food that causes no return of symptoms can remain in the diet.

Expert guidance is needed to ensure that you are eating the re-introduced foods in the right form and quantity and at the right time. Ask your GP to refer you to a nutritionist for advice.
SEE ALSO *Food allergies and intolerances*

Emaciation

Emaciation is a wasting of the body, with loss of muscle as well as fat. The cause can be related to malabsorption syndromes, as in cases of intestinal surgery, **coeliac disease**, **Crohn's disease**, **irritable bowel syndrome** and other diseases that impair absorption of nutrients across the gut wall.

Other causes of emaciation range from a drastic reduction in food intake, as occurs in starvation or **anorexia**, to conditions such as **diabetes** and some cancers, where metabolic disturbances drastically affect the rate at which nutrients are absorbed by the tissues.
SEE ALSO *Malnutrition; Nutritional disorders*

Embolism

An embolism occurs when part of a blood clot detaches and travels to lodge in an artery, cutting off an organ's blood supply. The lung and brain arteries are commonly affected. A blockage may occasionally be caused by fat (after a crush injury to bone) or air (after a diving accident or error in injecting into a vein).

Unless the circulation is quickly restored, the tissue may die (infarction).
SEE ALSO *Heart and circulatory system; Pulmonary embolism*

Embryo research

Embryo research involves performing medical tests on embryos nurtured outside the mother's body during fertility treatment. Some people see this as unethical, but for others it is a key to tackling serious disease.

Embryo research, with all its potential and all its ethical implications, has come about as a side effect of test-tube fertility treatment. In vitro fertilization (IVF), as it is also known, has a very low average success rate – worldwide, only about 20 to 30 per cent of IVF treatments succeed. Women undergoing IVF take fertility drugs to make them produce more eggs than they would otherwise. All the eggs are then fertilized, so that if the first attempt at implantation in the uterus fails, there may be some left over that can be used for further attempts. Fertilized eggs not used in the first attempt can be kept in a deep freeze so that they are ready for later use if necessary.

The ethical problem of what to do with any 'surplus' embryos after implantation succeeds has provoked a major controversy. Many scientists call for the embryos to be thawed and used in research programmes. The embryos consist of stem cells, unspecialized cells that have the facility to grow into any of the body's specialized cells – muscles, nerve, skin and so on. But opponents of the process believe that human embryos created in this way should be accorded rights and should not be treated as raw material for medical research, however useful it might be. Despite the opposition, most countries have agreed that such surplus embryos can be used for research under strict regulation (see box, below).

GENETIC SCREENING OF EMBRYOS

Development of IVF techniques has also made it possible for an embryo to be screened before placing it in the mother's uterus. This process, known as pre-implantation genetic diagnosis, is used to ensure that an embryo has not inherited any serious genetic defect, or that when born it will make a suitable donor for a living child in need of a transplant (see box, page 433).

If there is a possibility that an embryo will develop into a baby that could serve as a donor of stem cells for therapeutic use, a cell is removed from the embryo and checked twice: once to make sure that any baby born will be free of disease, and once more to make sure that the baby's genes make it a compatible donor. If it is suitable, the embryo is placed in the mother's womb, hopefully resulting in pregnancy. Then, when the new baby is born, doctors take stem cells from its umbilical cord – which can

IVF and stem cell research

Medical research using embryos created in IVF is tightly regulated.

The embryos used in stem cell research are virtually undifferentiated balls of cells with no brain or nervous system. After the human egg cell has been fertilized in IVF treatment, it is allowed to multiply until it is a small bundle of cells (a blastocyte). At this point it is placed in the uterus of the mother or may be frozen, in which case it could later be taken for research. Between 1991 and 1998, 48,000 embryos created in IVF treatments in the UK were donated for research.

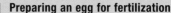

1 Preparing an egg for fertilization
A round human egg is separated from the corona radiata cells that normally nourish it (to the above left of the egg). This process makes it easier to fertilize the egg.

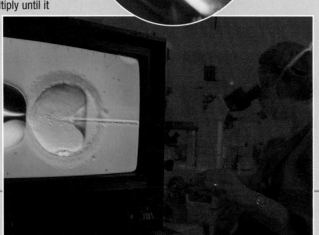

2 The egg is fertilized
A doctor injects a single sperm into an egg cell. She uses a pipette to hold the egg in position and a super-thin microneedle to pierce the egg and deliver the sperm. The doctor views the procedure through a microscope and its image is magnified on the blue screen. Once the egg's first cell divisions have taken place, it will be placed in the mother's uterus.

regenerate bone marrow – and inject those cells into the sick child. The new baby is not harmed.

Screening embryos in this way for specific useful genetic characteristics has attracted criticism from some anti-abortion campaigners and others who believe that it is wrong to bring a child into the world for anyone's benefit but its own. Other critics are concerned that embryo selection is the first step towards an acceptance of 'designer babies' – embryos chosen on the basis of intelligence or beauty or other desirable attributes. They also oppose the practice of discarding of any unsuitable embryos.

DONATED EGGS

Another controversial aspect of embryo research focuses on donated eggs – an issue that affects some of the many thousands of women who suffer from premature **menopause**. If a woman cannot have a baby of her own because she cannot produce her own eggs, she may be able to undergo a normal pregnancy by having IVF treatment using another woman's fertilized eggs. Adopting an egg that is hers almost from conception is often more attractive to a woman than adopting someone else's child after birth.

In cases of medical need approved by doctors, a woman can either have an egg fertilized by her own partner (egg donation) or, when the partner is unable to fertilize the egg, have it fertilized by sperm from another person before implantation (early embryo donation).

THE EMBRYO SUPERMARKET

Critics fear that, once we accept the principle that a woman may nurture an embryo when she is not the biological parent, we take an irrevocable step towards a hypothetical 'embryo supermarket'. According to this scenario, well-paid independent women would select an embryo with genes chosen for health, intelligence and good looks, possibly with none of their own genes or those of their partner.

Potential problems multiply in this area. A child conceived from a donated egg may feel that he or she has two female parents, and if the donor is known may look towards her at times of strife with the legal mother – for example, in the teenage years. An egg donor, who remains in contact with the 'birth' family may come to feel strongly that she could look after 'her' child better than the woman who adopts the egg. A father may start to develop inappropriate feelings towards any known donor of eggs that he has fertilized.

More problems are raised by wealthy post-menopausal women in their 50s or even 60s who request egg donation. Gynaecologists generally regard this as medically inadvisable as well as unethical, and most egg donors strongly oppose the idea.

SEE ALSO *Cells; Cloning; Ethics, medical; Genetics and genetic disorders; Infertility; Research, medical*

CONTACT **Human Fertilisation and Embryology Authority** 21 Bloomsbury Street, London WC1 3HF (020) 7291 8200 (www.hfea.gov.uk)

Creating a donor

Genetic screening can save the lives of children who need bone marrow transplants.

In early 2002, the Human Fertilisation and Embryology Authority (HFEA) offered a lifeline to a young boy with the blood disorder **thalassaemia major**. His parents were allowed to select a specially screened embryo of their own, offering an 80 per cent chance of a genetic match being found, compared to only a 20 per cent chance from a brother or sister conceived naturally.

4 The future
Scientists have shown that the specialized tissues grown from stem cells can be used for transplants. This tissue might be used to repair injuries to the spinal cord or to replace parts of the heart following a heart attack. Research on the cells might also open the way to finding cures for Parkinson's disease or diabetes or to investigating infertility and improving IVF's success rate.

3 Stem cells
Stem cells from embryos are put in culture in an incubator. When a few days old, an embryo consists entirely of stem cells, which can be grown into specialized tissues.

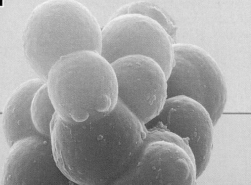

Emetics

Emetics are **drugs** that cause vomiting. Emetics are used to treat certain types of poisoning, especially drugs taken in overdose, but not poisoning by petroleum substances or by corrosive substances such as acids. Some emetics work by acting at the vomiting centre in the brain and/or by irritating the gastro-intestinal tract. They are used only when a patient is fully conscious and not convulsing. The best-known and most-used emetic is ipecacuanha, or ipecac syrup. Although ipecac syrup can be administered at home, it is best to seek medical advice at the earliest opportunity. When poisoning results from harsh chemicals, vomiting can further damage the digestive system and, in this case, a stomach pump is a much safer treatment.

SEE ALSO *Poisoning and gassing*

EMG

An EMG (or electromyogram) is a test in which the electrical impulses generated by muscle contraction are amplified and recorded. It is used in the diagnosis of nerve and muscle disorders, such as **muscular dystrophy** and **myasthenia gravis**.

The EMG involves inserting a needle electrode, attached to a recorder, into the muscle, or placing disc electrodes on the skin over the muscles being investigated. The electrical output is then displayed as a trace image on a computer screen or the trace is marked on paper. The trace indicates whether contraction is weaker than usual, and whether a weakness is due to degeneration of the muscle or damage to the nerves involved in its contraction.

Emphysema

Emphysema is a chronic obstructive pulmonary disease (COPD), a progressively disabling and life-threatening disease of the lungs. The disease is almost always associated with smoking cigarettes.

Smoking damages the tiny air sacs (alveoli) in the lungs, making breathing difficult. It is thought that only one in four cases of emphysema are diagnosed. It mainly afflicts men over the age of 45, although diagnosis in women is rising because increasing numbers of women smoke. Smokers in their late 20s may already have emphysema but attribute their symptoms to 'smoker's cough'.

SYMPTOMS
- Breathlessness, mild at first.
- Wheezing.
- Increasing disability.
- Anxiety and depression.

CAUSES
In nearly all cases – about 98 per cent – smoking is the sole cause, though sometimes alpha-1 antitrypsin deficiency, an inherited condition, contributes. This is a disorder in which the liver produces too little or none of the protein alpha-1 antitrypsin, which protects the lungs. Without this protection, the lungs are damaged very easily by smoking.

TREATMENT
There is no cure, but treatment to relieve symptoms includes drugs to widen the airways and reduce inflammation, **oxygen** therapy, surgery to remove areas of damaged lung and fitness programmes.

What you can do
- Stop smoking.
- Avoid polluted air.

When to consult a doctor
See a doctor if you suffer from shortness of breath, wheezing, or if your symptoms become worse.

Complementary therapies
The following may help to ease symptoms:
- blowing up balloons (see **Breathing exercises**);
- **relaxation techniques**;
- **massage**.

PREVENTION
Do not smoke.

OUTLOOK
Emphysema is a progressively debilitating disease that over many years results in increasing breathlessness, disability and eventually respiratory failure and death.

SEE ALSO *Bronchitis; Lungs and disorders; Smoking*

CONTACT **The British Lung Foundation (Breathe Easy club)** (020) 7688 5555 (www.britishlungfoundation.org)

Encephalitis

Encephalitis is a serious and sometimes fatal inflammation of the brain, usually caused by a viral or bacterial infection.

SYMPTOMS
A person with encephalitis usually has a feverish illness followed, perhaps days or weeks later, by varying degrees of disability as the infection spreads to the brain tissue. Symptoms may include drowsiness, confusion,

convulsions, involuntary movements, **paralysis** and **coma**.

The symptoms of encephalitis may be similar to those of **meningitis, encephalomyelitis** and encephalopathy, which is brain inflammation occurring as a result of drug overdose, liver failure and diseases such as brain cancer.

CAUSES

Encephalitis usually occurs as the result of a viral infection, but it can also be due to infection by bacteria and parasites. It may occur as a rare complication of the common viral infections **measles, mumps** and **rubella**, although an effective vaccination programme has caused this incidence to fall. Vaccination can also help prevent encephalitis caused by the rabies virus, Japanese encephalitis (a mosquito-borne viral disease that is widespread in Asia and to which travellers are vulnerable) and tick-borne encephalitis, which is common in forested parts of Europe and Scandinavia.

TREATMENT

Treatment usually focuses on alleviating symptoms. But encephalitis caused by the virus herpes simplex may be helped by the antiviral agent aciclovir.

OUTLOOK

Encephalitis may resolve itself completely, but some people suffer from permanent memory loss or muscle weakness. In severe cases, particularly those caused by the herpes simplex virus, the condition can be fatal.

SEE ALSO *Brain and nervous system*

Encephalomyelitis

Encephalomyelitis is an inflammation of the brain and spinal cord. Its symptoms are similar to those of **encephalitis** and myelitis (an inflammatory disease of the spinal cord).

SYMPTOMS

Encephalomyelitis usually begins with a feverish illness, headache and neck stiffness. Inflammation of the brain causes confusion, convulsions and **coma**, and inflammation of the spinal cord leads to paralysis in the limbs. Eyesight may also be affected.

CAUSES

Viral infections such as measles, smallpox, chickenpox, rubella and rabies can cause encephalomyelitis. Vaccination against these diseases can prevent the disease, but, extremely rarely, vaccination can also actually lead to encephalomyelitis. In the case of smallpox, vaccination is therefore no longer recommended because the disease has been eradicated from the world.

OUTLOOK

Most cases improve completely, but others may experience long-term weakness and memory loss.

TREATMENT

Treatment is mainly directed at relieving the symptoms.

SEE ALSO *Brain and nervous system; Viral infections*

Endocarditis

Endocarditis is a rare but serious, and sometimes fatal, infection of the lining of the heart cavity (endocardium), especially that of the heart valves. It is more common in developing countries.

SYMPTOMS

■ Persistent fatigue, weakness and night sweats.
■ Later there may be high fever, rashes, breathlessness and a rapid or irregular heartbeat.

DURATION

The infection can last several weeks.

CAUSES

■ Bacteria or other micro-organisms enter the bloodstream (often during dental or medical procedures) and infect the heart.
■ The infection usually affects people with pre-existing heart damage.
■ People with lowered immune systems and intravenous drug users are also at risk.

TREATMENT

A cure may be possible with early treatment so seek medical advice at the earliest opportunity.

When to consult a doctor

Seek medical advice if you have any of the symptoms listed here, or a high temperature without apparent cause.

What a doctor may do

■ Arrange tests, including blood analysis for bacteria.
■ Refer you to hospital for intravenous **antibiotics**.
■ Recommend heart valve surgery.

PREVENTION

People with pre-existing heart damage should take antibiotics before undergoing dental or surgical procedures.

COMPLICATIONS

■ Heart failure.
■ Kidney or other organ damage.

OUTLOOK

If the infection is treated early enough, a cure is often possible. However, about 25 per cent of sufferers die as a result of endocarditis.

SEE ALSO *Heart and circulatory system*

Endocrine system and disorders

The endocrine system is a complex communication network that governs the chemical processes behind our emotions and physical reactions. The hormones produced by the endocrine system control the way we grow and develop, as well as basic appetites such as hunger, thirst, sex drive and sleep.

The endocrine system is a sophisticated and sensitive system made up of a number of different organs or glands that secrete hormones. Hormones are chemical messengers, usually carried in the bloodstream, which speed up or slow down the activity of cells in other organs and tissues.

Hormones are responsible for a range of bodily reactions including response to stress, feelings of hunger or thirst, energy levels, mood, temperature and sexual desire. In childhood and adolescence hormones are essential for both growth and development. In adulthood, they control reproductive functions, including ovulation, menstruation, pregnancy and milk production in women and sperm production in men.

▼ **Thyroid hormones**
The large molecule (in orange) is a hormone producer called a thyroglobin, which produces two thyroid hormones. These hormones are then carried into the blood-stream via the capillary network (in blue).

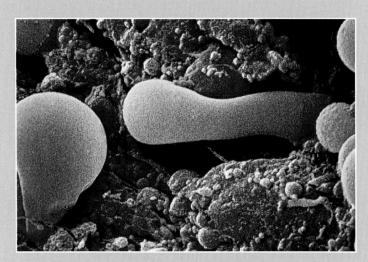

Most hormones are produced by the endocrine glands, but some are also produced by other body tissues. The major endocrine glands are the pituitary, thyroid, parathyroid, adrenal glands, and the reproductive organs. The pancreas, the hypothalamus and pineal gland also contain endocrine tissue that produces hormones. Pockets of hormone-producing cells are also located in the small intestine, stomach, kidneys and the heart.

Hormonal levels rise and fall throughout the day. The stress hormone, cortisol, for example, peaks in the early hours of the morning, whereas growth hormone peaks while we sleep. Because hormones cannot be stored in large quantities,

the brain programmes glands to produce them as needed in a biochemical cycle designed to keep our bodies in a state of balance. Hormonal production is controlled by a series of 'feedback loops', which operate in a similar way to the thermostat on a central heating system to raise or lower levels of hormones. The system is sensitive to many different factors. These can range from the food we eat, the amount of exercise we take, our feelings, illness, changes in body chemistry, pregnancy, ageing, temperature and even the time of day or season.

Although hormones are carried to almost all the body's tissues they can act only on specific 'target cells'. They do this by locking on to structures called receptors on the surface of or inside cells – like a door key fitting into a particular lock – and switching on or turning off the cell's activity. For example, when the stress hormone adrenaline binds to receptors on muscle cells in blood vessel walls it causes them to contract, preparing our bodies to fight or flee danger. All this takes place very quickly: a maximum of 11 seconds is needed for the blood to travel around the body and deliver a particular hormone.

THE MIND-BODY CONNECTION
The tiny pituitary gland at the base of the brain is often referred to as the 'master gland' because it plays a key role in co-ordinating the activities of the endocrine system. The pituitary looks rather like a pea on a stalk. The stalk is connected to the hypothalamus, an area of the brain about the size of a grape, which sends and receives hormonal messages between the brain and the rest of the body. The hypothalamus picks up information from the brain about a person's external or internal state and relays this by means of hormones to the pituitary down the 'stalk'. This triggers the pituitary into stimulating or inhibiting the action of other glands (including the reproductive organs).

Not all glands are controlled by the pituitary. Some react to concentrations of chemicals such as glucose, fatty acids and minerals in the bloodstream, while others respond to neurohormones, chemical messengers produced by the nervous system.

The glands and organs that produce hormones

More than 50 different hormones are produced within the body. The majority are produced by the endocrine glands, but several other organs, such as those in the reproductive system, also contain hormone-producing tissue.

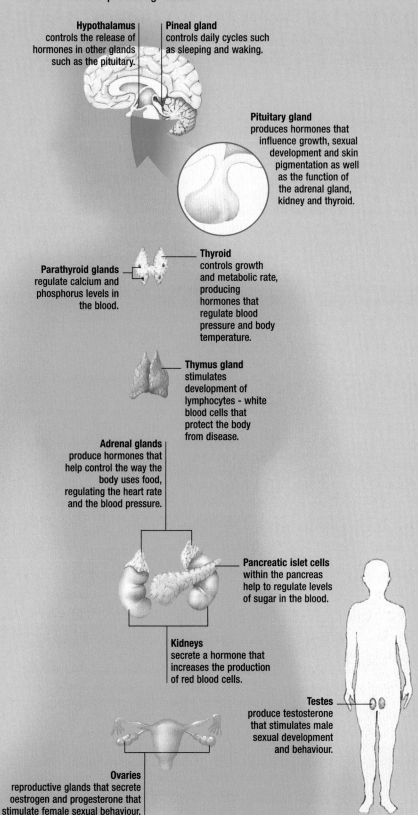

Hypothalamus controls the release of hormones in other glands such as the pituitary.

Pineal gland controls daily cycles such as sleeping and waking.

Pituitary gland produces hormones that influence growth, sexual development and skin pigmentation as well as the function of the adrenal gland, kidney and thyroid.

Parathyroid glands regulate calcium and phosphorus levels in the blood.

Thyroid controls growth and metabolic rate, producing hormones that regulate blood pressure and body temperature.

Thymus gland stimulates development of lymphocytes - white blood cells that protect the body from disease.

Adrenal glands produce hormones that help control the way the body uses food, regulating the heart rate and the blood pressure.

Pancreatic islet cells within the pancreas help to regulate levels of sugar in the blood.

Kidneys secrete a hormone that increases the production of red blood cells.

Testes produce testosterone that stimulates male sexual development and behaviour.

Ovaries reproductive glands that secrete oestrogen and progesterone that stimulate female sexual behaviour, development and menstruation.

DISEASES AND DISORDERS

Endocrine autoimmune disorders are conditions caused by the body's defence mechanisms turning against themselves. This involves antibodies attacking certain tissues within the body, believing them to be foreign material. Examples include Hashimoto's disease (a form of thyroid failure), Graves' disease (when the thyroid is overactive) and diabetes.

Tumours of the pituitary gland may occur. These are generally benign but may interfere with the normal functioning of the gland.

Multiple endocrine neoplasia (MEN) is an inherited disorder affecting 3 to 20 people in 100,000 in the UK. Tumours, usually benign (non-cancerous), develop, often all at the same time in a number of different endocrine glands. One common type involves the parathyroid, pituitary glands and the pancreatic islets.

CUTTING EDGE

Growing recognition of the links between hormones and the brain has led to the emergence of a field of study called psychoneuroendocrinology, dedicated to researching the links between hormones and our feelings and behaviour.

This field of research is throwing new light on medical conditions such as premenstrual syndrome (PMS), chronic fatigue syndrome and irritable bowel syndrome (IBS). These have been recognized but insufficiently understood by the medical profession. Psychoneuroendocrinology is also offering fascinating insights into the interaction between brain chemicals and bodily hormones, suggesting that mind and body are linked and do affect each other measurably.

SEE ALSO *Adrenal glands and disorders; Diabetes; Digestive system; Kidneys and disorders; Ovaries and disorders; Pancreas and disorders; Pituitary gland and disorders; Puberty; Reproductive system; Thyroid and disorders*

CONTACT **The Pituitary Foundation** PO Box 1944, Bristol BS99 2UB; helpline 0870 774 3355 (www.pituitary.org.uk)
British Society for Paediatric Endocrinology and Diabetes (www.bsped.org.uk)
Climb CAH UK Support Group Congenital Adrenal Hyperplasia UK Support Group (01270) 259375; helpline 0800 652 3181 (www.cah.org.uk)
British Thyroid Association (www.british-thyroid-association.org)
The Child Growth Foundation Write to 2 Mayfield Avenue, London W4 1PW.

Endometriosis

With endometriosis, fragments of the uterine lining (endometrium) are deposited elsewhere in the body – typically in or on the Fallopian tubes, on the ovaries, behind the uterus, or on the bowel, bladder or pelvic wall, but sometimes in abdominal scars or even the lungs.

These fragments respond to monthly hormonal changes, growing and bleeding during each cycle. But, unlike the lining of the uterus, they have no means of escape, and this leads to inflammation and a build up of scar tissue.

Endometriosis can begin at any time from the onset of menstruation to the menopause. You are more at risk if you have a family history, a menstrual cycle shorter than 28 days and if your periods last more than a week. It is the second most common gynaecological condition, affecting about 10 per cent of women in their reproductive years – about 2 million women in the UK.

SYMPTOMS

The main symptom is pelvic pain. Other symptoms include bloating, fatigue, painful periods, painful sex, painful bowel movements, constipation, painful and frequent urination or blood in the urine during periods, and infertility. Diagnosis is confirmed by **laparoscopy.**

TREATMENT

There is no cure for endometriosis, but it usually disappears at the menopause. Treatment is aimed at relieving pain, shrinking or slowing the development of endometrial deposits, preserving or restoring fertility, and preventing or delaying recurrence. It may include hormonal drugs designed to stop ovulation and allow endometrial deposits to shrink; the combined oral contraceptive pill; and the Mirena, a T-shaped device made of light plastic that releases small doses of a progestogen.

Sometimes endometrial deposits are surgically removed or vaporized with a laser. In severe cases hysterectomy may be necessary.

What you can do

Relaxation and stress management techniques may help to reduce stress and fatigue. Acupuncture, aromatherapy, herbal treatments, homeopathy, reflexology, naturopathy and osteopathy may also help.

COMPLICATIONS

- Endometriosis may stick organs together with strands of tissue, called 'adhesions'.
- 'Chocolate cysts' filled with dark blood may form.
- Fragments of the endometrium may block the Fallopian tubes, making it difficult to become pregnant.

OUTLOOK

Research is being carried out into genes that may play a part in endometriosis and this could lead to new treatments.

SEE ALSO *Reproductive system*

CONTACT **Women's Health** (www.womens-health.co.uk) **The National Endometriosis Society** helpline 0808 808 2227 (www.endo.org.uk) **OBGYN.Net** (www.obgyn.net)

Endorphins

Endorphins are a family of proteins that act as the body's natural painkillers. Endorphins are released in response to painful stimuli and bind to proteins called opiate receptors on nerve cells to exert their pain-relieving effects. The same receptors are used by morphine and morphine-like drugs when administered for the treatment of severe pain. Similarly, the painkilling effects of acupuncture may work by stimulating the release of endorphins.

Related chemicals, called enkephalins, are also thought to be involved in the body's natural methods of pain control.

SEE ALSO *Pain*

Endoscopy

Endoscopy is a technique used by doctors to investigate and treat health problems by looking directly into the patient's body through a flexible fibre-optic viewing instrument known as an endoscope. Many major surgical procedures have now been replaced by endoscopy, allowing faster recovery time.

WHY IS ENDOSCOPY USED?

Endoscopy may be recommended for:
- diagnosis of medical problems through inspection of internal organs – **ulcers,** for example, are readily revealed from an examination of the stomach lining;
- taking specimens for pathological analysis – for instance, in colon disease;
- performing **keyhole surgery,** such as removal of the gallbladder, by attaching miniature surgical instruments to the endoscope.

WHAT'S INVOLVED?

The endoscope is passed through the mouth, anus or penis, or through a miniature incision made in the abdomen. Since endoscopy often causes some degree of discomfort, the patient will usually be sedated during the procedure. New electronic endoscopes allow doctors to view almost any part of the body, including the

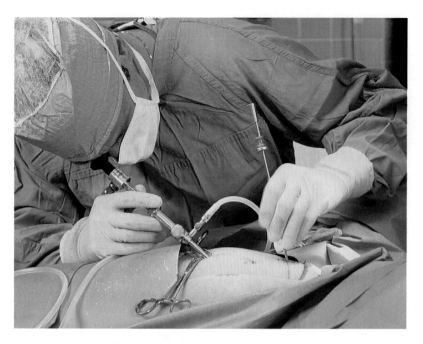

▲ Endoscopy
Surgical procedures such as endoscopy allow doctors to investigate and treat internal organs through small incisions – a technique known as keyhole surgery. These procedures are minimally invasive and allow a quicker recovery time.

digestive tract, the lungs, bladder, abdominal cavity, nasal cavity, and joints. Some endoscopes have a camera attached to them, allowing images of the interior of the body to be projected onto a large screen.

Enema

An enema is the introduction of fluid into the rectum. It may be given to relieve **constipation**, to clear the lower bowel before surgery, as part of an investigation (see **Barium investigations**) or as a means of introducing drugs.

HOW AN ENEMA IS GIVEN
A lubricated tube is introduced gently into the rectum while the recipient lies on his or her side with hips raised up by a pillow. Then the fluid, which has been warmed, is slowly pushed through the tube. Soap and water were used in the past, but nowadays special enema fluid is available. The procedure is not painful, although there may be some discomfort.

POSSIBLE RISKS
Enema equipment is widely available, and some people give themselves enemas regularly, in the belief that doing so is conducive to good health. Frequent home enemas are inadvisable because both the lining and the muscles of the lower bowel may become damaged or infected.

Enteric fever

Enteric fever is an alternative name for both **typhoid fever** and **paratyphoid fever**. Typhoid is caused by infection with the bacterium

Salmonella typhi, which can be transmitted to human beings via food or drinking water contaminated with faeces or urine from a carrier. A vaccine is available, which is needed when travelling to at-risk countries. Paratyphoid, caused by the bacterium *Salmonella paratyphi*, is similar to typhoid, but is usually much less severe.
SEE ALSO *Infectious diseases*

Enteritis

Inflammation of the small intestine, known as enteritis, can result in acute **diarrhoea**, loss of appetite, abdominal pain and, sometimes, vomiting. Possible causes include **food poisoning, salmonella**, exposure to contaminated water and **Crohn's disease**. Enteritis usually clears up without treatment in two to three days, although fluids should be taken to prevent **dehydration**.

Entropion

Entropion is an inward turning of the eyelid or lids, towards the eyeball. The condition may be present from birth, but it is most common in elderly people whose muscles around the eye have lost their elasticity. It may also result from scarring, usually of the surrounding facial skin, a common complication of **trachoma**.

With entropion the eyelashes tend to rub against the cornea (see **Inturned eyelashes**), causing irritation, discomfort or more severe pain, blurred vision and watering of the eye. There is also an increased risk of conjunctivitis.

Special lubricants for the eye or artificial tears provide temporary relief. Taping the lid in the required position may reposition the lid margin and prevent further irritation but a more permanent solution usually requires surgery to realign the eyelid.
SEE ALSO *Ectropion; Eye and problems*

Enuresis

Enuresis is the involuntary passing of urine in a child who is at an age when bladder control should have been obtained. Most children can stay dry during the day between the ages of two and three years and many are dry at night as well. **Bedwetting** is defined as nocturnal enuresis and is normal in many children up to the age of about five years, and in some cases for far longer.
SEE ALSO *Child care*

Environmental Health

Our health and well-being can be boosted or damaged by our surroundings. Keeping aware of possible threats and taking a few precautions inside and outside the home helps us to stay healthy.

▼ Hi-tech waste
Electronic goods such as computers are quickly superseded by new models and dispatched to landfill sites for domestic waste. But such equipment can be donated to community groups in the UK and abroad. Local councils hold information on these recycling schemes.

Health scares connected to food or the atmosphere suggest that citizens of the urbanized modern world face assault from a bewildering range of hazardous substances. But the threat is exaggerated. In the UK, regulators appointed by central and local government protect the quality of our air, water, land and food. They also offer advice on ways to avoid or reduce the health impact of the hazards that do exist.

AIR POLLUTION

Air pollution derives mainly from car, bus and lorry exhausts, but industrial emissions and the burning of solid waste also contribute to the problem. Nitrogen oxides, hydrocarbons, carbon monoxide and microscopic particles can aggravate respiratory problems such as **asthma**, **bronchitis** and **emphysema**.

Air particles
Particulate matter (PM) is the general term used to describe solid particles and liquid droplets of smoke, fine ash and dust found in the air from traffic and industrial emissions. PM10 particles (10 micrometres in diameter or less) can pose a potentially significant health risk in urban areas. They can be carried deep into the lungs, causing inflammation and exacerbating heart and lung conditions.

Carbon monoxide
Carbon monoxide is released from car exhausts, and regular intake can make people feel generally lethargic and unwell. Carbon monoxide is also released from faulty gas appliances in the home. If allowed to accumulate in an unventilated room it can be fatal (see **Carbon monoxide poisoning**). For this reason you should have your gas appliances checked annually by a certified technician. Seek technical help at once if you see an orange-yellow flame or soot deposits in your gas appliance. (See also **Passive smoking**.)

WATER POLLUTION

Polluted water can spread disease-causing viruses from treated sewage and bacteria, and other micro-organisms from untreated sewage. Heart, circulation and blood disorders can be caused by sodium and nitrogen in industrial wastes in river water. In the UK, Environment Agencies are responsible for limiting pollution of water sources by regulating land use.

Water companies clean, filter and disinfect water before supplying it to homes. There are standards for water quality, enforced by the government's Drinking Water Inspectorate. For example, nitrates – which are present in all waters but may be concentrated to dangerous levels by run-off because of fertilizers from farm fields – must not be present in a concentration greater than 50mg per litre of tapwater.

If you live in a house built in the 1960s or earlier, you may have lead water pipes. These can boost lead in water to unhealthy levels. If you are concerned, ask your water company for a free test. If levels are high, it is worth considering replacing lead pipes with copper or plastic ones. If you cannot replace the pipes, avoid drinking water that has been standing in the pipes. If the cold tap has not been used for a few hours, run the water for a few minutes before drinking it or using it for cooking. The initial water flow can be used to water plants.

WASTE

Each person in England alone produces 500kg of household waste each year – and the volume is rising by 4 per cent annually. Household and commercial wastes used as landfill generate methane gas, which can cause poisoning. Waste that is incinerated releases ash and poisonous chemicals into the air, which can cause severe respiratory illnesses. Under the UK's licensing system, waste operators have to demonstrate that they dispose of rubbish in ways that protect human health and the environment. It is helpful to try to reduce the amount of household waste sent to landfill or to be incinerated by recycling or composting it – one-third of the contents of a typical dustbin in the UK comprises paper and one-fifth is vegetable matter.

RADIATION

Radioactive radon gas emitted by the uranium in rocks and soil can enter houses through the floor. In some areas, houses built on certain types of rock can contain high levels of radon, which may increase the risk of developing lung cancer. If you are concerned, contact the National Radiological Protection Board for advice and to arrange a test of radon levels in your home.

Accidental emissions from nuclear power stations, nuclear reprocessing plants and research facilities are the most common sources of a potentially harmful form of radiation (ionizing radiation) in the atmosphere. Ionizing radiation may have adverse effects on health, such as increasing rates of cancer, but the difficulty of setting up controlled statistical studies makes it impossible to determine this conclusively. Doses of radiation from man-made sources are low compared to those from natural sources such as rocks and the 'cosmic radiation' that hits the Earth from space. If you are concerned, the Committee on Medical Aspects of Radiation in the Environment publishes advice and surveys. (See also **Radiation sickness.**)

Among other, non-ionizing forms of radiation in the atmosphere are magnetic and electrical fields beneath power lines, radio frequency and the ultraviolet radiation emitted by the sun. **Ultraviolet radiation** is an undoubted health risk. Studies have shown that due to the depletion of the ozone layer around the poles, more ultraviolet radiation is reaching the Earth, and there is an increased risk of skin **cancer** among populations exposed to high levels of solar radiation.

Everyone – especially children – should wear sunblock creams and protective clothing when in direct sunshine. Loose, light clothing should be worn when in the shade to protect from **sunburn.**

Mobile phones

There is well-publicized concern that excessive use of mobile phones poses a threat to health, especially to children. The phones receive and emit radio waves, and there is evidence that radio waves cause heating in the body when emitted above a certain level. All mobile phones offered for sale in the UK meet international guidelines that keep exposure below the safety level.

However, it also appears that in some people radio waves below the safety level can cause changes in brain activity. For this reason, it is sensible to keep your calls short and to choose phones that have a low specific absorption rate (SAR), a measure of how much radio energy each mobile phone emits. Ask about the SAR of a phone before buying it. Research has shown that living near a base station through which mobile phone signals pass also poses no health threat.

Microwave ovens

Microwave radiation leaking from ovens can cause heating of body tissue. There is a theory that it also causes warming of the testes, producing temporary infertility, but this has not been proved or disproved. Always make sure that the microwave door is firmly shut before trying to

> The UK recycles 15.6 per cent of household waste, compared with 31 per cent in the United States, 64 per cent in Austria, 52 per cent in Belgium and 48 per cent in Germany.

Maintaining a safe environment

In the UK several major government agencies are responsible for planning and maintaining standards of environmental health.

■ The Department of Health is responsible for microbiology and toxicology (poisons) in the environment; control of communicable diseases; health promotion; and food safety. Environmental health officers (formerly called public health inspectors) are consulted on matters relating to public and environmental health.

■ The Department for the Environment, Food and Rural Affairs is responsible for housing, waste management, air and noise pollution, the quality of drinking water, sewage disposal and energy efficiency. It also covers food standards and labelling; imported food controls; pest control; animal health and welfare; and food science and technology. The Food Standards Agency is an independent food safety watchdog.

■ The Department for Transport maintains a Marine Pollution Control Unit and assists with cleanup after accidents.

■ Local authorities are responsible for collecting and disposing of domestic waste; cleaning and maintaining the streets; food safety; and controlling air pollution, noise and other nuisances.

■ The Environment Agency controls water quality in rivers, lakes, estuaries and coastal waters. It is responsible for flood protection, and manages the fish stocks and fishing rights.

■ In addition, the World Health Organization enforces international sanitary regulations to control epidemics and runs international health programmes.

Detox your home

Cleaning and DIY products generally contain poisonous chemicals. When used to excess, they can turn a home into a 'sick building'.

To reduce the pollution in your home, be careful in your use and disposal of chemical cleaners. Try using natural alternatives such as washing soda and lemon juice. Contact your local authority for advice on disposing of harmful chemicals.

Wood preservatives can be toxic. Try using non-toxic alternatives such as borax-based products for indoor application. Also using softwood instead of particle board or chipboard can prevent the release of formaldehyde fumes several years after installation.

Cleaning products often contain chemicals that can be harmful in high concentrations. Try to use cleaning products based on natural ingredients.

Decorating materials can be toxic. Use water-soluble paints, varnishes, paint thinners, strippers and adhesives, which are kinder to the environment.

Insecticide sprays may contain harmful chemicals. Use insect traps or insect-repellent lamps to trap flies.

In the garden, many pest-control treatments contain toxic chemicals. Use non-toxic alternatives.

---

use the oven and replace any microwave that has a cracked or faulty door. Check the seal regularly, and replace it or the whole oven if it appears faulty. (See also **Electromagnetic radiation**.)

FOOD PROBLEMS

Outbreaks of **food poisoning** can be caused by campylobacter, a bacterium usually acquired by eating raw or undercooked poultry or drinking unpasteurized milk or untreated water. Symptoms including abdominal pain and diarrhoea may occur up to one week after the initial infection.

Species of the **salmonella** bacterium can survive for long periods in human and animal faeces, on vegetables and in eggs. Salmonella grows quickly in food at 10–40°C (50–104°F), causing severe illness in anyone who eats it. *Escherichia coli* (**E. coli**) is a bacterium that may be transferred to food via the hands from human faeces. It causes gastroenteritis, especially in children, plus urinary tract and other infections (See also **Additives, food**.)

BSE and vCJD

The practice of feeding animal products to cattle in the 1980s may have led to the appearance of bovine spongiform encephalopathy (**BSE**). The European Community imposed rigid controls on the sale of beef and beef cattle, but not before what is thought to be a human form of BSE, a variant of Creutzfeldt Jakob disease, had appeared in the UK (See **CJD**).

SEE ALSO *Allergies; Immune system and disorders; Noise; Occupational health; Passive smoking; Poisoning and gassing; Safety; Smoking*

CONTACT **Chartered Institute for Environmental Health (CIEH)** (020) 7928 6006 (www.cieh.org) **Department of Health** www.doh.gov.uk **Department of the Environment, Food and Rural Affairs** 08459 335577 (www.defra.gov.uk) **Environment Agency** 0845 933 3111; incident hotline for the public to report damage and danger to the natural environment 0800 807060 (www.environment-agency.gov.uk) **Food Standards Agency** (020) 7276 8000 (www.foodstandards.gov.uk) **National Radiological Protection Board** (now includes Medical Aspects of Radiation) (01235) 831600 (www.nrpb.org.uk) **Pesticide Action Network UK** (020) 7274 8895 (www.pan-uk.org)

Enzymes

Enzymes are proteins that act as catalysts for the biochemical reactions of the body's cells. The human body contains some 40,000 enzymes, which are under the control of genes. Enzymes enable us to metabolize food and drugs, help to carry away waste, aid the delivery of hormones to the cells, balance levels of blood fats and help to control clotting. The presence or absence of certain enzymes can be used to diagnose illness. For instance, tests for levels of cardiac enzymes help to diagnose heart attacks and determine the amount of damage to heart muscle.

ENZYMES AND DISEASE

Many metabolic disorders result from enzyme deficiencies or malfunction. **Albinism**, for instance, is often caused by a deficiency of tyrosinase, an enzyme needed to produce the pigment melanin. **Phenylketonuria** is caused by a lack of the enzyme phenylalanine, which can cause severe mental retardation if left untreated.

The involvement of enzyme reactions – both good and bad – in many other disease processes is being increasingly recognized. Enzymes are thought to play a role in:
- causing the development of brain plaques in **Alzheimer's disease**;
- triggering cancer cells to invade other tissues;
- reducing the oxidation of 'bad' **cholesterol**, and therefore the risk of coronary heart disease;
- helping to stop the joint destruction that is a feature of **rheumatoid arthritis**.

Research into the interaction between genes and enzymes is paving the way for the development of 'designer drugs' tailored to the biological make-up of individuals.

SEE ALSO *Metabolism and disorders*

Epidemic, epidemiology

An infectious disease that is normally rare in a community becomes epidemic when it spreads to affect many people or into new areas. Epidemiology is the study of the occurrence, transmission and control of epidemic diseases.

HOW INFECTION SPREADS

Infection is spread by:
- droplets – **influenza** and children's diseases such as **mumps** and **measles** are commonly spread by droplets released into the air by coughing, sneezing and breathing;
- contact – infection can also be spread by touching an infected person or something that the person has touched. **Sexually transmitted diseases** are spread by sexual contact;
- insects – **malaria**, dengue and **yellow fever** are all spread by the bite of a mosquito;

Medical detectives

Increasing availability and accuracy of medical statistics enable epidemiologists to compare a wide range of illnesses on a worldwide basis.

In the 20th century epidemiologists were instrumental in investigating the origins and spread of newly discovered illnesses, such as Legionnaire's disease, Lassa fever, Hepatitis B and AIDS and to focus on non-infectious diseases, such as cancers, that affect many people. They constantly collect and update information about new strains of infectious diseases, such as influenza, so that vaccines remain effective. Epidemiologists largely established the connection between cigarette-smoking, heart disease and cancers of the mouth, throat and lungs, and the relationship between diet and heart disease.

Epidemiologists need investigative skills to track diseases to their source. In the 1980s Australian physician Barry Marshall doubted the prevailing belief that stomach ulcers are caused by emotional stress. He analysed tissue from the stomachs of patients with stomach ulcers and discovered a new bacterium, *Helicobacter pylori*. He found that people without stomach ulcers, do not have this bacterium in their stomachs. Antibiotics are now the cure for stomach ulcers, and *Helicobacter pylori* has been found to have a major role in stomach cancer.

- oral contamination – **cholera, typhoid, E. coli** and **salmonella** are usually transmitted when bacteria from an infected person's urine or faeces contaminate food or drink;
- household pests – typhus is caused by rickettsia, a parasite in rat faeces, which is spread by the bites of fleas, lice, mites and ticks.

PREVENTING EPIDEMICS

Infectious diseases spread rapidly through populations with no immunity, but their virulence often abates naturally. In most industrialized countries, diseases such as the plague, cholera, typhoid and typhus are controlled primarily by public health measures that ensure clean water supplies and sewage disposal, hygienic food production, healthy housing, and the elimination of rodents and other pests. Other diseases, such as measles and whooping cough, are controlled by **immunization**.

Diseases that are kept in check by immunization can reappear if many people choose not to be immunized – usually because a disease no longer seems a threat, or because of side effects or fear of complications. In the 1970s in the UK, rumours that **whooping cough** immunization caused brain damage reduced vaccinations from 85 per cent to 31 per cent of

A pandemic is an epidemic that spreads from country to country. The 1918 flu pandemic killed more than 20 million people worldwide.

the population, resulting in two whooping-cough epidemics during the 1980s.

The failure of so many patients to finish courses of **antibiotics** to treat **tuberculosis** has contributed to the appearance of drug-resistant tuberculosis strains. These are now infecting susceptible populations such as homeless people and drug users in the United States and the UK.

Epidural

An epidural is a form of pain relief in which the nerves in the spine are anaesthetized. It is most often used during childbirth. A tiny needle or catheter is inserted between two of the vertebrae in the small of the back. This is used to inject anaesthetic into the epidural space – the cavity that surrounds the spinal cord. A needle is used for a single dose or a catheter is left in place in case a top-up is needed. An epidural numbs the entire area below the waist, and some women find it reduces their ability to push. It also increases the risk of subsequent **back pain**.

SEE ALSO *Anaesthesia and anaesthetics; Birth and problems*

Epiglottitis

Epiglottitis is a relatively rare but serious illness that strikes suddenly. It mostly affects children aged between two and six years, but sometimes occurs in older children and adults. The infection causes inflammation of the voice box (**larynx**) and swelling of the epiglottis, the flap of cartilage at the back of the tongue. This obstructs breathing and, if not treated promptly, can cause death by suffocation.

Epiglottitis is usually caused by the bacterium *Haemophilus influenzae*. A vaccine against this micro-organism (which can also cause meningitis) is now included in children's routine vaccinations (see **Immunization**).

SYMPTOMS

Symtoms, similar to those of croup, include:
- fever;
- severe throat pain;
- hoarseness;
- difficult or noisy breathing, which is not relieved by steam inhalation;
- excess mucus in the mouth, with drooling.

TREATMENT

Always seek prompt medical treatment if a child has fever or breathing difficulties. If epiglottitis is suspected, the child will be admitted to hospital, where **X-rays** of the neck will be taken to confirm diagnosis. A tube may be passed into the windpipe to aid breathing,

and **oxygen** may be necessary. Antibiotics will probably be given. The patient should begin to recover within 24 hours, once the breathing obstruction has been cleared.

Epilepsy

Epilepsy affects one in 130 people in the UK today and is characterized by recurrent **seizures** that occur suddenly for no apparent reason. The seizures are the result of excessive and disordered electrical activity in the brain, which

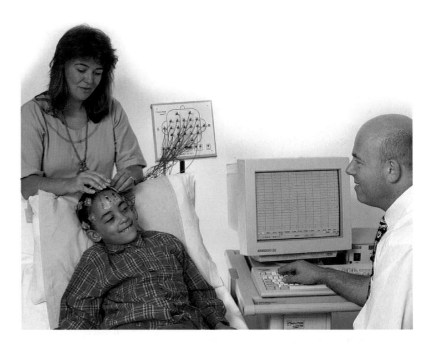

▲ **Brain wave activity**
An EEG machine can be used to detect tiny characteristic electrical impulses of brain activity that can help diagnose epilepsy.

produces a brief change in consciousness, behaviour, emotion, movement or sensation. Seizures are triggered by alcohol, stress, illness, skipping meals or occasionally by flashing lights, although they can occur without an identifiable trigger.

Each year, up to one person in ten with epilepsy experiences prolonged or repetitive seizures, with no recovery between attacks. This is called status epilepticus and can be fatal when the seizures are generalized.

There are also a number of epilepsy syndromes (for example, Lennox-Gastaut syndrome) in which people have a mixture of seizure types or have large numbers of seizures each day. In children, these can be associated with learning difficulties.

SYMPTOMS

Symptoms range from small areas of numbness and tingling to widespread muscle spasms and convulsions, depending on the type of epilepsy. However, such symptoms can be due to other conditions – for example, certain heart conditions, **panic attacks** and breathing problems – and so anyone who is experiencing epilepsy-like seizures should be referred as soon as possible to a neurologist or other epilepsy specialist.

Some people with epilepsy know when they are about to have a seizure because they experience an aura – restlessness or an unpleasant feeling – before an attack. There are two types of epileptic seizures: generalized and partial.

Generalized seizures

The whole body is affected by generalized seizures, which are the result of abnormal electrical activity over a wide area of the brain. There are several types of generalized seizure.

■ Tonic-clonic (grand mal) seizures cause a person to lose consciousness and fall to the ground. At first the muscles contract and the body stiffens (the tonic phase), then the limbs twitch rhythmically for a time (the clonic phase) as the person goes into a deep sleep. Gradually the person regains consciousness, remembering nothing about what has happened. About 60 per cent of people with epilepsy have this type of seizure.

■ Absence seizures (also known as petit mal) occur mainly in children. There is a sudden, brief loss of conscious activity. The condition can easily go unnoticed as it may appear as though the sufferer is merely daydreaming. Other subtle symptoms include small chewing movements, fluttering eyelids or trembling of the hands.

■ Myoclonic seizures produce a sudden brief single or repetitive muscle contraction, involving the whole body or just one part.

■ Atonic seizures are known as drop attacks because the brief loss of consciousness that they bring on causes children to drop to the ground for short periods. The sudden falls may result in head or other injuries.

Partial seizures

Partial seizures, also called focal seizures, are caused by abnormal activity in a small part of the brain. The location of the seizure in the body depends on which part of the brain is affected. However, a seizure can start in one part of the body and then spread.

Partial seizures are subdivided into simple and complex types. During a simple partial seizure, there is no loss of consciousness – a person may have muscle spasms, numbness or tingling for several minutes, but remains aware throughout. During a complex partial seizure, a person loses conscious contact with his or her surroundings for one or two minutes. The person may stare into space, move purposelessly and repetitively, make unintelligible sounds or appear confused.

Usually the person will not be able to recall the episode.

CAUSES

A tendency to develop epilepsy can be inherited, but there are numerous other causes, including strokes, brain tumours, head injury and meningitis. Epilepsy can also be brought on by alcohol and certain drugs. It is most common among children and the elderly. Some children stop having seizures as they get older.

DIAGNOSIS

Epilepsy is diagnosed mainly by the doctor listening carefully to a description of the way the seizure occurred, preferably by someone who saw it. An **EEG** (electroencephalogram) of electrical activity in the brain and a brain scan, usually by **magnetic resonance imaging** (MRI), provide additional information.

TREATMENT

People with epilepsy get to know which situations bring on a seizure and so to some extent can reduce the frequency of attacks by avoiding their own particular triggers. All but the mildest of cases will need treatment of some form.

Medication

The aim of drug treatment is to control seizures with minimal side effects, preferably with a single drug. The exact choice and dose depends

Epilepsy affects one in 130, or 300,000 people in the UK. It is the second most common neurological condition, after migraine.

Living with epilepsy

Between attacks, most people with epilepsy lead perfectly normal lives, and can work or go to school or college, and take part in everyday sports and activities.

■ Drug therapy stops seizures in about one-third of people with epilepsy and reduces their frequency in another third. The drugs are reduced gradually over time and about two-thirds of people with well-controlled seizures can eventually stop their drugs without having a relapse. It is not known why some people stop having seizures while others continue.

■ Women taking anti-epileptic drugs should take medical advice before becoming pregnant as their treatment may need to be changed to avoid harming the unborn child.

■ Very few jobs are unsuitable for people with epilepsy, although many of those affected find it hard to overcome employer fears and prejudices. Driving restrictions may make some jobs difficult. Anyone who has just been diagnosed with epilepsy must not drive by law. Anyone affected must inform the DVLA (Driver and Vehicle Licensing Authority) in Swansea, and can only reapply for a licence after he or she has been free of seizures for a year.

Helping a person during a fit

When someone is having an epileptic fit follow these basic procedures.

Do

✔ Roll the person onto his or her side, loosen clothing around the neck and place a pillow under the head.

✔ If the person recovers naturally within a few minutes, ask them to tell you what, if any, additional help is needed.

✔ Call for emergency help if the person does not recover within 10 minutes.

Don't

✘ Try to restrain someone during a seizure, unless the person is in real danger. Instead, move furniture or anything else that might injure them out of the way.

✘ Attempt to put anything in the mouth of a person having a seizure.

on the type of seizures, but most patients are likely to start with either sodium valproate or carbamazepine. Other drugs that may be used include the newer anti-epileptic drugs, lamotrigine and gabapentin. The older drug phenytoin tends to be reserved for hard-to-treat cases because of its unpleasant side effects.

Other drugs used in the treatment of epilepsy include tranquillizers and antidepressants, either to help to control primary symptoms or to relieve the side effects of treatment. Some types of complementary therapy, such as **relaxation techniques**, **massage**, **yoga** and **aromatherapy** may be helpful in this respect.

Surgery

A growing number of people are having surgery for epilepsy. This is especially true of younger people with simple partial seizures, originating in the temporal lobes of the brain cortex, which do not respond to drug treatment. MRI scans and other tests help to locate the precise area of the brain affected so that it can be removed.

SEE ALSO *Brain and nervous system; Fits; Seizure*

CONTACT **British Epilepsy Association** New Anstey House, Gate Way Drive, Yeadon, Leeds LS19 7XY; helpline 0808 800 5050 (www.epilepsy.org.uk)

National Society for Epilepsy Chesham Lane, Chalfont St Peter, Buckinghamshire, SL9 0RJ (01494) 601300 (www.epilepsynse.org.uk)

Episcleritis

Episcleritis is an inflammatory condition of the episclera, the outer layer of the white fibrous wall of the eyeball. It causes redness and discomfort. Common among young adults, it usually settles without treatment within a week or two. Episcleritis may recur. If concerned, you should see a doctor or optometrist to exclude other more serious causes of redness.

SEE ALSO *Eye and problems*

Episiotomy

An episiotomy is a small incision in the area between the anus and the vagina (the perineum), which may be performed to enlarge the vaginal opening during childbirth, to prevent more serious tearing or in the event of an assisted delivery using forceps or a ventouse (vacuum extractor). Local **anaesthetic** is given beforehand, and the cut is stitched immediately after the delivery. The site of the incision may be uncomfortable for a few days, usually healing within a week, but pain may persist.

SEE ALSO *Birth and problems*

Erectile dysfunction

More commonly known as **impotence**, erectile dysfunction is a condition in which a man is unable to produce or maintain an erection adequate for his chosen sexual activity. One in 10 men are affected at any one time and although the likelihood increases with age, the immediate trigger may be a variety of physical or psychological causes or usually both.

Erosion

Erosion is the wearing away of a tissue surface. Dental erosion reduces the protective enamel surface of teeth, caused by physical damage from excess brushing, or acid attack. Acid is present in carbonated drinks and citrus fruits, which also contain sugar. When sugar is present it is converted to acid by the bacteria that live in the mouth. In **bulimia nervosa**, when self-induced vomiting is frequent, the enamel on the back of the front teeth is attacked by stomach acid.

Cervical erosion is where the velvety lining of the cervical canal has become turned out and is visible at the opening to the vagina. The term 'erosion' isn't strictly correct; a more accurate name is 'ectropion', meaning 'turning out'.

Erysipelas

Erysipelas is a bacterial infection of the skin that spreads rapidly; it is a form of **cellulitis**. The infection starts as a small red patch, which is painful and swollen. It spreads within hours and blisters may form in the centre of the inflamed area. Other symptoms include a sudden fever, headache, shivering and vomiting. Erysipelas is caused by the bacterium *Streptococcus*, which may enter the skin via a wound, skin abrasion or ulcer, or fungal infection. Before the advent of **penicillin**, erysipelas caused many deaths; today, with prompt treatment, recovery can be rapid. If untreated, the infection may spread, causing **blood poisoning**, an **abscess** or **gangrene**, so it is important to see a doctor as early as possible.

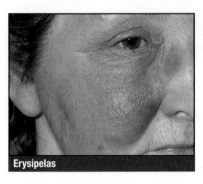

Erysipelas

Erythrocyte

An erythrocyte is a red blood cell, full of **haemoglobin**, whose function is to transport oxygen to the tissues and carry waste carbon dioxide from the tissues to the lungs. Each erythrocyte is a flattened disc, providing a maximum area for oxygen and carbon dioxide to come into contact with haemoglobin. Adults have some 30 million in circulation.
SEE ALSO *Anaemia; Blood and disorders*

Erythrocyte sedimentation rate

The erythrocyte sedimentation rate (ESR) is the speed at which red blood cells fall through blood **plasma**. The faster the ESR, the greater the likelihood of significant inflammation within the body, indicating infections, cancers or autoimmune disorders. GPs routinely perform ESR tests on people with non-specific symptoms such as tiredness, joint pains and weight loss to see if more specific investigations are advisable.

Essential amino acids

Amino acids are the basic building blocks from which proteins are made. Most can be produced by the body, but eight cannot be made by the body and must therefore be provided by the **diet**. Having been broken down from protein, amino acids are carried in the bloodstream to the liver and other sites in the body. They are then re-assembled to make the specific forms of protein required by different cells and tissues.

Essential fatty acids

Essential fatty acids are unsaturated fatty acids that are essential for growth. The body must obtain them in their natural form in food because it cannot synthesize them.

There are two 'essential' fatty acids: linoleic acid and linolenic acid. The body requires these in a ratio of roughly 2:1 linoleic to linolenic. They play important roles in the structure of cell membranes, the brain and myelin sheath of nerves, and in fat transport in the blood. A typical Western diet has a good level of linoleic acid from seed oils and blended margarines, but is often very low in linolenic acid. Good sources are pumpkin seeds, linseeds (flaxseeds) and the seed oils.

▶ **The power of seeds**
Adding a variety of seeds such as pumpkin, linseed or sunflower seeds to your diet may help reduce cholesterol and offer protection against coronary heart disease.

Ethics, medical

Medical ethics are founded on a set of principles or rules of professional conduct that help to govern the increasingly complex relationship between patient and doctor or other healthcare staff.

An ethical code is necessary because doctors and other healthcare professionals exercise considerable power over their patients. Patients may be vulnerable or in need, and they have a right to feel that they can trust their carers – to the point of life-or-death decisions. The duties of a doctor were first laid down by the Greek physician Hippocrates in the 5th century BC. Although very few doctors now take the Hippocratic oath, its core idea – that the good of the patient is paramount – is still present in the World Medical Association's International Code of Medical Ethics, adopted in 1949. The code embodies some universally agreed standards and states that a doctor has an ethical duty to:
■ act in the patient's best interests;
■ keep confidential what is revealed in the consulting room, including all medical records;
■ ensure that the patient agrees to any examination, treatment or procedure, preferably in the full knowledge of what it involves (see **Informed consent**);
■ avoid negligence, sexual impropriety and any other abuses of the patient's trust.

DECIDING WHAT IS ETHICAL
The principles of medical ethics were once the sole concern of the medical profession. They were passed down along with the practical teaching of medicine, and patients were generally confident that their doctors were acting in good conscience. But medical paternalism – the notion that 'doctor knows best' – is in decline. Modern medical ethics tend to stress 'patient autonomy' – the idea that people have an absolute right to determine what happens to their own bodies, even if it means rejecting medical opinion.

This broadening of the ethical debate means that doctors' decisions are increasingly scrutinized by people outside the profession – by lawyers and moral philosophers as well as the press and the general public. Many practical ethical issues are the subject of passionate and wide-ranging discussion. They include – among others:
■ **abortion** – under what circumstances, if any, should it be allowed?
■ **embryo research** – is it acceptable to use cells from aborted fetuses or 'spare' embryos created in the IVF process in research to find cures for disease?
■ the use of animals in **clinical trials** – is it right to subject animals to pain to relieve human suffering?
■ **euthanasia** – when is it right to hasten death?
■ medical negligence – how far is a doctor to blame if treatment fails? And how far should doctors be held accountable before the law if they make mistakes?
■ organ donation – should people be presumed to consent to donation of their organs after death?
■ brain death – who should decide whether to discontinue life support for someone in a persistent vegetative state?
■ **genetics** – should doctors agree to help couples using fertility treatments to select the sex or other characteristics of their child?

Many of these questions touch on fundamental ideas about the value of human life and the values of human society. For this reason, most doctors and non-medical professional people agree that the burden for resolving them ought not to be borne by medical professionals alone.
SEE ALSO *Death and dying; Doctor; Donors; Embryo research; Infertility; Research, medical; Transplants*

'I will follow that system of regimen which, according to my ability and judgment, I consider for the benefit of my patients ... I will give no deadly medicine to anyone ... Whatever, in connection with my professional practice or not in connection with it, I see or hear, in the life of men, which ought not to be spoken of abroad, I will not divulge, as reckoning that all such should be kept secret.'

From the ancient Hippocratic oath

Euphoria

The term 'euphoria' describes a feeling of intense happiness and elation. It can be caused by very positive life events, but also appears in psychiatric disorders: for example, the manic phase of **manic depression** (bipolar disorder). Euphoria is characteristically the first effect of the 'high' experienced by misusers of opiates.

Eustachian tube

The Eustachian tube connects the middle ear to the nasal passage and allows equalization of pressure on both sides of the eardrum. If it becomes swollen or blocked – by infection or inflammation – air in the middle ear spaces becomes trapped, resulting in a feeling of fullness in the ear and perhaps some hearing loss. Treatment by **decongestants** usually brings relief. The patient should avoid air travel or diving, which involve sudden pressure changes.

Euthanasia

Euthanasia means ending a life to relieve suffering. The term covers both the practice of helping a terminally sick person to die, and the act of choosing assisted suicide for oneself.

In the debate on this highly emotive subject, four types of euthanasia have been identified, each of which raises subtly different issues. They are:

- active euthanasia – doing something to hasten death, such as giving a lethal drug;
- passive euthanasia – inducing death by failing to act, for example, by withholding medication;
- voluntary euthanasia, which means that death was requested by the individual;
- non-voluntary euthanasia, which means that someone decides to end life on behalf of a sufferer who is incapable of deciding himself.

THE MORAL DEBATE

Euthanasia has become an intensely debated issue, partly because the medical profession is increasingly involved in managing the process of dying (most deaths now occur in hospital), and partly because medical technology has made it possible to prolong life artificially, in some cases extending the period of terminal suffering.

The opposition to euthanasia comes from religious groups and others who claim that the 'sanctity of life' is paramount. They argue that no one has a right to take a life: not their own, and certainly not someone else's. Non-voluntary euthanasia, they say, is morally and legally indistinguishable from murder.

Factfile

A right to choose

Supporters of euthanasia believe that people have a right to choose their time of death.

- One-third of doctors comply when asked to offer active euthanasia.

- It is estimated that around 10,000 people die through assisted suicide in the UK each year.

- In 1999, a GP who had injected a patient with a lethal dose of heroin and admitted helping patients to die 'pain-free' deaths was found not guilty of murder.

- Voluntary euthanasia and assisted suicide are legal in Belgium, Oregon, the Netherlands and Switzerland.

Supporters of voluntary euthanasia counter that 'quality of life' is the key: someone in such pain that life is unbearable has the right to end their suffering. Support is growing for the legalization of 'assisted suicide' or helping others to kill themselves if they want to die but are physically incapable of acting on their wish.

DOCTORS AND THE LAW

All forms of active euthanasia, including assisted suicide, are illegal in the UK. It has been argued that this discriminates against disabled people, and creates a cruel and absurd situation in which people with degenerative diseases are forced to commit suicide while they still can, but before they really want to.

Patients cannot insist that a doctor actively helps to end life – if a doctor did so, technically prosecution could follow; however, anyone can refuse treatment. Also, doctors may withhold or withdraw treatment they consider futile, including life support and tube feeding. They may also, by invoking the doctrine of 'double effect', give drugs intended to relieve suffering, even if, as a 'side effect', the patient's life is shortened.

SEE ALSO *Advance directives; Death and dying; Ethics, medical*

Ewing's sarcoma

Ewing's sarcoma is a type of malignant tumour of bone. It is a **cancer** most commonly found in the long bones, especially the thigh bone (femur) and shin bone (tibia), and is more likely to occur in children, although adults may be affected. Typical symptoms include pain and swelling. Ewing's sarcoma is very resistant to treatment and so the cure rates are low.

Exercise and health

Our bodies are designed to be active. Even a small amount of regular exercise delays the processes of degeneration and decay, and boosts our long-term health and our resistance to disease.

As you become fitter, so does your heart. The pulse rate slows down because each beat pumps blood more efficiently round your body.

Watch a group of two-year-old children and they never seem to stop; they are always on the go. Some teenagers retain this natural tendency to be active. But most adults, whether 21 or 81, live sedentary lives. We sit for hours behind a desk or supervise machines that do the work. Trains, cars and buses take us home, where we watch television, surf the Internet, or play computer games. Over the past five years in the UK there has been a 20 per cent reduction in 'foot miles'. If this trend continues we won't be walking anywhere by the year 2025 – except from the front door to the car.

Taking regular exercise has numerous benefits, and we all need to build some form of exercise or physical activity into each day. Unfortunately for some people, it is not until their health is taken away, perhaps after a heart attack or a near-fatal accident, that they begin to value it. You only have one body, so it's worth looking after it.

THE BENEFITS OF EXERCISE

Exercise makes the heart muscle more elastic, so that it fills with blood more easily and forces out more blood with each beat. This means that fewer beats are needed each minute to pump the same amount of blood to your legs. Your pulse rate is therefore a useful measure of your fitness. Once you begin taking regular exercise, you will become fitter and your heart rate will decrease.

The increase in circulation during exercise means that more oxygen is delivered to your

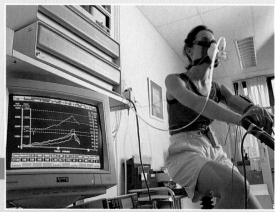

Test your own fitness

Your resting pulse rate is a good rough guide to fitness: by and large, the slower your resting pulse rate, the fitter you are.

Take your pulse as soon as you wake. Hold your left hand out, palm upwards. Put your right hand under your wrist and curl your fingers round to the pulse point. Count the rate for 15 seconds and multiply by four to get the rate per minute – then check it against the charts.

Being aware of your general fitness is important before undertaking any kind of new exercise. Many health clubs use hi-tech equipment to assess fitness levels before devising a tailor-made exercise plan for you.

Male resting pulse rate

AGE	18–25	26–35	36–45	46–55	56–65
Excellent	49–55	49–54	50–56	50–57	51–56
Good	57–61	57–61	60–62	59–63	59–61
Above average	63–65	62–65	64–66	64–67	64–67
Average	67–69	66–70	68–70	68–71	68–71
Below average	71–73	72–74	73–76	73–76	72–75
Poor	76–81	77–81	77–82	79–83	76–81
Very poor	84–95	84–94	86–96	85–97	84–94

Female resting pulse rate

AGE	18–25	26–35	36–45	46–55	56–65
Excellent	54–60	54–59	54–59	54–60	54–59
Good	61–65	60–64	62–64	61–65	61–64
Above average	66–69	66–68	66–69	66–69	67–69
Average	70–73	69–71	70–72	70–73	71–73
Below average	74–78	72–76	74–78	74–77	75–77
Poor	80–84	78–82	79–82	78–84	79–81
Very poor	86–100	84–94	84–92	85–96	85–96

brain. This helps to make you more alert and able to think more clearly. Regular exercise improves the ratio of the beneficial HDL cholesterol compared with the harmful LDL type. Several studies have shown that running for 2–3 hours per week cuts the risk of a heart attack by 40 per cent compared with a sedentary lifestyle.

Moderate activity boosts your **immune system**. Research shows that people who exercise on a regular basis have less sickness than their sedentary colleagues. In one US study, the number of days off work with the common cold was reduced by half in those who walked briskly for 30–45 minutes, five days a week. During this type of moderate exercise, several positive changes occur in the immune system. For example, levels of antibodies rise, and stress hormones such as adrenaline and cortisol, which can suppress immunity, are kept low.

Regular exercise also helps you to sleep better. Refreshed and recharged after a good sleep, you have more energy.

GETTING STARTED

If you are unfit, try to build more activity into your everyday lifestyle. Walk to the local shops instead of taking the car. Park further away from the supermarket entrance and use the stairs instead of escalators in shops, offices and railway stations. Then, depending on your level of fitness, aim for a minimum of 30 minutes of moderate-intensity exercise, five days a week. This might be brisk walking, cycling on flat roads, gently swimming, gardening, golf, brisk housework or cleaning a car. The activity should make you slightly breathless.

You don't have to do 30 minutes of exercise in one session. Build up slowly and do, for example, a 10-minute walk and 20 minutes of gardening. After about ten weeks, you should feel fitter. Increase the total time spent in moderate exercise to an hour each day, five days a week to maintain fitness.

Make it fun

Unless exercise is something you want to do rather than a chore, you will not keep it up. Take exercise for positive reasons – as a break from daily routine, as a means of social contact, for relaxation, as part of a weight-management programme to get fit, or to help reduce blood pressure. Above all, find a form of exercise that suits you.

The best exercise – and the one that will do you the most good – is one you enjoy doing, not one you endure. Aerobics classes, circuit training and jogging are popular forms of exercise, but so are line dancing, ice-skating and roller-blading, which bring the same health benefits.

How different sports and hobbies rate as exercise

Choose a physical activity that you enjoy and do it regularly. Whether it's playing squash or digging the garden, you will soon feel the benefit.

ACTIVITY	STAMINA	SUPPLENESS	STRENGTH
Aerobics	★★★	★★	★★
Badminton	★★	★★	★★★
Circuit training	★★★	★★	★★★
Climbing stairs	★★	★	★★★
Cricket	★	★	★
Cycle touring	★★★	★	★★
Dancing (salsa)	★★★	★★	★
Dancing (ballroom)	★	★★	★
Digging the garden	★★	★	★★★
Football	★★	★★	★★
Golf	★	★★	★
Hockey	★★	★★	★
Jogging	★★★	★	★
Judo	★★	★★	★
Mowing the lawn	★	★	★
Rope skipping	★★★	★	★
Rowing	★★★	★★★	★★
Running	★★★	★★	★★★
Squash	★★★	★★★	★
Swimming	★★★	★★★	★★★
Step aerobics	★★★	★	★★
T'ai chi ch'uan	★★	★★★	★
Tennis	★★	★★	★★
Walking/trekking	★★	★	★
Weight training	★	★★	★★★
Yoga	★	★★★	★

If you want to do aerobics or circuit training, find a class with an instructor who makes the session fun. Forget the notion that if a little exercise is good, then a lot must be better. A certain exercise pattern for one person might help to reduce stress, but in another will only add to it.

Find your own level

As with eating habits, exercise is an individual matter. Listen to your body and let it dictate the pace. Some people push their bodies too hard – and pay the price. The optimum level of exercise for an individual will give his or her immune system a slight boost, but too much will suppress the immune function. This is because exercise produces a chemical called glutamine (the fuel for white blood cells which help to fight bacteria) and stimulates the immune system. But extreme exertion, such as over-training – running 50 miles a week, say, when your body is only ready to cope with 25 – causes glutamine levels to plummet, leaving you more prone to infection. Enjoy exercise at a level that suits you.

The frequency of exercise is important too. A brisk 30-minute walk with your dog every day is much better for you than a strenuous session in the gym once every three weeks.

PREGNANCY AND EXERCISE

Pregnancy is often thought of as a time to rest and take it easy. But if you are accustomed to taking regular exercise before you conceive, there is no reason not to continue to keep fit after you become pregnant. However, since the weight of the baby alters your centre of gravity, be sure to choose activities that do not put extra strain on posture and cause backache.

Swimming is particularly good during the later stages of pregnancy when doing anything bouncy is uncomfortable because the baby is pressing on the lungs (making breathing difficult) or putting pressure on the bladder.

The increase in circulation during exercise helps to reduce many of the common pregnancy-related conditions such as piles,

▶ **Fit for two**
Adopting the tailor's position during pregnancy strengthens your thigh muscles and tones your pelvic floor. Sit with your back straight and ease your heels together and towards your perineum. Use your arms to push down on your thighs.

Exercising: dos and don'ts

It is never too late to start exercising. Whatever your age, you will soon start to feel the benefits of a gentle, regular fitness programme.

Do

✔ Start gradually. If you are unfit, slowly build up to 30-minute sessions.

✔ Get advice from your doctor if you suffer from diabetes, dizziness, any heart condition, back pain or joint problems.

✔ Drink plenty of fluids. Water or unsweetened fruit juice diluted with water are best.

✔ Wear several layers of clothing if conditions are cold. Warm muscles are less prone to injury.

✔ Buy shoes suitable for your activity; they can help to prevent injury.

✔ Eat more fruits and vegetables (preferably fresh, but also canned, frozen and dried). All vegetables, except potatoes, are good sources of antioxidant nutrients. These neutralize the damaging free radical molecules produced as a normal byproduct of energy metabolism.

Don't

✗ Measure yourself against others; it's your own achievement that counts.

✗ Exercise if you are feeling unwell, or have a cold or a chest or throat problem. Respiratory infections will make proper breathing difficult.

✗ Cut down on starchy carbohydrate foods (breakfast cereals, wholemeal bread, brown rice, pasta, baked potatoes, porridge, oatcakes). These provide fuel for working muscles.

Self-help
Exercises you can do while seated

Being unable to get to a gym is no excuse for not keeping yourself as fit as possible. There are many stretching exercises you can practise in the office to help you staysupple, even when sitting in a chair. The exercises shown below are especially useful if you spend long periods of time typing or sitting at a computer screen.

1 Keeping your back straight, stretch your arms in front of you, with your hands clasped together. Hold for 10 seconds then relax.

2 Next, hold your left shoulder with your right hand and clasp your right elbow with your left hand. Repeat on the opposite side.

1 Enjoy a hand stretch and help prevent repetitive strain injuries. Place your hands an inch or two above your keyboard and flex your fingers as wide as possible.

2 After stretching your fingers to their full extent, curl up the top parts of your fingers before repeating both steps of the exercise 10–20 times.

constipation, varicose veins, cramps and water retention. Exercise also promotes good circulation, which supplies more oxygen and nutrients to the baby via the placenta.

One of the many hormonal changes during pregnancy is the production of relaxin, which softens ligaments and improves suppleness. This means that you may find your joints are more flexible during pregnancy. A daily routine of stretching will develop strong abdominal and back muscles, which in turn help to promote good posture and prevent backache.

An active childhood

Small children exercise naturally out of sheer exuberance so provide plenty of opportunities.

■ The garden, or any outdoor green space, is an ideal environment for uninhibited exercise.

■ Walk everywhere with your child, to shops, letterbox, or with a dog.

■ Helping to sweep the floor, push a toy vacuum cleaner or rake leaves in the garden are all much more fun than watching television.

■ Indoor spaces where little ones can run and jump include toddler groups, health centres and organized baby-gym or music and movement groups.

CHILDREN AND EXERCISE
Children learn by example. They mimic and follow the behaviour patterns of adults. A good way to encourage children to be active and include exercise as a normal part of their daily routine is to be active yourself.

Play active games, combine a walk with a picnic, and encourage children to join in with gardening, car washing or dog walking.

With older children, encouraging activity can be difficult. Teenagers often rebel against their parents. Many are not motivated to get out and exercise, although some young adults are inspired by friends, teachers, elite athletes or sportspeople.

But although these external factors play a role, it is the inner passion that will keep motivation to exercise high – and sustain the love of it through various life stages. This inner passion is developed in early childhood.

Fit for anything

Exercise may not rank that high on many teenagers' lists of priorities, but it can help you to feel good, and look good, too. It can also help keep at bay many of the health problems that people experience later in life.

■ If you hate organized school sports, try other things like kick-boxing or salsa.

■ Your friends might not think it's cool to exercise, but it hasn't done David Beckham or Tiger Woods any harm. Although we can't all be the best – and may not even want to be – there is a lot to be gained from being fitter.

■ If you have moved to a new area, a good way to make local friends is to join a fitness studio or a sports team.

■ There's no need to stop doing what you enjoy – whether it's playing computer games, watching TV or hanging out with your friends; do all those things but find ways to be active, too.

■ If you are diabetic or suffer from asthma; keep your medication or inhaler nearby when you are exercising, but use them only if you really need to.

■ Girls may feel less inclined to take part in exercise during their periods. If you feel self-conscious or uncomfortable about the clothes you are asked to wear, talk to your PE teacher or parents about it. If your periods are causing a problem, discuss it with any teacher who you feel will understand. Some people suffer with cramps each month, while others have a painful period only every now and then.

▶ **The new cool**
It is no fun being unfit, and even the most sluggish of teenage metabolisms can be revitalized in just a few weeks.

Exercise can help with period pain, but sometimes all you want to do is curl up in bed with some aspirin and a hot water bottle.

■ Drink plenty of water, especially when exercising indoors or in hot weather. For every half-hour of strenuous exercise aim to drink at least 30cl (half a pint) of water.

■ Recent research shows that girls are getting fatter; they may eat fewer calories than boys but they are less active. You may not be interested in school sports, but you could look at activities outside school such as dance, martial arts or horse riding.

■ Earning money while you exercise is a great incentive to get going. Washing cars, gardening and delivering newspapers (watch your posture when carrying a heavy bag) all count as exercise.

TEENAGERS AND EXERCISE

The teenage years are a stage of life in which the individual is searching for self. Being accepted as part of a peer group and keeping up with all the physical changes brought on by hormones are two major challenges of the teenage years.

You know when you are unfit. Your friends out-run you to the bus, or you find yourself panting after a walk with the dog. Everything is an effort. Being physically unfit is embarrassing. Aim to do some sort of activity that leaves you slightly breathless on most days.

Although you may feel awful to start with, after a month or so you will feel better. For the next ten weeks, choose any activities that push up your heart rate and make you breathe harder. You will then be in the 'super fit' league, and ready to take up an activity seriously or join a team.

GOING TO THE GYM

Most local sports centres have a gym and there are numerous private fitness studios. All charge fees, and you will probably have to buy a 6-month or 1-year membership. Gyms are strictly regulated. Before you are allowed to use the equipment, a trainer will test your fitness and draw up an exercise plan tailored to suit you. He or she will then teach you how to warm up properly and how to use the equipment safely. This process is known as induction, and you will probably be given a membership card to prove that you have been shown the ropes.

Most gyms recommend at least three sessions a week – several short sessions are much better for you than one marathon work-out. Wear cotton clothing in layers so you can strip off as you warm up, and take a towel for the shower.

Stretching exercises

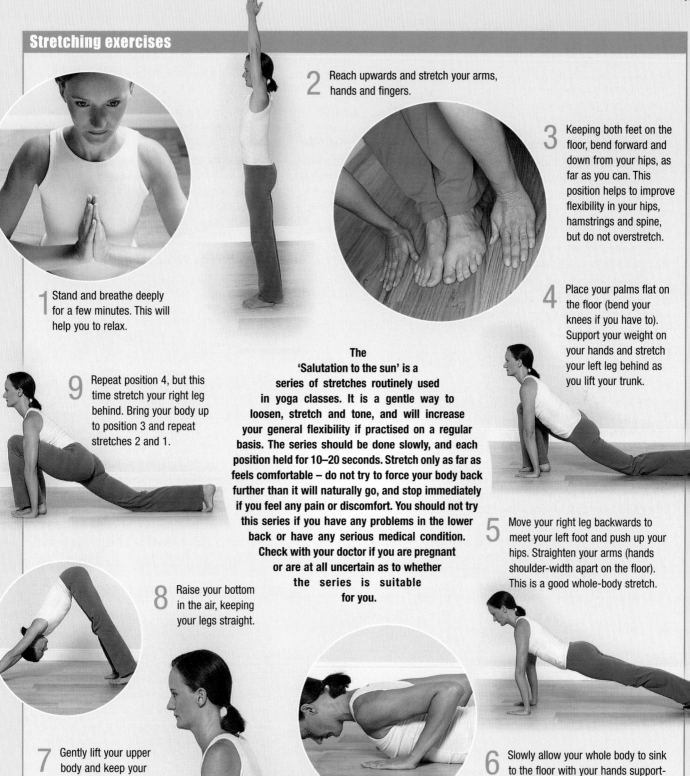

2 Reach upwards and stretch your arms, hands and fingers.

3 Keeping both feet on the floor, bend forward and down from your hips, as far as you can. This position helps to improve flexibility in your hips, hamstrings and spine, but do not overstretch.

1 Stand and breathe deeply for a few minutes. This will help you to relax.

4 Place your palms flat on the floor (bend your knees if you have to). Support your weight on your hands and stretch your left leg behind as you lift your trunk.

9 Repeat position 4, but this time stretch your right leg behind. Bring your body up to position 3 and repeat stretches 2 and 1.

The 'Salutation to the sun' is a series of stretches routinely used in yoga classes. It is a gentle way to loosen, stretch and tone, and will increase your general flexibility if practised on a regular basis. The series should be done slowly, and each position held for 10–20 seconds. Stretch only as far as feels comfortable – do not try to force your body back further than it will naturally go, and stop immediately if you feel any pain or discomfort. You should not try this series if you have any problems in the lower back or have any serious medical condition. Check with your doctor if you are pregnant or are at all uncertain as to whether the series is suitable for you.

5 Move your right leg backwards to meet your left foot and push up your hips. Straighten your arms (hands shoulder-width apart on the floor). This is a good whole-body stretch.

8 Raise your bottom in the air, keeping your legs straight.

7 Gently lift your upper body and keep your legs straight and toes stretched.

6 Slowly allow your whole body to sink to the floor with your hands supporting your body under your shoulders.

Exhaustion

Exhaustion is a state of extreme tiredness. It is often experienced in both a physical and psychological sense, although the original cause may be either physical or psychological, and sometimes both. Physical causes include excessive exercise, dehydration, starvation, prolonged labour in childbirth, uncontrolled diabetes, and thyroid disease. Psychological causes include intense stress for longer than the individual can manage, uncontrolled psychotic illness and severe depressive illness.

Sleep deprivation has direct physical and psychological effects on the body because it deprives the muscles and joints of rest, as well as bringing on mental exhaustion.

Expectorant

Expectorants are drugs intended to aid the coughing up and expulsion of phlegm (sputum). They are used to relieve symptoms such as **catarrh** and bronchial congestion and are incorporated into medicated liquids, including over-the-counter cold remedies. But it is not known exactly how expectorants work and there is doubt about their effectiveness. Drugs called mucolytics have similar actions in that they 'disintegrate' mucus and make phlegm more watery. They are sometimes used by people with chronic asthma or bronchitis.
SEE ALSO *Cough; Drugs, medicinal*

Exposure

Exposure is the term used to describe the physical effects of being subjected to extreme weather – usually to intense cold, or cold combined with damp and wind. Exposure also covers the ill effects of extreme heat, radiation and pollutants such as pesticides.

The human body is capable of surviving intense cold as long as it is warmly wrapped, fed and adequately sheltered. Clothing provides insulation, trapping air warmed by body heat. Since cold increases the rate at which the body uses energy, the body requires food to generate heat to keep warm.

Well-fed adults can maintain their core temperature of 37°C (98.6°F) for a long period in still air temperatures of -29°C (-20.2°F) or lower. If there is wind, however, it replaces the warm air around the body with cold, so the skin freezes and the core temperature drops. Water conducts heat away from the body faster than air, so if the clothing is wet from rain, snow

or immersion in water of a temperature lower than 20°C (68°F), the core body temperature falls and death from **hypothermia** follows.

Medical treatment focuses on restoring the normal body temperature as a gradual process in order to maintain an even blood temperature.
PREVENTION
If you are at risk of exposure from cold, there are some things you can do to protect yourself.
■ Find or construct a shelter.
■ Cover your body, head and extremities to insulate them from cold.
■ If immersed in cold water, keep still. Moving prevents the body from warming a surrounding layer of water that could protect you.
■ Drink water or other non-alcoholic drinks.
SEE ALSO *Environmental health; Frostbite; Heatstroke*

Extradural haematoma

Extradural haematoma is a life-threatening brain haemorrhage resulting from a severe blow to the head. It often occurs at the same time as a skull fracture. The trauma causes a tear in a major artery, which leaks blood into the outer covering of the brain (the extradural space), producing pressure on the brain. Brain swelling may cause the pupil of the eye on the affected side to dilate. The concussed patient recovers initially until deepening **coma** occurs minutes or hours later, necessitating prompt surgical treatment. This involves making a hole in the skull (burr hole) over the injury, removing the clot and tying the leaking artery.
SEE ALSO *Brain and nervous system*

Extrasystoles

Extrasystoles are extra heartbeats arising as a result of spontaneous electrical activity in the heart. They may interrupt the normal rhythm, producing the sensation of a 'missed beat'. This gives the heart longer to fill up, so the next scheduled beat becomes stronger and a 'thump' is felt. Extrasystoles can be identified by an **ECG** (electrocardiogram).

Some types of extrasystole are common in healthy people, and may be triggered by stimulants such as caffeine or stress. Ventricular extrasystoles may also be normal, but can also be a sign of heart disease. Frequent extrasystoles may be the forerunner of other abnormal rhythms.
SEE ALSO *Arrhythmia; Heart and circulatory system*

Eye and problems

Problems affecting the eye range from infections and injuries to impaired vision and blindness. Any of the structures of the eye may be poorly developed or become diseased during a person's lifetime.

The eye has two main parts: an image-forming system consisting of the cornea, iris and lens, and the retina, which converts images falling onto it into electrical signals that are passed to the brain by the optic nerve.

Each eyelid acts as a protective shutter for the eyeball and, like the visible part of the eye itself, is lined by the conjunctiva, a thick membrane filled with blood vessels. Behind the lids lies the cornea – the 'window' through which light enters – and the sclera, or white of the eye. The conjunctiva and cornea are constantly bathed in tears secreted by the lacrimal and other glands to keep the front surface lubricated and protected.

The amount of light that enters the eye is controlled by the pupil, a hole of variable diameter in the centre of the iris (the coloured part of the eye). The light is then focused by the lens, a firm, transparent, convex body behind the iris. The lens may be made thinner or thicker by the action of a ring of muscle around it called the ciliary muscle. This focusing ability reduces throughout life (see also **Presbyopia**) due to a loss of elasticity of the lens – hence the need for reading glasses as we grow older.

The space between the cornea and the lens is filled by a watery fluid called the aqueous humour, which is constantly secreted and drained to maintain the eye's shape and internal pressure. If the drainage is blocked, it causes a rise in pressure in the eye, which can lead to **glaucoma**.

Light passes from the lens through the vitreous humour – a transparent, jelly-like substance that fills the interior of the eyeball.

From there, the light is focused onto the retina, a light-sensitive sheet of nerve cells and fibres lining the interior of the eyeball. Behind the retina is the choroid, a layer of blood vessels supplying

Organ of vision
The eye is a complex and delicate structure that measures only 25mm (1in) in diameter. It supplies the brain with more information about the outside world than any of the other senses.

Sclera A tough outer coating forming the white of the eye.

Choroid A layer of blood vessels that nourishes the retina.

Retina A light-sensitive membrane where light waves are converted into nerve impulses.

Iris The coloured part of the eye.

Conjunctiva A membrane lining the eyelids and the white of the eye.

Lens A transparent body that focuses light onto the retina.

Pupil An opening in the iris that admits varying amounts of light.

Aqueous humour A narrow water-filled chamber that nourishes the cornea and lens.

Vitreous humour A watery gel that fills the main part of the eye and maintains its shape.

Optic nerve A nerve that transmits signals from the retina to the brain.

Eye muscles Muscles that move the eyeball.

Ciliary body A ring of muscle that adjusts the shape of the lens to focus the eye.

Cornea A transparent layer through which light enters the eye.

the retina with nutrients. The retina contains light-sensitive cells called photoreceptors that convert light into electrical signals. There are two types of photoreceptor cell: cones and rods. The cones are primarily responsive to colour and detail (and are faulty in **colour blindness**) and the rods respond to lower light levels and movement. The signals pass through retinal nerve fibres to a small area called the optic disc. Here the nerve fibres leave the eye and pass down the optic nerve. They carry the electric signals to the visual cortex on each side of the brain, where they are processed to allow perception of the image.

COMMON EYE PROBLEMS

External eye infections are usually related to **conjunctivitis**, an inflammation of the mucous membranes that line the eyelids. Other causes of redness and irritation are a persistent scaliness on the eyelid edges (**blepharitis**) and inflamed, painful bumps at the base of the eyelashes (**styes**). Inflammation may also result from injuries to the eye, allergies or irritants such as smoke.

Common problems affecting the lids and lashes include a turning out of the eyelid (**ectropion**), a turning in of the eyelid (**entropion**), **inturned eyelashes**, and swelling of a gland in the eyelid (**chalazion**). Tear problems are also common, and drainage of the tears may be disrupted, as happens with a blocked tear duct.

The cornea is vulnerable to damage by foreign bodies or abrasion and may become ulcerated (see **Cornea and disorders**). The sclera may become inflamed (scleritis or **episcleritis**). The iris and ciliary body may become inflamed (**iritis**).

Diet and smoking

One of the keys to healthy eyes is general well-being – so, to keep your eyes in good condition, you need to maintain a balanced diet, take plenty of exercise and avoid smoking.

■ There is increasing evidence that a diet rich in antioxidants – contained in fresh fruit and vegetables, for example – may reduce the risk of degenerative diseases such as age-related macular degeneration.

■ A deficiency of vitamin A may lead to night blindness, so eat plenty of green vegetables and carrots.

■ A high-sugar diet has been linked with diabetes, the most common cause of blindness in people of working age.

■ Smoking increases the risk of age-related macular degeneration, which can cause blindness as well as cardiovascular disease.

Practical eye care

Some work and leisure activities expose the eyes to various dangers, but there are a number of practical steps you can take to minimize any risk.

■ Wear sunglasses with an adequate filter or tint, especially when skiing or taking part in other prolonged outdoor activities. Exposure to ultraviolet radiation can increase the risk of disorders such as corneal problems, cataracts and conjunctival degeneration.

■ Always wear eye protection when carrying out a task such as welding or garden strimming, which could result in injury.

■ When doing close work, ensure that you have good lighting and take regular breaks to reduce eye strain, which may cause discomfort and headaches.

■ If your work involves long hours in front of a computer screen, give your eyes plenty of opportunities to refocus by gazing into the distance at 20-minute intervals.

■ Have an eye test at least every two years to monitor the health of your eyes.

VISION PROBLEMS

If the eye is not the right shape to allow normal focusing on the retina, a refractive error exists. For example, if the length of the eye from front to back – from the cornea to the retina – is too short, or the cornea is too flat, the eye will find it hard to focus on close targets; this is known as **long-sightedness** or hypermetropia.

If the focal length is too long or the cornea is excessively curved, the eye will have difficulty perceiving distant objects; this is called **short-sightedness** or myopia. If the eye is not spherical, **astigmatism** will result.

All these refractive errors can be corrected with focusing lenses, the powers of which are determined by the results of an **eye test**. **Laser surgery** can also be effective in correcting many refractive errors.

Double vision – seeing two images in place of one – when looking in certain directions indicates a **squint**, which can sometimes be corrected by a treatment programme that may include special eye exercises. An uncorrected squint in childhood can lead to **amblyopia**, in which the eye never achieves normal levels of vision.

The retina is vulnerable to many disorders, with symptoms ranging from **night blindness** to total blindness in conditions such as a **detached retina**.

The central area of retina with the highest concentration of photoreceptor cells is called the macular, and this often degenerates with age. Age-related macular degeneration is estimated to be responsible for about half of all registered sight loss in the UK.

Damage to the nerves carrying the signal out of the eye may occur, for example, in glaucoma or **optic neuritis**. Such damage is sometimes seen as a paleness of the fibres (**optic atrophy**).

Problems of the blood supply to the eye, its muscles or the structures within the visual pathway – as can occur in people with diabetes or high blood pressure, for example – may result in loss of normal eye function. In later life, the lens may lose its transparency (see **Cataract**).

SEEKING HELP

Optometrists, who are qualified to undertake **eye tests**, are listed in the Opticians Register, available from the General Optical Council. Most registered optical practices display a sign indicating the presence of a qualified optometrist on the premises.

Although the content of an eye test may vary depending upon the nature of the presenting problem, all tests should include an assessment of your vision and an eye health check.

Consult a doctor or optometrist if you experience any of the following:
- pain in the eyes;
- blurred vision;
- discharge;
- redness;
- visual phenomena, such as flashing lights or **floaters**.

See a doctor or report to your nearest eye casualty unit urgently if you experience:
- sudden loss of total vision or a portion of peripheral vision, with or without pain;
- severe pain;
- severe headaches, with or without loss of vision;
- sudden flashing lights or many floaters;
- haloes around lights;
- visual loss when general ill health is felt;
- sudden onset of double vision.

SEE ALSO *Blindness; Contact lenses and problems; Eye test; Subconjunctival haemorrhage*

CONTACT General Optical Council
41 Harley Street, London W1G 8DJ
(020) 7580 3898 (www.optical.org) Holds a list of optometrists qualified to undertake eye tests.
College of Optometrists 42 Craven Street, London WC2N 5NG (020) 7839 6000
The Eyecare Trust 0845 129 5001
(www.eyecare-trust.org.uk)

Eye test

An eye test is designed to assess an individual's level of vision and, if necessary, to prescribe spectacles or contact lenses. The health of the person's eyes is checked at the same time.

Such a test will generally be carried out by an optometrist (a specialist in vision defects) or an ophthalmologist (a specialist in eye diseases).

Regular tests are advisable because everyone's level of vision changes over time. This applies especially to elderly people, in whom conditions such as **cataract** and **glaucoma** are more common. Generally, a test every two years is adequate, but more frequent assessment may be advised, especially if you have **diabetes**.

Eye examinations are free on the NHS for children, full-time students up to the age of 19 and people over 60 – as well as those receiving certain health and social security benefits, those with glaucoma or diabetes, those over 40 who have a parent or sibling with glaucoma, and those who need a very strong correction.

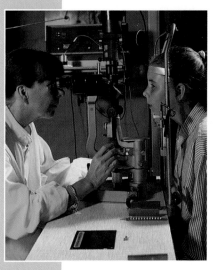

▲ **Health check**
As well as assessing your level of vision, an eye test can identify a variety of health problems.

WHAT'S INVOLVED

An eye test takes between 20 minutes and one hour, depending on the number of tests required. You will be questioned about your vision and any history of visual problems or symptoms. You will also be asked about your general health, and about any family members with eye or general health problems.

A series of tests will be carried out to check all aspects of your vision and to assess the health of your eyes. The optometrist will explain the results and advise you on general care of your eyesight, such as avoiding eye strain. He or she will also tell you when you should have your next eye test.

If you need help with your vision, you will be given a prescription specifying the strength of any spectacles or contact lenses required. You can take it to any optician where prescription spectacles are made up. Most opticians have a very wide selection of frames suitable for prescription lenses. If a health problem has been detected, the prescription will also indicate whether you should see your GP for further investigation.

SEE ALSO *Eye and problems*

Face and problems

The face is made up of 14 bones, including the two parts of the jaw. These are overlaid with specialized muscles that allow an enormous complexity of expression and communication. Women's faces are smaller than men's, with smaller teeth and jaws, more rounded contours, smoother facial bones, less prominent eyebrow ridges, sharper upper margins to the eye sockets and a more vertical forehead. The overall effect is that women are more 'baby-faced'; as with infants, such features tend to evoke protective instincts in adults – both men and women. Facial attractiveness is closely linked with facial symmetry: the more closely the two halves of the face match each other, the more a face is likely to be rated as attractive by observers.

The face is the front we present to the world and has vital importance to our sense of 'self',

to emotional expression and to interactions with others. Any cosmetic deficiencies – whether real or imagined – can cause self-consciousness, low self-esteem, withdrawal from normal relationships and teasing or bullying from others.

SKIN COLOURING

Facial colouring is determined by the skin pigment melanin, which individuals have in varying amounts. This accounts for variations in skin tone among people of the same race, as well as for the differences in colour between people of different races. Alterations in skin pigmentation – either lightening or darkening – are sometimes much sought-after, but can cause considerable distress, particularly if the effects are patchy.

Factors that alter skin pigmentation include:

- patchy darkening (melanoderma) caused by hormonal changes in pregnancy or the contraceptive pill (chloasma), sunburn, menopause, old age or various diseases including diabetes and malaria;
- loss of pigment – known as vitiligo;
- discoloration caused by carotenaemia – in which sufferers develop an orange skin colour as a result consuming excessive quantities of carotene – or haemochromatosis ('bronzed diabetes'), a hereditary disorder in which iron is deposited in skin.

Facial bones and muscles

The facial skeleton consists of 14 stationary bones (6 paired and 2 single) that provide attachments for the muscles that control facial movements.

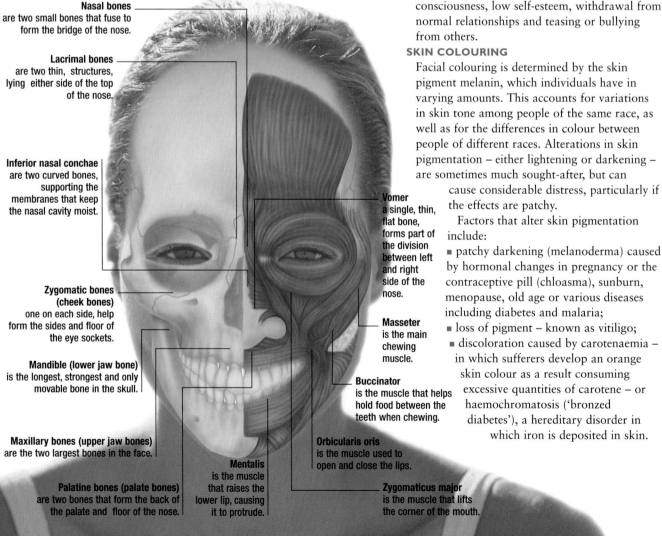

Nasal bones are two small bones that fuse to form the bridge of the nose.

Lacrimal bones are two thin, structures, lying either side of the top of the nose.

Inferior nasal conchae are two curved bones, supporting the membranes that keep the nasal cavity moist.

Zygomatic bones (cheek bones) one on each side, help form the sides and floor of the eye sockets.

Mandible (lower jaw bone) is the longest, strongest and only movable bone in the skull.

Maxillary bones (upper jaw bones) are the two largest bones in the face.

Palatine bones (palate bones) are two bones that form the back of the palate and floor of the nose.

Mentalis is the muscle that raises the lower lip, causing it to protrude.

Vomer a single, thin, flat bone, forms part of the division between left and right side of the nose.

Masseter is the main chewing muscle.

Buccinator is the muscle that helps hold food between the teeth when chewing.

Orbicularis oris is the muscle used to open and close the lips.

Zygomaticus major is the muscle that lifts the corner of the mouth.

FACIAL DISFIGUREMENTS

Facial malformations evident at birth include **cleft palate and hare lip** and **birthmarks** such as strawberry marks (haemangioma) and port-wine stains. Malformations may be caused by more extensive disorders such as foetal alcohol syndrome, congenital syphilis, cretinism (lack of thyroid hormone), Down's syndrome, and some forms of muscular dystrophy. Causes of facial disfigurement developing after birth include:

- bulbous red nose (rhinophyma) in **rosacea**;
- deformity caused by fractures, especially of the nose;
- drooping eyelids – many causes, including **myasthenia gravis**;
- drooping of one side of the face due to muscle paralysis – **Bell's palsy**;
- melanoma;
- protruding or misaligned teeth;
- **rodent ulcer** – a slow-growing skin tumour;
- scarring due to **burns** or trauma;
- **squint**.

'Invisible' facial problems include facial pain or frontal headache from **sinusitis**, trigeminal neuralgia, temporal **arteritis** and temperomandibular joint problems.

ENLARGED ADENOIDS

If left untreated, enlarged adenoids stop a child breathing through the nose. This tends to produce a characteristic facial expression – a gaping mouth with a vacant expression – associated with a nasal voice. Prolonged mouth breathing has been shown to reduce the levels of oxygen reaching the brain and can impair intelligence. (See also **Adenoids and problems**.)

PLASTIC SURGERY

Reconstructive surgery is used to repair or restore damage to the facial structure or skin. For example, people with severe burns

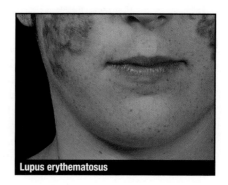

▶ **Diagnostic clue**
Red scaly patches on the face may be a sign of lupus erythematosus, a condition in which the connective tissue in the skin breaks down. The drug chloroquine (often used against malaria) can help, though most cases will improve with time.
Lupus erythematosus

to the face may need a number of skin-grafting operations or a badly broken jaw may need to be surgically rebuilt.

FACIAL CLUES TO BODILY AILMENTS

Many diseases are linked with facial features that can give doctors vital clues to diagnosis:

- acromegaly – enlarged, coarse features;
- Addison's disease and some cases of poisoning – dark pigmentation;
- alcoholism – broken blood vessels on the nose;
- anaemia – pale skin;
- chronic bronchitis – blueish complexion;
- Cushing's syndrome or steroid treatment – enlarged 'moonshaped' face;
- cyanosis – blue lips, dusky cheeks;
- emphysema – reddish complexion;
- hypothyroidism – coarse puffy skin and eyelids in myxoedema;
- jaundice – yellow skin and 'whites' of eyes;
- lupus erythematosus and rosacea – butterfly rash;
- mitral stenosis – prominent blood vessels on the cheeks;
- thyrotoxicosis – staring, protruding eyes.

SEE ALSO *Cosmetic and plastic surgery;*
Endocrine system and disorders; Eye and
problems; Mouth and disorders; Nose
and problems; Skin and disorders; Teeth and
problems; Thyroid and disorders

Cosmetic surgery

Cosmetic surgery involves remoulding the skin and sometimes the deeper structures of the face to enhance appearance.

Purely aesthetic surgery, commonly described as cosmetic surgery, is becoming increasingly popular. Its aim is to correct perceived defects or lessen their prominence. Cosmetic surgery on the face may involve cutting and reshaping facial structures. Procedures include reducing a large nose, reversing the effects of ageing (as in a facelift), skin grafting, using lasers to remove blemishes, plumping out wrinkles by injecting collagen into deep skin creases, or paralysing facial muscles with injected botox (botulinum toxin) to stop particular muscle actions such as frowning.

CONTACT **Cleft Lip and Palate Association**
235–237 Finchley Road, London NW3 6LS
(020) 7431 0033 (www.clapa.com)
British Association of Aesthetic Plastic Surgeons (for cosmetic procedures) and
British Association of Plastic Surgeons
(for cosmetic and reconstructive surgery)
Royal College of Surgeons of England,
35–43 Lincoln's Inn Fields, London WC2A 3PE;
BAAPS adviceline (020) 7405 2234;
(www.baaps.org.uk; www.baps.co.uk)
Changing Faces 1 and 2 Junction Mews,
London W2 1PN 0845 4500 275
(www.changingfaces.co.uk) Help and advice for people suffering from facial disfigurement.

Face lift

A face lift is a cosmetic operation to give the face a more youthful appearance. Under general **anaesthetic**, an incision is made at the temples and extended behind the earlobes and around the back of the scalp. The skin and underlying muscles are then tightened and any excess fat removed. The procedure can be combined with forehead, eye and cheek surgery.
SEE ALSO *Cosmetic and plastic surgery*

Faeces

Faeces are the waste products of the digestive process. Material that has not been absorbed into the body builds up in the large intestine and is expelled as faeces from the anus during defecation. On average, the bowels contain around 225g (8oz) of faeces, which take about 50 hours to pass through from the top of the small intestine to the anus in men and about 67 hours in women. This time difference is due to the fact that women have a lower resting **metabolism** than men.

Water accounts for around 85 per cent of faeces. The remainder consists of food residues that cannot be digested, such as vegetable fibres, as well as carbohydrates, proteins, fats and mineral salts. As faeces pass through the **colon** water and salts are absorbed through the intestinal walls, while large numbers of bacteria – there are around 100 billion and almost 100 different types in each gram – break down carbohydrates and proteins. Some of their constituents are absorbed and others are expelled during defecation. In addition, the faeces contain mucus from the intestinal walls, and chemicals that are waste products of the processes of metabolism.

Examination of passed faeces (stools) can be an important diagnostic tool. Pale faeces may indicate a **gallbladder** disorder, while dark, tarry stools may indicate bleeding in the bowel (although they may also be the result of drinking red wine or taking iron tablets). Greasy, smelly stools (**steatorrhoea**) may indicate a bowel disorder, such as **coeliac disease**.

In small children and elderly people, especially, prolonged constipation can cause faeces to become impacted – small hard faeces become lodged in the rectum. The result can be cramps, pain in the rectum and sometimes a type of diarrhoea in which liquid faeces push past the impaction and leak from the anus. A doctor may try to dislodge the faeces using a lubricated, gloved finger, or prescribe glycerin **suppositories** or an **enema**.

Fainting

Fainting is when a person collapses due to loss of consciousness following a temporary reduction in blood supply to the brain. The effect of falling in a faint is to reduce the vertical distance between the heart and the brain, thereby helping to restore normal blood flow. Known medically as syncope, fainting is extremely common and can happen to anyone. Causes include emotional trauma and prolonged standing, particularly in hot, stuffy conditions – or a faint may follow injury or haemorrhage.

SYMPTOMS
There are common warning signs of an impending faint. The person feels lightheaded, giddy and sweaty, and vision may be blurred. Onlookers may notice that he or she looks pale, grey, clammy or sweaty. Eventually the person will become unsteady, lose consciousness and fall to the ground.

TREATMENT
Within a few minutes of being horizontal, most people recover consciousness and there are usually no after effects, unless the person is injured by falling. If fainting follows an injury, if other symptoms are present, or if repeated attacks occur with no obvious cause, medical advice should be sought.

PREVENTION
Someone who is about to faint should lie down or sit with the head between the knees, and breathe some fresh air.
SEE ALSO *FIRST AID*

Faith healing

Faith fealing has been used in religious and magical practice in nearly every culture and country in the world. One common type is the 'laying on of hands'. Reports of miraculous cures are mostly anecdotal but clinical research studies have found that faith healers can improve tension headaches, lower blood pressure and anxiety levels, speed up wound healing and improve the recovery rates of cardiac patients.

There is little rational scientific explanation for how faith healing works, but some doctors point to the **placebo** effect. Practitioners say that they simply act as channels for spiritual energy and direct this into the person's system. Faith healers work on the basis that a patient must believe in the practitioner's ability or in the power of God for healing to take place. **Spiritual healing** works in a similar way but without the emphasis on religious faith.

WHAT'S INVOLVED

The healing may take place at a healing clinic, at the healer's home or at a church or other religious meeting place. The healer may ask why you have come, and ask about your basic medical history.

For a healing session involving the laying on of hands, you sit fully clothed in a chair or lie back on a couch. After taking a few moments to 'attune' to your presence, the practitioner will pass his or her hands over you, often keeping them a short distance from your body. You may notice warmth or a tingling sensation emanating from the healer's hands, and you may feel peaceful or sleepy during and after the session.

A first session might last 30–45 minutes; subsequent sessions are usually 20–30 minutes. You may start to feel an improvement right away, or it may take two or three sessions before you are aware of the benefits, if any. The number of sessions you will need depends on the problem itself.

Avoid a healer who:
- charges a high fee (most don't charge or work on a donation basis only);
- promises a cure for a specific disease or disorder;
- implies that if you do not get better, it is because of your lack of faith.

SEE ALSO *Healing; Reiki*

Fallen arches

Fallen arches (also known as flat fleet) can cause poor posture as well as easily tired muscles in the feet and legs, low back pain and a burning sensation in the soles. In the long term, fallen arches can also lead to **arthritis** in the feet, knees and hips.

The feet have a natural arch shape at the insole, which acts as a shock absorber to protect the knees, hips and back. This arch can 'fall' as a result of the person being overweight, or if he or she stands relatively still for long periods of time.

Painless flat feet rarely need treatment. If the condition causes aching when standing or walking, individually moulded arch supports can be fitted inside the shoes. Exercises to strengthen the ligaments and muscles can help.

SEE ALSO *Foot and problems*

Fallopian tubes

The two Fallopian tubes are part of a woman's reproductive system. They carry eggs (ova) from the ovaries to the uterus. Each of these muscular structures is about 10cm (4in) long. The ovarian end opens into the abdominal cavity through a funnel-shaped structure edged with fringe-like projections called fimbriae. These direct the egg into the tube. Muscular contractions of the walls of the tube and the 'waving' of specialized lining cells then move the egg to the uterus.

The Fallopian tubes can be damaged by pelvic infection; abnormalities in the tubes account for up to 50 per cent of female infertility.

A fertilized egg sometimes implants itself in one of the Fallopian tubes rather than in the uterus. This is called an **ectopic pregnancy** and requires emergency medical intervention.

SEE ALSO *Infertility and fertility; Pelvis and disorders; Reproductive system*

Fallot's tetralogy

Fallot's tetralogy is a form of congenital heart disease in which an affected child is born with four heart defects that occur together. This results in the child appearing blue (cyanosis).

The condition develops progressively, usually from birth, and is usually diagnosed in the first month or two of life. The defects are a hole in the heart (ventriculoseptal defect), narrowing of the pulmonary valve, displacement of the aorta and a thickened right ventricle. Symptoms include **clubbing of the fingers and toes**, underdevelopment, and shortness of breath.

Fallot's tetralogy can often be treated with surgery, which is carried out before the child is five years old.

SEE ALSO *Congenital disorders; Heart and circulatory system; Heart surgery*

Farmer's lung

Farmer's lung is a lung disease caused by an allergy to the spores of fungus growing in mouldy hay or straw. It is a form of alveolitis, an inflammation of the tiny air sacs in the lungs. Farmer's lung occurs when someone who has developed a hypersensitivity to the fungi spores inhales them. The inflammation makes the lungs less efficient, causing breathlessness, fever, headache and muscle ache. Repeated exposure can make the condition chronic (long term). If it is not diagnosed early on, the lungs may be permanently scarred.

The risk of farmer's lung is reduced by ensuring that stored hay or straw is kept dry, and that farm workers work in dry, well-ventilated areas and wear protective masks.

SEE ALSO *Lungs and disorders*

Fat

Fat is one of the three main constituents of food, along with carbohydrate and protein. The body needs dietary fat to supply essential fatty acids as well as the fat-soluble vitamins (see **Diet**). Fat is also a concentrated form of energy that the body needs to run its metabolic process. Food that is surplus to requirement is converted by the body into fat and stored in adipose tissue. This is found under the skin, around the kidneys and in the buttocks. Excessive build-up of fat in the body leads to obesity.

SATURATED AND UNSATURATED FATS

Fats are divided according to their chemical make-up into saturated and unsaturated types. A diet high in saturated fats – found mainly in animal products such as meat, cheese, butter, cream – increases blood cholesterol levels and the risk of heart disease. Monounsaturated and polyunsaturated fats, found in vegetable oils, provide essential fatty acids that the body cannot make for itself. **Fish oils** are another good source of polyunsaturates.

Fatigue

Fatigue is a state of tiredness, which often becomes a normal part of everyday life. Its extreme stage is **exhaustion**. Causes include sleep deprivation, jet lag, prolonged stress or depression, work, exercise and illness.

Febrile convulsion

Also called **seizures** or fever fits, febrile convulsions are fits associated with a fever, and usually caused by a viral infection. They look like epileptic fits, but are not in fact a sign of **epilepsy**. Febrile convulsions may occur in a child aged between six months and five years if the child's temperature rises either too high or too quickly. The child may turn blue, the eyes may roll, and the limbs or whole body may start jerking or twitching.

In rare cases, a child may suffer febrile convulsions after receiving the **MMR vaccine**. In such a case, convulsion occurs eight to ten days after the vaccination. They are caused by the measles component of the vaccine, but catching measles itself is more likely to cause febrile convulsion than receiving the vaccine.

Although they last for only 2–3 minutes, fits can be very alarming for parents. A child who has a fit should lie on his or her side on the floor. Do not insert anything into the child's mouth, and when the fit is over call a doctor. To reduce a high temperature, give your child plenty of cool clear fluids, remove all clothing except a nappy or pants and vest, and keep the room cool.

Feldenkrais technique

The Feldenkrais technique is a system of physical training that promotes bodily self-awareness, coordination and movement re-education. Based on gentle exercises that are designed to reprogramme a person's patterns of movement, it was developed in the 1940s by Dr Moshe Feldenkrais, a Russian-born Israeli physicist, judo expert and engineer.

People with chronic or acute pain in the back, neck, shoulders, hips, legs or knees can benefit from Feldenkrais sessions, as can anyone who has multiple sclerosis or cerebral palsy, or who has suffered a stroke. Some musicians, actors and artists use the technique to extend their abilities and enhance creativity, and elderly people use it to retain or regain their mobility.

Feldenkrais can be taught individually or in groups. The practitioner takes you through a sequence of movements in basic positions – sitting, lying, standing – showing you how to do them more easily and smoothly, guiding you verbally. In the one-to-one sessions, props such as rollers or pillows may be used to help to support your body and facilitate certain movements, but mostly you are guided by gentle touch. You remain fully clothed for the 60-minute sessions.

THE ORTHODOX VIEW

Most doctors are prepared to acknowledge the neurological rationale for the Feldenkrais technique, and are unlikely to object to its use alongside conventional **physiotherapy**.

CONTACT The Feldenkrais Guild UK
The Bothy, Auchlumies Walled Garden, Blairs, Aberdeenshire AB12 5YS 07000 785 506 (www.feldenkrais.co.uk)

Fertility

Fertility is a man's or woman's physical capability of conceiving a child. Female fertility, governed by the menstrual cycle, decreases with age, ending at the menopause, whereas men are fertile for most of their adult lives.

Factors that may impair fertility include pelvic infection, injury, some medicines and treatment for cancer.

SEE ALSO *Conception; Infertility*

Fetal alcohol syndrome

A woman who drinks too much alcohol during pregnancy may give birth to a child with a collection of characteristics and abnormalities known as fetal alcohol syndrome.

Every week in the UK, 14 babies are born with fetal alcohol syndrome, and there is concern that this figure will rise as a result of increasing alcohol consumption among women.

SYMPTOMS

A baby affected by fetal alcohol syndrome may exhibit a number of problems, including:
- a small size for its estimated delivery date;
- small wide-set eyes, flattened cheekbones and bridge of the nose, and a shallow or non-existent groove between the nose and upper lip;
- heart defects;
- skeletal abnormalities such as fused joints, deformed fingers and toes, or curvature of the spine;
- alcohol withdrawal after the birth, which may make the baby fretful.

▶ **Uncertain future**
A child born with fetal alcohol syndrome has distinctive facial features and is likely to suffer from poor physical coordination.

PREVENTION

Fetal alcohol syndrome is most commonly associated with heavy drinking, but the 'safe' level of alcohol consumption during pregnancy is not known. Only a small number of babies born to women with alcohol problems suffer from fetal alcohol syndrome; the pattern of consumption and the mother's nutrition and genetic susceptibility also influence the risk.

Total abstention from alcohol throughout pregnancy prevents fetal alcohol syndrome, but some women drink alcohol before they realize that they are pregnant. This is unlikely to cause serious harm and should not lead to undue anxiety.

OUTLOOK

Fetal alcohol syndrome is the leading cause of non-genetic mental retardation in the world, and children affected by the condition have irreversible damage to the central nervous system. They are likely to have developmental delays and learning and behavioural difficulties, as well as poor physical coordination.

CONTACT Fetal Alcohol Syndrome Trust
PO Box 30, Walton, Liverpool L9 8HU
(0151) 284 2900

Fetus

Eight weeks after conception, a fertilized egg has developed into a recognizably human form and, from this point until the birth, it is known as a fetus. In legal terms, a fetus is considered capable of survival (viable) if born 24 weeks after conception, as long as it receives specialized intensive care.

SEE ALSO Conception; Pregnancy and problems

Fever

Known medically as pyrexia, a fever is defined as a body temperature above 37°C (98.6°F), measured in the mouth.

Most fevers are triggered by the body's defence mechanism against either viral or bacterial infections, including typhoid fever, tonsillitis, influenza and measles. In these cases, proteins called pyrogens are released when the body's white blood cells fight the micro-organisms responsible for the illness. These pyrogens act on the temperature-controlling centre in the brain, causing it to raise the body's temperature in an attempt to destroy the invading micro-organisms.

Sometimes conditions that are non-infectious may be accompanied by a fever. These include dehydration, heart attack and lymphoma (a tumour of the lymphatic system). Why fever should be a feature of such conditions is not yet properly understood.

TREATMENT

Most fevers will not require any treatment, but drink plenty of fluids while the temperature lasts. Aspirin (for adults) and **paracetamol** may help to relieve fevers caused by infections.

When to consult a doctor
- If your temperature remains raised for longer than 48 hours or rises above 40°C (104°F).
- If there are accompanying symptoms such as severe headache with a stiff neck or abdominal pain, which may be a sign of **meningitis**.

Complementary therapies
Feverfew is an old herbal treatment for the relief of fever, but it should not be taken by pregnant women.

SEE ALSO Temperature

Fibre

Dietary fibre, also known as roughage, is that part of our food which is not broken down by the body's digestive enzymes and theoretically contains no nutrients. Yet fibre is a vital part of a healthy **diet**, absorbing water in the large intestine. This makes stools soft and easy to pass, which aids a healthy digestive system.

There are two types of fibre: soluble and insoluble. Both help to prevent constipation and other **bowel** disorders, **diverticular disease**, **obesity** and certain forms of cancer. In addition, soluble fibre slows down glucose absorption, helping to prevent surges in blood sugar levels.

Highly refined foods contain no dietary fibre. Oats and beans are good sources of soluble fibre; wholewheat, bran and brown rice are rich in insoluble fibre (but too much bran may cause flatulence or diarrhoea); root vegetables, wholegrain cereals and fruit are good sources of both.

Soluble fibre helps to reduce blood cholesterol levels by binding with cholesterol in the gut.

Fibrillation

Fibrillation is characterized by cardiac muscle fibres contracting at different rates, producing a quivering effect instead of coordinated heartbeats. Atrial and ventricular fibrillation may be due to heart damage or other diseases; ventricular fibrillation after a heart attack or electrocution is often rapidly fatal. Drugs or electric shock treatment may restore normal rhythm.

SEE ALSO *Atrial fibrillation; Heart and circulatory system; Ventricular fibrillation*

Fibrynolytics

Fibrinolytic **drugs** break up blood clots in blood vessels (thrombi) and so act as 'clot-busters'. They activate the process that dissolves fibrin, a mesh-like protein which is the main component of many thrombi. They are given by intravenous infusion in conditions such as **pulmonary embolism** or to re-open the blocked coronary artery after a heart attack (**myocardial infarction**).

Fibroadenoma of the breast

Fibroadenoma of the breast is a benign (non-cancerous) breast tumour made of fibrous and glandular tissue, which forms an easily movable, smooth, rubbery lump in the breast. Fibroadenomas are most common in women under 30. If the diagnosis is confirmed, fibroadenomas can be safely left in place.

SEE ALSO *Breasts and disorders*

Fibroids, uterine

Also known as fibromyomas, uterine fibroids are benign (non-cancerous) tumours of the wall of the uterus. They consist of smooth muscle fibres and fibrous connective tissue. Their growth is stimulated by the hormone oestrogen and they vary considerably in size.

About 30 per cent of women over the age of 35 have fibroids. Childless women are at greater risk than women with children, and Afro-Caribbean women are at higher risk than white women. Fibroids do not develop before puberty and shrink after the menopause.

SYMPTOMS
■ Fibroids usually cause no symptoms and are often found during a routine pelvic examination.
■ The most common symptom of fibroids is heavy periods. There are other less common symptoms, which can include abdominal swelling, pain, frequent urination caused by pressure on the bladder, and **infertility**.

TREATMENT
Treatment is rarely needed for small fibroids that do not cause any symptoms.
■ Women with problematic fibroids are usually offered a **hysterectomy**. If women hope to bear children, an operation to remove the fibroid while leaving the uterus intact (known as a myomectomy) is sometimes possible.
■ Uterine artery embolization, a procedure that blocks the blood supply to the fibroid, may be offered as an alternative to surgery. This causes the fibroid to degenerate and form scar tissue.

OUTLOOK
Therapies currently being tested include using laser or an electric current to shrink the fibroid, and a treatment that combines a procedure to reduce oestrogen production with removal of the womb lining (endometrium) to control heavy periods.

SEE ALSO *Pelvis and disorders*

Fibromyalgia syndrome

Fibromyalgia syndrome is a disorder in which sufferers experience widespread pain in the muscles, ligaments and tendons, as well as sleep disturbance and fatigue. It has no known cause, but possible triggers include viral or bacterial infection or the development of other disorders, such as **rheumatoid arthritis**, **lupus** or **hypothyroidism**. It does not cause permanent damage, but it may last for years. There are no outward signs, so a person suffering from fibromyalgia may look well but feel terrible.

SEE ALSO *Fibrositis*

Fibrosis

Fibrosis is the irreversible thickening and scarring of connective tissue, usually caused by inflammation or injury. Fibrosis is normal in scar tissue, but becomes a problem in some types of scarring. In **connective tissue disorders** such as scleroderma, for example, the skin and other tissues progressively tighten and harden. In some cases disfigurement may occur, and when the underlying joints and muscles are severely affected there may be disability.

Fibrositis

Fibrositis is a common, sometimes severe, condition, also termed fibromyalgia, in which fibrous tissues and muscles are affected by pain and tenderness. Sufferers also experience sleep disturbance. Fibrositis may persist for months or years, but does no permanent damage.

SYMPTOMS
- Aching in muscles, tendons and ligaments.
- Stiffness in muscles.
- May affect one or more parts of the body.
- Fatigue or lack of energy.

If symptoms closely resemble those of **ME** (**myalgic encephalomyelitis**), consult a doctor as soon as possible.

TREATMENT
Treatment usually focuses on relieving symptoms.

What a doctor may do
- Advise or prescribe painkillers and non-steroidal anti-inflammatory drugs (NSAIDS).
- Administer steroid injection.

What you can do
- Avoid alcohol, tea and coffee late at night.
- Eat healthily and watch your weight.
- Identify and eliminate stresses.
- Exercise progressively.

Complementary therapies
Physiotherapy, **massage**, **acupuncture**, **homeopathy** and **chiropractic** may all help.

CONTACT Fibromyalgia Association UK helpline 0870 220 1232.

Fish oils

Oils from fatty or oily fish (salmon, mackerel, herring and sardines) belong to a group of essential polyunsaturated fatty acids derived from linolenic acid. Necessary for healthy eyes and brain function, they help to alleviate inflammatory conditions such as rheumatoid **arthritis, psoriasis** and **dermatitis**, and can reduce the risk of heart disease or stroke. A healthy diet should include three or four portions of oily fish a week. Fish oils are also available in supplement form.

SEE ALSO _Diet; Nutritional supplements_

Fistula

A fistula is any abnormal channel between the interior and exterior of the body or two body organs. The most common form is an anal fistula, in which a channel between the rectum and anus allows mucus, pus and sometimes faeces to leak. The cause may be an injury, an abscess or **Crohn's disease, ulcerative colitis** or **colorectal cancer**.

Fits

Fits or seizures result from excessive nerve activity in the cortex of the brain. They can last for anything from a few seconds to several minutes. Fits may be recurrent or isolated and non-recurrent. Recurrent fits occur in **epilepsy**, for example. Non-recurrent fits can be caused by, for example, a head injury, **eclampsia** during pregnancy, or a childhood infection resulting in a high temperature (febrile seizure).

SYMPTOMS
Symptoms include altered consciousness and usually convulsions in which the body goes rigid and the limbs move rhythmically.

TREATMENT
Anyone experiencing a fit for the first time should seek urgent medical help.

Treatment of febrile seizures focuses on reducing fever. Seizures caused by infections, such as **meningitis** and **rabies**, are treated with anti-microbial therapy. In eclampsia, it may be necessary to deliver the fetus. A variety of **drugs** are available to treat epileptic seizures.

PREVENTION
Vaccines are available against rabies and some forms of meningitis. Epileptic seizures may be prevented by regular medication. Alcohol- and cocaine-induced seizures may be prevented by reduction or withdrawal of intake.

COMPLICATIONS
Severe, prolonged or recurrent fits can cause brain damage.

SEE ALSO _Brain and nervous system; Epilepsy; Seizure_

CONTACT British Epilepsy Association New Anstey House, Gate Way Drive, Yeadon Leeds LS19 7XY; helpline 0808 800 5050 (www.epilepsy.org.uk)

Flat feet

Flat feet, also known as fallen arches, is a condition characterized by an absence of the normal arches of the feet, so that the soles lie flat on the ground. It is normal in toddlers, but should not persist into later childhood.

The condition can also develop in adulthood as a result of prolonged standing or obesity, and can lead, in the long term, to **arthritis** in the feet, knees and hips.
SEE ALSO *Foot and problems*

Flatulence

Flatulence – which affects everyone at times – is excess gas or wind in the digestive tract. Wind is brought up from the stomach through the mouth in a belch or passed through the anus.

CAUSES

The most common cause of gas in the stomach is swallowed air, which may be taken in while eating and drinking. Air swallowing is also often associated with nervous tension.

Gas in the bowel stems from bacterial fermentation of food, especially beans, peas eggs and some vegetables, in the digestive tract.

Flatulence can be a sign of a gastro-intestinal disorder such as **gastroenteritis**, **gastric ulcer**, **hiatus hernia** or **irritable bowel syndrome**, or a condition affecting the **gallbladder**.

TREATMENT

Charcoal, available from pharmacies in tablet form, can be taken to absorb excess gas. Over-the-counter antacids or indigestion remedies may help.

When to consult a doctor

■ If flatulence becomes socially troublesome.
■ If it is accompanied by persistent pain, **constipation** or **diarrhoea**.

What a doctor may do

■ Advise on diet.
■ Prescribe an antacid liquid for belching.
■ Check for any underlying causes.

PREVENTION

Avoid wind-producing foods, fizzy drinks, hurried meals and nervous tension.
SEE ALSO *Digestive system*

Floaters

Floaters are dark spots or specks in the field of vision. Most people see them occasionally, especially when looking at a light, even background, such as an overcast sky. Floaters are commonly remnants of the many blood vessels that filled the now transparent jelly in the chamber behind the eye lens (the vitreous humour) when the eye was developing in the womb. They may also be caused by damage to the retina or an inflammation of the eye.

ONSET AND DURATION

Once floaters are present, they remain, although they may not be noticed after a while. They are more noticeable when they drift into the centre of the eye, which is why people complain of intermittent floaters. Floaters are often reported after eye surgery, such as a **cataract** operation.

DIAGNOSIS

Any floaters seen for the first time (even if not in large numbers) should be investigated by a thorough eye examination in case there is an underlying disease that needs treatment, but most floaters are harmless.

■ The sudden appearance of a large cobweb-like floater may be a result of the jelly inside the eye shrinking (a vitreous detachment). Consult a doctor or optometrist as soon as possible to rule out any damage to the retina.
■ A sudden shower of floaters, accompanied by flashing or sparkling lights, may indicate retinal detachment. Report to your nearest eye casualty unit for urgent treatment.
■ A gradual increase in large floaters together with a reduction of vision and a general feeling of malaise could indicate an inflammation in the eye. See a doctor if you have this combination of symptoms.
SEE ALSO *Eye and problems*

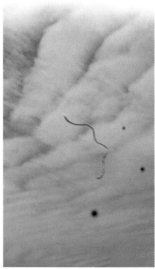

▲ **Spotted vision**
Floaters cast a shadow on the retina and are therefore seen as dark shapes. A large floater passing across the line of gaze may intermittently affect vision.

Flooding

Flooding is a psychological technique used in the treatment of a **phobia**. A phobia is an exaggerated, irrational fear of objects – for example, dogs – or a situation, such as being in enclosed spaces. People with pronounced phobias may go to extreme lengths to avoid the source of their fear.

Treatment for a phobia is based on teaching the affected person how to react differently to the stimulus, or the source of the problem. The person is exposed to the feared stimulus, either in the imagination or reality. Sudden intense exposure is called flooding. A gradual exposure to the stimulus using graded small steps is called systematic desensitization. Both techniques have successful outcomes. Once the fear has been overcome, anxiety-management techniques such as **relaxation** and **creative visualization** may also help to maintain desensitization.

TREATMENT

If you suffer from a phobia, your GP will refer you to a specialist clinical psychologist for treatment. For any psychological therapy to be effective, it is important to feel comfortable with your therapist; you should be able to discuss the proposed treatment and set goals that you feel you can manage.

SEE ALSO **Cognitive behaviour therapy**

Fluid retention

Fluid retention is the accumulation of fluid in body tissue. It most commonly affects the feet and ankles, but can also affect the hands and face, in severe cases the legs, and sometimes the entire body. It occurs in many diseases in which sluggish circulation is a factor. Gravity tends to pull the fluid to the lowest point of the body. Fluid retention is common in premenstrual syndrome, occurring the week before the start of a period (see also **Oedema**).

SYMPTOMS
- Swelling of soft tissues.
- Weight gain.
- In severe cases, breathlessness and swelling of the entire leg.

DURATION

In premenstrual syndrome, fluid retention is resolved when the period begins. Otherwise the duration of the problem depends on what has caused it and what treatment is given.

CAUSES

Apart from premenstrual syndrome, there are several other causes of fluid retention:
- prolonged standing or sitting;
- varicose veins;
- pregnancy;
- heart, kidney or liver disease;
- malnutrition;
- allergy;
- side effects of some drugs, especially steroids and non-steroidal anti-inflammatory drugs (NSAIDs) such as aspirin or ibuprofen.

TREATMENT

If you suffer from fluid retention, keep your legs elevated while sitting. Take a mild diuretic, available from pharmacies. Avoid prolonged standing or sitting – if this is impossible, walk around for a few minutes every half-hour, and exercise the calf muscles by stretching the feet out and down, then back and up. This is especially important in any long-distance travel.

When to consult a doctor
- If the symptom is troublesome.
- If leg swelling is new, especially if it affects only one leg.
- If you are unwell.

What a doctor may do
- Examine and treat you as appropriate, refer you to a specialist, or admit you to hospital, urgently if necessary.
- Prescribe medication to alleviate premenstrual syndrome. Diuretics, evening primrose oil, hormones and vitamin B$_6$ (pyridoxine) can help. The **antidepressant** fluoxetine, which is useful in relieving the psychological effects of premenstrual syndrome, may also be prescribed.

PREVENTION

Regular evening primrose oil or Vitamin B$_6$ can ease premenstrual syndrome generally and reduce the incidence of fluid retention.

Complementary therapies
- Herbal remedies include evening primrose oil and natural diuretics such as dandelion leaves and asparagus.
- A naturopath would recommend a wholefood, low-salt diet and greater consumption of foods containing gammalinoleic acid (the active ingredient in evening primrose oil). These include blackcurrants, redcurrants, gooseberries, oats, barley and borage oil.
- A homeopath would recommend Lacheis muta (lachesis) and Natrum chloratum (Nat. mur.) to relieve bloating in premenstrual syndrome.

SEE ALSO **Menstruation and problems; Oedema**

Fluoride and fluoridation

Fluoride, a compound of the element fluorine, occurs naturally in water supplies in some areas and has a remarkable strengthening effect on tooth enamel. It makes teeth more resistant to acids in the mouth and reduces the incidence of decay in children's teeth. For this reason, most toothpastes contain added fluoride, and fluoride is also added to water supplies in some areas of the UK and the USA. The optimum amount for fluoridation of water is one part fluoride to 1 million parts water.

If fluoride is not added to the water in your area, fluoride rinses and supplements may be advisable. Check the situation with your water authority and consult your dentist.

Fluoride supplements should always be treated with care because too much fluoride can be harmful. Children who absorb excessive fluoride by swallowing toothpaste or being given too many fluoride drops can develop fluorosis, an unsightly (though usually treatable) mottling of the teeth.

When cleaning teeth, use no more than a pea-sized blob of toothpaste and spit foam and remaining toothpaste out after brushing.

SEE ALSO **Dentists and dentistry; Teeth and problems**

Folic acid

Folic acid is a B vitamin. It works alongside vitamin B_{12} to produce the genetic materials DNA (deoxyribonucleic acid) and RNA (ribonucleic acid). It also promotes the breakdown and use of proteins, and helps to form blood cells. Good dietary sources of folic acid include beans, green leafy vegetables, egg yolks, whole wheat, lamb's liver and salmon. For adults, the UK recommended daily intake is 200mcg. But women planning to get pregnant and those with a high risk of neural tube defects may be advised to take 400mcg a day.

SEE ALSO *Nutritional supplements*

Fontanelle

A fontanelle is one of two soft spots on a newborn baby's head, overlying gaps between the plates of bone. These gaps later fuse together as the skull grows. During childbirth they allow a degree of overlap and movement of the bones so that the baby's head can pass through the birth canal.

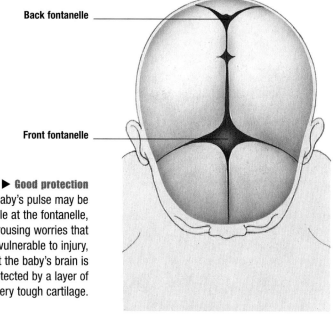

Back fontanelle

Front fontanelle

▶ **Good protection**
A baby's pulse may be visible at the fontanelle, arousing worries that it is vulnerable to injury, but the baby's brain is protected by a layer of very tough cartilage.

The rear fontanelle is small and closes within six weeks of a baby being born. The front fontanelle is a larger, diamond-shaped area, measuring about 4cm (1½ in) by 2cm (¾ in), which closes at around 18 months of age. A fontanelle that appears sunken or depressed is a sign of dehydration – the baby should be offered more breast milk or small quantities of boiled and cooled water from a sterilized bottle.

SEE ALSO *Babies and baby care*

Food allergies and intolerances

Food allergy is different from food intolerance. An allergy is an adverse reaction to food that causes a rapid response of the immune system and obvious symptoms. An intolerance, on the other hand, may be slower to manifest itself and is not an immune response. An example is lactose intolerance in someone who lacks or has low amounts of the enzyme lactase: that person will have an adverse reaction to milk, but tests for allergy will prove negative.

A food allergy often causes a severe reaction within seconds or minutes. It usually happens when the susceptible person eats the food, but it can happen through contact with someone else who has eaten a food containing the allergen.

A severe allergic reaction that constricts the throat making breathing difficult is known as **anaphylactic shock**. Many foods can trigger it, but the most common culprits are peanuts, tree nuts (such as almonds, hazelnuts and cashews), seeds, shellfish, eggs and milk. Anaphylaxis is a life-threatening emergency requiring immediate medical intervention.

But even apparently mild symptoms of allergy, such as a tingling of the lips or tongue, should not be ignored because there is a chance that future symptoms may be more severe. If you experience any symptoms of allergy, consult a GP and ask to be referred to an NHS allergy clinic. (See also **Allergies**.)

SYMPTOMS
The symptoms of a food allergy include:
■ itching, redness and swelling of the lips, mouth and tongue;

Tests for food allergy

Tests for food allergy may include a skin-prick test or a blood test called a RAST.

In a skin-prick test, a small needle is used to prick the skin, usually in the forearm, and introduce a drop of fluid containing a known allergen. The test is not painful and results are available within a few minutes. The existence of an allergy is indicated when the skin around the needle prick becomes itchy and red and a white swelling called a weal develops. A negative reaction means that the person does not have an allergy to that particular allergen.

Among laboratory tests used to confirm a diagnosis is a blood test called a RAST (radio-allergosorbent test), which measures the quantity of antibodies to various food allergens that are present in the blood.

Distinguishing between intolerance and allergy

Food intolerance frequently has less drastic consequences than food allergy, but in the case of intolerance it is much more difficult to identify the culprit food(s).

FOOD INTOLERANCE	FOOD ALLERGY
Reaction is delayed – hours to days	Reaction is usually immediate
Much larger amounts of culprit food are needed to provoke reactions	Reactions provoked by tiny quantities of food
No direct starting point; masked onset	Has an obvious starting point; link between food and symptoms is usually obvious
Some may be outgrown or disappear if culprit food is not eaten for a while	Usually persist for years (perhaps a lifetime)
Symptoms and their severity very variable	Symptoms very similar in susceptible people

■ nasal irritation and conjunctivitis;
■ urticaria or hives (marked by a sudden outbreak of intense itching and a raised rash);
■ eczema;
■ asthma;
■ vomiting;
■ diarrhoea;
■ stomach cramps;
■ throat swelling;
■ in severe cases, difficulty with breathing, collapse or unconsciousness.

The symptoms of food intolerance are usually delayed or masked, and are generally much less severe than those of an allergy. Any food that is eaten regularly can be responsible, which makes it very difficult to identify the culprit. There will be no clear-cut mechanism underlying the symptoms, as there is with food allergy. One laborious but effective way to find out which foods are producing intolerance or sensitivity reactions is for the person affected to undergo a diagnostic **elimination diet**.

WHAT HAPPENS IN AN ALLERGIC REACTION

All allergies are triggered by allergens – tiny particles of matter which are found in the environment or in food. Allergens are normally harmless in themselves, but the body of a susceptible person will see the particles as hostile invaders. It then responds to the threat by mounting an immune response, which involves releasing a host of antibodies into the bloodstream or tissues.

This leads in turn to the release of a cocktail of chemical messengers (mediators) one of which is histamine. The normal function of

mediators is to organize a more effective immune response – by increasing blood flow to the areas under attack, for example – but when such chemicals reach certain levels they produce the damaging symptoms of allergy.

The immune response is characterized by dilation of blood vessels, increased 'leakiness' of blood vessels, allowing white blood cells to move into the tissues, and contraction of the smooth muscle in lungs, stomach, intestine, bladder and blood vessel linings.

FOODS THAT ACT AS ALLERGENS

Most allergens in foods are proteins. Common foods and ingredients that cause reactions include:
■ cereals containing gluten – wheat, rye, barley, oats and spelt;
■ crustaceans such as shrimps and prawns;
■ eggs;
■ fish;
■ peanuts, nuts and nut products;
■ soya beans;
■ milk and dairy products;
■ sesame seeds;
■ mustard.

CONTACT **Allergy UK** Deepdene House, 30 Bellegrove Road, Welling, Kent DA16 3PY (020) 8303 8583 (www.allergyuk.org)
National Society for Research into Allergy PO Box 45, Hinckley, Leeds LE10 1JY (01455) 250715

Avoiding nuts in food

Check ingredients labels thoroughly. Look out for the words 'may contain traces' which can appear on crisps or supermarket breads, for example. Foods likely to contain nuts include:

■ cakes, biscuits, pastries, ice cream and desserts;

■ sweets, chocolate bars and cereal bars;

■ confectionery products such as marzipan and praline;

■ Chinese, Thai, Indonesian or Indian dishes;

■ salads, dressings made with nut oils and pesto;

■ many vegetarian dishes.

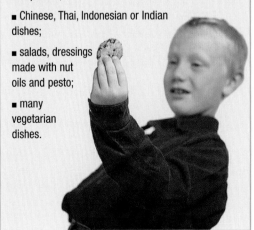

Acknowledgments

The Reader's Digest Complete A–Z of Medicine and Health was published by the Reader's Digest Association Ltd, London. It was commissioned, edited, designed and typeset by Librios Publishing, 21 Catherine Street, London WC2B 5JS (email: bookcreation@librios.com)

FOR LIBRIOS PUBLISHING

PROJECT MANAGER	Finny Fox-Davies
DESIGN MANAGER	Justina Leitão; Stefan Morris
SENIOR DESIGNERS	Keith Miller; Beatriz Waller
EDITORIAL ASSISTANT	David Popey
EDITORS	Liz Clasen; Antonella Collaro; Celia Coyne; Kim Davies; Henrietta Heald; Jude Ledger; Sam Merrell; Marion Moisy; Charles Phillips
DESIGN ASSISTANTS	Elisa Merino Cuesta; Anthony Morgan; Austin Taylor
PICTURE RESEARCH	Elizabeth Loving
INDEXER	Marie Lorimer
PUBLISHING DIRECTOR	Hal Robinson
EDITORIAL DIRECTOR	Ali Moore
ART DIRECTOR	Peter Laws

FOR THE READER'S DIGEST

COMMISSIONING EDITOR	Jonathan Bastable
ART EDITORS	Louise Turpin; Joanna Walker
PRE-PRESS ACCOUNT MANAGER	Penny Grose
EDITORIAL ASSISTANT	Lucy Murray

READER'S DIGEST GENERAL BOOKS

EDITORIAL DIRECTOR	Cortina Butler
MANAGING EDITOR	Alastair Holmes
ART DIRECTOR	Nick Clark
DEVELOPMENT EDITOR	Ruth Binney
SERIES EDITOR	Christine Noble

CONTRIBUTORS

Elizabeth Adlam MA; Harriet Ainley BSc; Susan Aldridge MSc PhD; Dr Michael Apple BA MBChB MRCGP; Toni Battison RGN RSCN PgDip; Glenda Baum MSc MCSP SRP; Nikki Bradford; Dr Sarah Brewer MA MB BChir; Pat Broad; Dr Harry Brown MBChB DRCOG MRCGP; Jenny Bryan BSc; Rita Carter; Dr Alex Clarke DPsych MSc BSc AFBPsS; Drew Clode BA; Geraldine Cooney BA; Dr John Cormack BDS MB BS MRCS LRCP; Dr Christine Fenn BSc PhD; Dr Vincent Forte BA MB BS MRCGP MSc DA; Dr Judith Hall BSc PhD MBPS; William Harvey BSc MCOptom; Caroline Holland BA; John Isitt BA; Dr Gillian Jenkins BM DRCOG DFFP BA; Georgina Kenyon BA; Dr Laurence Knott BSc MB BS; Dr Jim Lawrie MBBS FRCGP MA (Oxon) MBE; Dr Patricia Macnair MA MBChB Dip Aneasth; Oona Mashta BA; Sheena Meredith MB BS MRCS (Eng) LRCP (Lond); Denise Mortimore BSc PhD DHD; Dr Ian Morton BSc PhD MIBiol; John Newell MA (Camb); Dr Louise Newson BSc MB ChB MRCP MRCGP; Nigel Perryman; Jim Pollard BA MA PCGE; Dr Ann Robinson MBBS MRCGP DCH DRCOG; Dr Christina Scott-Moncrieff MB ChB FFHom; Helen Spence BA; Dr Jenny Sutcliffe PhD MB BS MCSP; Jane Symons; June Thompson RN RM RGV; Helen Varley BA; Patsy Wescott BA; Ann Whitehead MB BS MRCS LRCP MFFP; Dr Melanie Wynne-Jones MB ChB MRCGP DRCOG

CONSULTANTS & ORGANISATIONS

Alcohol Concern; Alzheimer's Society; Dr Keith Andrews MD FRCP, The Royal Hospital for Neuro-disability; Arterial Disease Clinic; Association of British Insurers; Association for Postnatal Illness; BackCare; Toni Battison RGN RSCN PgDip; Blood Pressure Association; British Dental Health Foundation – Dr Nigel L. Carter BDS LDS (RCS); British Dyslexia Association; British Lung Foundation; British Red Cross; Cancer Research UK; Candle Project – St Christopher's Hospice; Dr A Cann, University of Leicester; Chartered Institute of Environmental Health; CJD Support Network – Alzheimer's Society; Charles Collins MA ChM FRCS Ed – Member of Council for the Royal College of Surgeons of England; Dr Carol Cooper MA MB BChir MRCP; Cystic Fibrosis Trust; Mr R D Daniel BSc FRCS FRCOphth DO; Mr Dai Davies FRCS (plas); Department of Health – Public Awareness; Diabetes UK; Down's Syndrome Association; DrugScope; Eating Disorders Association; The Eyecare Trust; Family Planning Association; Food Standards Agency; Dr Vincent Forte BA MB BS MRCGP MSc DA; Professor Anthony Frew MA MD FRCP; Dr Judith Hall BSc PhD MBPS; International Glaucoma Association; Dr Rod Jaques DRCOG RCGP Dip. Sports Med. (Dist.); Dr Laurence Knott BSc MB BS; Dr Richard Long MD FRCP; Dr John Lucocq MB BCh BSc PhD; Mr W.A. Macleod MBChB FRCSE; Pamela Mason BSc PhD MRPharmS; ME Association; Meningitis Research Foundation; Migraine Action Association; Ian Morton BSc PhD MIBiol; Motor Neurone Disease Association; Multiple Sclerosis Society; National Addiction Centre; National Asthma Campaign; National Autistic Society; National Blood Service; National Eczema Society; National Hospital for Neurology and Neurosurgery; National Kidney Research Fund; National Society for the Prevention of Cruelty to Children; Pituitary Foundation; RADAR (The Royal Association for Disability and Rehabilitation); RELATE; Dr Ann Robinson MBBS MRCGP DCH DRCOG; Royal College of Anaesthetists; Royal College of Speech and Language Therapists; Royal National Institute for Deaf People; Royal National Institute of the Blind; Royal Society for the Prevention of Accidents; Society for Endocrinology The Society of Chiropodists and Podiatrists and Emma Supple FCPodS; SCOPE; Speakability; Penny Stanway MB BS; Terrence Higgins Trust; Dr Mark Westwood MA(Oxon) MRCP

ILLUSTRATORS

Antony Cobb Associates; Ian Atkinson; Joanna Cameron @ Antony Cobb; Michael Courtney; Chris Forsey; Kevin Jones Associates; Andrew Laws; Katie Laws; Keith Miller; Michael Saunders; Beatriz Waller; Martin Woodward